ANOTHER OPENING, ANOTHER SHOW

A LIVELY INTRODUCTION TO THE THEATRE

● ●

Second Edition

Tom Markus   Linda Sarver

Florida State University and The American University in Cairo

Illustrations by Linda Sarver

Boston Burr Ridge, IL Dubuque, IA Madison, WI New York
San Francisco St. Louis Bangkok Bogotá Caracas Kuala Lumpur
Lisbon London Madrid Mexico City Milan Montreal New Delhi
Santiago Seoul Singapore Sydney Taipei Toronto

Higher Education

ANOTHER OPENING, ANOTHER SHOW: A LIVELY INTRODUCTION TO THE THEATRE
Published by McGraw-Hill, an imprint of The McGraw-Hill Companies, Inc., 1221 Avenue
of the Americas, New York, NY 10020. Copyright © 2005, 2001. All rights reserved. No part
of this publication may be reproduced or distributed in any form or by any means, or
stored in a database or retrieval system, without the prior written consent of The McGraw-
Hill Companies, Inc., including, but not limited to, in any network or other electronic storage or transmission, or broadcast for distance learning.

This book is printed on acid-free paper.

8   9   10   11   12   DOC/DOC   1 5 4 3 2

ISBN-13: 978-0-07-256260-6
ISBN-10: 0-07-256260-9

Editor in Chief: Emily Barrosse
Publisher: Lyn Uhl
Sponsoring Editor: Caroline Ryan
Marketing Manager: Zina Craft
Developmental Editor: Nadia Bidwell
Production Editor: Holly Paulsen
Manuscript Editor: Mary Roybal
Design Manager: Kim Menning

Text and Cover Designer:
    Caroline McGowan
Art Editor: Katherine McNab
Illustrators: Linda Sarver, Joan Carol, and
    Judy and John Waller
Photo Research: Alexandra Ambrose and
    Emily Tietz
Production Supervisor: Rich DeVitto
Media Project Manager: Kathleen Boylan

Composition: 9.5/12 Palatino by Thompson Type
Printing: 45# New Era Matte, R. R. Donnelley & Sons/Crawfordsville, IN

Cover: Hugh Jackman and performers from several Broadway shows dance in an opening
number at the 2004 Tony Awards. © Sara Krulwich/The New York Times.

Credits: The credits section for this book begins on page 336 and is considered an extension
of the copyright page.

Library of Congress Cataloging-in-Publication Data
Markus, Tom.
    Another Opening, Another Show: A Lively Introduction to the Theatre / Tom Markus
and Linda Sarver.—2nd ed.
        p.   cm.
    Includes index.
    ISBN 0-07-256260-9 (alk. paper)
        1. Theater.   I. Sarver, Linda.   II. Title.

PN2037.M327 2004
792—dc22

                                                            2004061126

The Internet addresses listed in the text were accurate at the time of publication. The inclusion of a Web site does not indicate an endorsement by the authors or McGraw-Hill, and
McGraw-Hill does not guarantee the accuracy of the information presented at these sites.

www.mhhe.com

CONTENTS

OVERTURE

● ● ● ● ● ● ● ● ● ● ●

Writers' Bios

Hi. We're Tom and Linda. We're two people who have made a happy life in the theatre and who've enjoyed teaching theatre for a long time. We wrote this book in the first person instead of in the vague, third-person voice of most textbooks because in addition to sharing the solid information and facts we've learned over the years, we wanted to include our opinions and observations and a lot of behind-the-scenes stories. And because we're exuberant theatre folks who enjoy nothing better than a good laugh (even at our own expense), we really needed to tell those stories in the first person. Also, we know that standing side by side we look like a comedy team. Tom's 6'2" and Linda is 5'1"—one tall, one short, just like Laurel and Hardy, Abbott and Costello, Penn and Teller, Bullwinkle and Rocky. You need a sense of humor if you're going to sustain a life in the theatre.

We take our *work* very seriously, but not ourselves. We're not celebrities or famous scholars, so you may wonder why you should pay attention to our observations and opinions. Since we've had one foot in the academic world and the other foot in the professional theatre (that's the foot with the banana peel under it), it's a fair question. Let us introduce ourselves.

I'm Tom Markus. I've been a professional director and actor for more than forty years and a professional educator for even longer. I'm not a celebrity face or a household name, but I've been able to make a living doing what I love. I have acted in films, on TV shows including *Touched by an Angel* and *Everwood*, and stage with some of the major actors of our time—I've even acted on Broadway. Being in a Broadway show is the career goal for most actors. It's like a singer cutting a major-label CD or a basketball player making an NBA team. You may not be at the top o' the heap, but not very many have done what you've achieved. I've been there—as an actor, a director, and a professor who has taught at Yale, at the University of California, and as far away as Flinders University in Australia. I have an alphabet soup of letters after my name—B.A., M.F.A., Ph.D.—but I use the title "doctor" only when I phone for a reservation at a trendy restaurant.

I'm Linda Sarver, the short one with the long hair—Tom's the tall guy with the beard. Tom can tell a string of theatre anecdotes that keep people continually chuckling, but I'm the quiet one who lets fly with the zinger that pops his balloon. Aside from cooking dinner for some famous theatre artists, I've earned my living as a costume designer—in Canada, in Hong Kong, and for professional theatres and Shakespeare festivals across America. I've also worked on TV shows and feature films. I was part of a team that won an Emmy Citation for costuming the TV miniseries *North and South*. I've worked from coast to coast as a dramaturg (that's a fancy name for someone who contributes historical and literary research to the production of a play), and I've been an educator for twenty-five years. I have a Master of Fine Arts degree, and I've enjoyed teaching at Florida State University and Marquette University. Tom and I each have a long pedigree of theatre awards and scholarly publications that we don't brag about. I've always believed that if we're not having fun then we're doing something wrong, and we had fun writing this book. Rest easy—you're in good hands.

We met working on a play in Florida. Ten years later, after collaborating at many theatres and after writing the first edition of this book, we got married. Tom always said he started acting in college plays because it was a good way to meet girls. It turns out he was right.

The Second Edition

Writing the second edition of *Another Opening, Another Show* has been like rewriting a musical during its out-of-town tryout—revising and refining until it's ready to open on Broadway. Entire songs are cut from musicals, new dances are inserted, characters are added, dialogue is changed, and the plot is rearranged time after time. Even the recent Broadway revival of the classic musical *Kiss Me, Kate* was revised and updated, though it retained the anthem to show business that gave this book its title:

> Another op'nin', another show
> In Boston, Philly, or Baltimoe
> A chance for stage folks to say "hello"
> Another op'nin' of another show.

Instead of reading the reviews of out-of-town critics while we were rewriting, we heeded the reviews of more than a dozen educators and the comments of hundreds of students. This second edition embraces their suggestions, and we're thankful that writing it has given us stage folks another chance to say "hello."

Classics from the first edition came from consulting students and learning what they wanted in a textbook for an introductory theatre course:

- A book that doesn't cost a lot
- A book that is fun to read
- A book that helps them understand and enjoy theatre
- An insider's look at theatre, not a scholar's critique of it
- An opportunity to learn about plays on a stage rather than plays on a page
- Pictures that illustrate the ideas in the text instead of just decorating it

Previews of this second edition:

- An opening by Aristotle
- Entirely new coverage on how to write about theatre
- A chance to be side by side with us as we work at the Colorado Shakespeare Festival
- Entertaining exercises at the end of each chapter
- Enriched discussions of cultural diversity in American theatre
- Up-to-date examples throughout the text—even a mention of Brad Pitt
- Dozens of new photos of current productions, including *Urinetown, Take Me Out, Hairspray,* and *The Producers*
- Entirely new coverage of the hidden world of backstage
- A greatly expanded glossary
- A reorganization of the text that allows you to read chapters in any order

All-New, Flexible Structure

We expect that many readers will follow the advice the King of Hearts offers in *Alice's Adventures in Wonderland:* "Begin at the beginning and go on till you come to the end; then stop." However, we recognize that some instructors will assign chapters in an order that best serves their unique approach to the subject, so we've followed their suggestions and have created a flexible structure. For example, if students are going to attend a play in the early weeks of the semester, they might be assigned chapters 11 and 12 right away. If an instructor likes to begin a course with an overview of theatre history, then chapter 15 might be the first assignment. We have ensured that each chapter can "stand alone," and we expect instructors to have fun and arrange the chapters to suit their own teaching style. *Another Opening, Another Show* is divided into five acts:

- *Understanding and Evaluating Theatre* begins by exploring what theatre is and then examines three established ways to analyze, understand, and evaluate theatre; it concludes with a description of how both beginning students and professional critics write about theatre. This should prepare students to write any papers that are assigned.
- *The Creative Process* discusses the work of playwrights, actors, directors, and designers and then describes a "case study" of how theatre artists create a production.
- *The Audience Joins In* brings students back into the action. It provides helpful hints about how to attend the theatre and what to look for when the curtain goes up, and it describes the wide variety of work people do in the theatre.
- *Theatre History* is the fourth act, and it includes a great many photos and drawings that illustrate how theatre was presented in the past as well as the variety of theatres students might attend today.

- *Theatre in America Today*, the fifth and final act, is where we explore the business of theatre; how theatre enriches our intellectual, political, and cultural lives; and the way theatre reflects the rich diversity of American society. The final chapter, on the American musical, celebrates what many people feel is America's unique and most exciting contribution to world theatre.

Special Features

- Sidebars are brief remarks written in *italics* and found in the margins of the pages. They comment on the main topic in the accompanying text.
- Boxes contain information that augments the main topics. Four kinds of boxes contain four different kinds of information:

  Asides are fun stories that illustrate a point.

  Foreshadowing prepares for what follows, usually in the form of a list.

  Exposition is background information that will enrich understanding of a topic.

  Review is a look back at what was just discussed, often in the form of a checklist to ensure that you didn't miss any important information.

Encore! Supplementary Material

We're very excited about the Online Learning Center for *Another Opening, Another Show,* www.mhhe.com/markus2. It provides multiple choice study quizzes and essays for each chapter, Internet Exercises related to the topics in the book, Web links for doing additional research, and other helpful items.

For educators, we've written an Instructor's Manual that includes sample syllabuses for fifteen-week and ten-week terms, a chapter-by-chapter list of new terms, suggestions for exercises ranging from field trips to Internet searches, and a list of audiovisual materials related to the content of the chapter. The Instructor's Manual also includes an extensive test bank of multiple-choice, true/false, and essay questions.

Applause and Special Thanks

We are deeply indebted to professional theatre artists Diane Hostetler, North Seattle Community College; Frank Kuhn, State University of New York at Brockport; Scott LaFeber, University of Southern Indiana; and Robert Potter, University of California, Santa Barbara, for their detailed and extensive suggestions on the entire book; to Jack Axelrod and the late John Harrop for their comments on the chapter "Actors and Characters"; to Walter Bilderback, Monique Bondeux, Beate Czogalla, F. Mitchell Dana, Richard Devin, Kevin Dunayer, Linda Essig, Eric Fielding, Angelo O'Dierno, Eric Sinkkonen, Michael Webb, Michael Wellborn, and Gage Williams for their advice and contributions on Act 2; and particularly to Joe Varga for the use of his many beautiful designs. We're grateful to the following instructors for their helpful reviews of the original manuscript:

Mark Adams, College of Mainland

Michael Corriston, Southeast Community College

Virginia Ludders, Glendale Community College

Joyce Porter, Moraine Valley Community College

Michelle Rebollo, St. Louis Community College at Meramec

Michael Severeid, Elizabethtown College

Larry Waters, University of Nevada, Reno

Thanks are also due to the many educators whose generous and insightful comments on the first edition helped us write the second:

Henry Bial, University of New Mexico

Elbin Cleveland, University of South Carolina

Mark Creter and Kurt Eisen, Tennessee Technological University

Daina Giesler, University of North Carolina, Charlotte

Cheryl Hall, University of Alabama, Birmingham

Corlis A. Hayes, Morgan State University

Susan Reid, Columbus State University

David Underwood, University of North Carolina, Pembroke

Our particular thanks to David Williams, Texas Tech University, for correcting our embarrassing errors in theatre history. Linda owes special thanks to Andrew Clark and Chelsea Smith at Kinko's for their invaluable technical assistance, and Tom and Linda smack their slapsticks together in appreciation of the contributions, support, wisdom, and patience of all the good folks at McGraw-Hill: Chris Freitag and Caroline Ryan, sponsoring editors; Nadia Bidwell, developmental editor; Alexandra Ambrose, photo research coordinator; Katherine McNab, art editor; Kim Menning, design manager; Holly Paulsen, production editor, Anu Sansi, editorial assistant; and Inge King and Emily Tietz, photo researchers.

Understanding and Evaluating Theatre

When you walk out of the theatre, somebody's bound to ask you if you liked the play. One of the things you'll learn from this book is how to tell them more than "two thumbs down" or "I give it five stars!" Act 1 will give you some tools to understand a play and evaluate *why* you liked it or hated it.

A professor we know jokes with his students that there are really only three kinds of theatre and that you can identify them by the audience's behavior.

If a play is exciting and compelling, he jokes, the audience sits on the edge of their seats and leans toward the stage.

If a play is mostly dull, the audience leans back in their seats with their hands in their laps.

And if a play is really boring, the seats are empty because the audience went home.

There's more to analyzing and evaluating a play than these three drawings suggest, of course, but they make us smile and they're a starting place.

The first chapter in Act 1 introduces you to what theatre is. The second chapter discusses the seminal essay of theatre, *The Poetics*, written by the ancient Greek philosopher Aristotle. Chapter 3 describes the six major genres of drama, and Chapter 4 describes the six most common theatrical styles. Act 1 concludes with an exploration of how students, scholars, and professional critics write about theatre.

• • • • • • • • • •

CHAPTER 1

What Is Theatre?

THEATRE IS FUN

For over two thousand years, people have gone to the theatre for entertainment. Each night on Broadway, thousands of people rush to the theatre to have a good time, and people in your home town and on your campus go to the theatre eager to be entertained. If you are an experienced theatregoer, the question "What is theatre?" will give you food for thought. If you have never seen a play, the question will prompt you to discover the excitement, the stimulation, and—yes—the fun of theatre.

Theatre is storytelling. Whether the stories are sad or happy, they capture our imagination. We all like to hear a good story, and theatre people are very skilled storytellers. If you stumble on a group of theatre students, you'll probably hear them laughing as they tell each other about their triumphs and mishaps. Actors' autobiographies are filled with comic incidents from their careers, and when actors are guests on TV talk shows, their "war stories" entertain millions. Your instructors will probably share with you some of their own favorite stories.

All these anecdotes reveal the joyous *playfulness* of theatre. But theatre stories also teach us something about the theatre as well as about human behavior, political ideas, social problems, or other aspects of our culture. The stories that begin this book will prepare you for the lighthearted tone of the frequently challenging ideas that follow.

FLYING FISH AND DYING VILLAINS

There are many funny stories that explain how theatre works. Here are two of our favorites.

I (Tom) was hired by the Oregon Shakespeare Festival to direct a production of Shakespeare's rollicking comedy *The Merry Wives of Windsor*. The central character is Sir John Falstaff, a fat and foolish middle-aged nobleman who attempts to seduce two very respectable married women in the city of

Windsor. He deludes himself into thinking that these women will adore him. They, however, find Falstaff ludicrous and decide to play tricks that will humiliate him. Mrs. Ford invites him to her home, but when he arrives she excitedly tells him that her insanely jealous husband is returning unexpectedly, so he'd better sneak out of the house before he's discovered. The two women hide Falstaff in a wicker basket of dirty laundry. Later, the audience learns that Falstaff was thrown into the river along with the soiled sheets and towels.

The actors and I decided to bring Falstaff back on stage for his next entrance dripping wet from his filthy dunking. We hoped the audience would laugh at the sight of him. In rehearsals, I suggested that the actor carry his boots, as though he had taken them off because they were wet. Then he could turn one boot upside down and pour out the water that had filled it. We hoped for a second laugh from this sight gag. Then someone suggested that Falstaff reach into the other boot and pull out a fish! We found some frozen rainbow trout at the grocery store, and when we thawed them out they flopped about in the actor's hand as if they'd just been pulled out of the river. We hoped for a third laugh when the audience saw the fish. The actor came up with the idea that Falstaff had caught a cold from having been tossed into the river, so he could give a big "Ah-choo!" to prompt more laughs. At one rehearsal I suggested, "Why don't you hold the fish by the tail, turn away from the audience, give a big sneeze, and toss the fish over your head and out into the audience?" "Are you *serious*?" the actor asked. "Nobody's going to want to get hit by a fish!" I replied, "Trust me; for the one person who might not like it, the other 999 will howl with laughter. Everybody loves to see someone else in trouble." We debated the idea, we rehearsed it, and on opening night the actor threw the fish (Figure 1.1).

The audience howled, but things didn't go exactly as planned. The actor turned, sneezed, and tossed the fish. The audience laughed, but while the actor waited for the laughter to subside, somebody tossed the fish back onto the stage. When the actor turned around, he saw the fish lying on the stage, mistakenly assumed he had failed to hit the audience with it, turned his back again, sneezed again, tossed the fish again, and turned back toward the audience. The fish came flying back onto the stage. The audience was exploding in laughter. The actor picked up the fish and carried it offstage when he exited. But he saved it for the curtain call, and when he took his bow, he tossed the fish back into the audience one final time. The comic business was a triumph. The production continued delighting large audiences for several performances, until one night a surprise occurred. Word had spread about the flying fish, and when Falstaff turned his back, sneezed, and tossed the fish over his head, *twenty fish came flying up onto the stage!*

Before you stop to consider what this first story illustrates, read the next one, an anecdote often told in theatrical circles. We don't know whether it really happened, but it's a funny story that illustrates the point we're trying to make. Johnny Weismuller, a movie star who played the role of Tarzan in

Figure 1.1   Falstaff's flying fish.

Figure 1.2 "I keel you weeth my poison ring!"

many films, was celebrated for his muscles, innocent charm, and monosyllabic dialogue that prompted parodies like "Me Tarzan, you Jane." The story goes that early in his career he performed some stage roles. Usually he was cast in melodramas, playing the honorable jungle boy so he could show off his physique by striding around in his loincloth before saving the virgin from the villain. One play required him to shoot the bad guy late in the third act. Weismuller wrestled the pistol from the villain and fired. Click! The stage gun misfired. The audience rustled its programs. A second click. This time the stage manager's offstage gun misfired. The audience smiled. Thinking quickly, Weismuller plucked his dagger from his waistband, leaped across the stage, and stabbed the villain—but the knife had a rubber blade, and the audience could see it bend against the villain's chest. By now the audience was laughing, and the villain wanted to be "dead" in the worst way. What to do? Looking about him wildly, Weismuller saw the curtains on the window, ripped them down, wrapped them around the bad guy's neck, and started to strangle him, with both actors using a lot of body English. But the flimsy curtain ripped apart in Weismuller's hands. By now, the theatre was rocking with laughter and the actors were fighting the giggles as they tried to find a way out of their problem. Weismuller was wringing his hands when he felt the large ring he was wearing. Confidently, he strode to the cowering villain, pressed his ring against the actor's forehead, and said in a full voice, "I keel you weeth my poison ring" (Figure 1.2).

Both stories are based on something going wrong, and we find the stories funny because we know how things are supposed to happen in the theatre. In both stories, things happened unexpectedly—and both the audience and the actors knew it. The stories illustrate two simple notions: learning about theatre can be fun, and the more you learn about how theatre works, the more you will understand and enjoy the experience.

DEFINING THEATRE

In this chapter, we'll analyze and explain each part of our definition of theatre. Don't try to memorize it; rather, use it as a reference point for the discussion that follows.

EXPOSITION
• • • • • • • • • • •

Theatre is a unique live event that involves actors and audience, that happens in a particular place at a particular time, that takes place in the present tense and yet has a predetermined structure, that uses understood conventions to communicate through all five senses, and that has a lasting impact on the audience.

• •

Have you figured out that our definition is a thinly disguised list? We admit it, and next we will explain each item on the list:

Ten Traits of Theatre

● *FORESHADOWING*

Ten Traits of Theatre

1. A live event
2. Actors
3. Audience
4. A particular place
5. A particular time
6. The present tense
7. A predetermined structure
8. Understood conventions
9. Communication through all five senses
10. A lasting impact

A Live Event   Theatre is a **live event** that takes place only once. It's like a rock concert or a religious service. No matter how carefully the play is rehearsed, each performance results in a different experience. That *experience* is what we call "theatre." Just as the guitarist's riffs change each time he plays a song, so too a theatrical experience is unique at each performance. The actors' timing changes, the audience's reactions vary, the light cues happen a second later. Your theatrical experience is, in small but important ways, very different from the one your friends will have at a different performance of the same play.

Much of the excitement of theatre results from the tension between what was rehearsed and what actually happens. Will the altar candle go out? Will the fish come flying up onto the stage? The excitement of the live event comes in part from the knowledge that something could go wrong, and that sense of unexpected possibilities has made theatre a popular form of entertainment for more than two thousand years.

Actors   Without **actors,** theatre can't happen. Whether the actor is playing Falstaff or Tarzan, throwing a fish or simulating a killing, someone has to play a part and imitate an action. Without actors, there is no action—and therefore no theatre.

Audience   Without an **audience,** theatre can't happen. Theatre is the experience you enjoy when you respond to the actions performed by actors in a gathering of strangers. You might enjoy watching a video on your own, but people enjoy theatre as part of a crowd. As **herd animals,** we get comfort and pleasure from being included in a crowd that has gathered together for a common purpose, whether for a football game, a religious ceremony, or a theatrical experience.

Theatre requires you to be more than a passive observer. It makes you into nearly the same kind of active participant as you are when you chant "DE-fense, DE-fense" at a basketball game. When you laugh or applaud, you become part of the event. Your laughter and applause influence the actors' performance, which in return shapes your experience, and so the cycle continues. Audiences who shuffle through their programs or rattle candy wrappers (and those rude people whose cell phones chirp) can have a negative influence on your theatre experience.

A Particular Place   Theatre happens in a **particular place.** We go to theatre; it doesn't come to us. In the same way religious services are normally held in churches and hockey games take place in arenas for ice skating, theatre is usually performed in places specially designed (or adapted) for it. When you were reading the funny stories at the beginning of this chapter, you probably imagined what the theatres looked like. The Oregon Shakespeare Festival's 1,000-seat outdoor theatre is very different from the tent in which Tarzan's archenemy died from a poisoned ring. Keep in mind that theatre happens in a particular place—a theatre.

A Particular Time   You can't just go to the theatre any time you'd like. Theatre happens only when the actors and audience convene in a particular place at the same time. Like a wedding or the Super Bowl, theatre is a special event that happens at a **particular time.**

ASIDE   The *New York Times* reported that when Madonna acted in David Mamet's play *Speed the Plow* on Broadway, some of her fans arrived late to a performance. After the curtain call, the audience left the theatre, reported the *Times,* but the ushers found a group of the singer's fans still in their seats. When asked why, they explained that they had arrived late and were waiting for the next show. Happily, you're taking a course and reading a book that will save you from making an embarrassing mistake like that.

The Present Tense   Theatre is a **present-tense** event. Yes, there are audio and video recordings of theatre, but these are past-tense events. Recordings can play back something that happened at an earlier time, but they're not the real experience of theatre any more than a boring video replay of a home run makes you cheer the way you would if you were in the stands when the ninth-inning hit won the game. Past-tense events can trick you into wondering what will happen next. But as soon as you remember that the drama you're watching is recorded and unchangeable, you lose the excitement and danger of the present-tense performance, where the scenery could fall down or the actor could forget his lines.

A Predetermined Structure   Theatre has an organized **structure.** When you attend a performance, you will recognize that the event usually is divided into lengthy segments called **acts** and sometimes is divided further into shorter segments called **scenes.** The acts have numbers, and sometimes the scenes have both numbers and names. For example, Act One, Scene Three of Tennessee Williams's *The Glass Menagerie* is titled "After the fiasco—." The printed program will usually give the number of acts and scenes and where the intermissions fall in the overall structure.

Understood Conventions   Theatrical **conventions** are the agreed-upon rules of the game, and you already know some of them. You know that the actors take a **curtain call** at the end of a performance (Figure 1.3). They bow to the audience, thanking them for their participation, and the audience applauds the actors, thanking them for their work. Here's another convention: when a character turns and speaks directly to the audience in what we call an **aside,** the other actors on the stage pretend that they don't hear what is being said, and the audience joins in the pretense.

An important theatrical convention was originally described by the nineteenth-century English poet and literary critic Samuel Taylor Coleridge. He called it the **willing suspension of disbelief.** It also applies to theatre, where the audience consciously sets aside its knowledge that what is happening on the stage is fiction and pretends for the duration of the performance to believe that what it's watching is really happening. The audience willingly (knowingly) suspends (sets aside) its disbelief (its objectivity). The

Figure 1.3 Broadway stars Marin Mazzie and Brian Stokes Mitchell take their curtain call at the end of the Broadway revival of Cole Porter's great musical *Kiss Me, Kate.* A DVD or video of this brilliant production is available in rental stores.

The theatrical experience requires the audience's "willing suspension of disbelief" (Samuel Taylor Coleridge).

result is that the audience derives an exciting experience from enthusiastically participating in the event. If the audience didn't understand this convention, disruptions might spoil the performance. For example, an excited spectator might run up onto the stage to stop the villain from kicking the hero in a wrestling match (Figure 1.4). This would be like a fan running out onto the field to tackle a football player and prevent a touchdown. As audience members in the theatre or in the stands, we agree to play the game by the rules.

The willing suspension of disbelief helps you understand the **convention of the fourth wall.** When plays are set in a living room or kitchen, the actors pretend that, in addition to the three walls of the room around them, a fourth wall exists on the side facing the audience. The audience also pretends that the wall is there. The audience can see through the wall, but the actors pretend that they can't. The characters can warm themselves at the fireplace located in that imaginary wall, and the audience can see the sunshine that comes through the windows in that (invisible) fourth wall.

Two other important theatrical conventions are **virtual time** and **virtual place.** These terms describe our understanding that the action on stage is happening in a time and place different from our own. You sit in the theatre from 8:00 P.M. to 11:00 P.M., watching characters in a play who age many years over

Figure 1.4 The wrestling match in Shakespeare's *As You Like It* must be carefully choreographed so that the actors don't hurt each other, although the audience can suspend its disbelief and pretend that the characters do. (Shakespeare Theater of Maine)

the course of the evening. While you continue living your three hours of real time in the twenty-first century, the virtual time of Shakespeare's *Hamlet* arcs over many years, and all the action happens centuries ago. You pretend to believe that the characters live in the virtual place called Denmark, while you sit in a theatre in your real America. Theatre happens in a virtual time and place that we escape to, a time and place where we can learn useful truths about our own lives in our own time and place.

The audience must understand the conventions of virtual time and virtual place.

Communication Through All Five Senses   Theatre is a form of communication, and because it is a live event, we receive it through all five of our senses simultaneously. We see and hear live theatre the same way we see and hear drama on TV, but we also experience live theatre through our other three senses: we smell it, taste it, and feel it. From our total experience, we derive a play's meaning.

A fascinating description of how we make meaning out of what we experience is found in some lyrics Stephen Sondheim wrote for the Broadway musical *Sunday in the Park with George.* The musical tells the story of the innovative nineteenth-century French painter Georges Seurat (Zhorzhe Sir-rot), and it makes the point that creating a work of art is hard. Seurat created paintings made up of thousands of tiny points of color that, when seen at a proper distance, create the illusion of a color that is not truly on the canvas (Color Plate 1). If you walk up close to Seurat's *A Sunday Afternoon on the Island of La Grande Jatte,* all you see are tiny dots of color; but if you back away from the canvas, all those dots fuse in your eye to make a glorious picture. *You* have created the colors. Sondheim's lyrics to the song "Color and Light" describe how Seurat creates that illusion with dots of color:

Color and light.
There's only color and light.
Yellow and white.
Just blue and yellow and white.
Look at the air, Miss—
See what I mean?
No, look over there, Miss—
That's done with green . . .
Conjoined with orange . . .

The sky in the painting appears to be blue, but the lyric tells us it is made up of tiny dots of blue, yellow, white, green, and orange. In the nineteenth century, the idea that our eyes could blend dots of color into a recognizable image was new, but today the idea is an everyday experience. When you look at the pixels on your computer screen, you put together thousands of dots of color, and your eyes see the image they conjoin to make.

In a song titled "Putting It Together," Sondheim explores the concept more fully and explains that the art of making art is putting things together "bit by bit." When you sit in the theatre, you put together not only bits of what you see, but also bits of what you hear—voices, sound effects, footsteps, slamming doors, as well as the silences that are like the rests in a piece of music. For a version of "Putting It Together" that Barbra Streisand recorded, Sondheim rewrote the lyrics to describe the aural instead of the visual "bits":

The art of making art
Is putting it together
Bit by bit,
Beat by beat,
Part by part,
Sheet by sheet,
Chart by chart,
Track by track,
Reel by reel,
Stack by stack,
By bit,
By reel,
By track,
By stack,
By sharp,
By flat,
And that is the state of art.

When you add the bits of sound you hear to the bits of images you see, you take a grand step toward putting the performance together—bit by bit.

When you experience a play, you also smell it and taste it. In the first act of *A Raisin in the Sun,* the character Ruth Younger cooks breakfast, and the

Figure 1.5 The audience for this recent revival of *A Raisin in the Sun* could actually smell and vicariously taste the coffee and eggs.

audience smells the coffee brewing and the eggs frying. When her husband eats those eggs, the audience tastes them, if only vicariously (Figure 1.5).

ASIDE In rare performances, the audience is given actual food to eat, and then the sense of taste is real and not vicarious. The cast of the Broadway production of *Nicholas Nickleby* threw real biscuits to the audience. Tom caught one. It was tasty.

The fifth of our senses is feeling, or touch. The English language doesn't make it clear what we mean when we say "He touched me." Do we mean "I felt the pressure of his hand," or do we mean "I felt sad when he told me his father died"? In the theatre, you can feel the arms of your chair, and that's a physical feeling you truly experience. Equally true are the emotions you feel when you are "touched" by the action on the stage. Your experience is called

empathy, a word that describes the human capacity for participating in another's feelings. In a performance, when a character scalds his mouth from drinking hot coffee, we flinch. We feel what he feels. We empathize with him.

Theatre communicates to us through all five senses. That is one of the reasons we value it so highly—it gives us a sensory experience we find exhilarating.

A Lasting Impact   Theatre is an experience that stays with us. We have all seen a performance that is so funny that we remember it when something similar happens in our own life. Perhaps you've seen a performance that is so sad that it pops back into your mind when something in your own life parallels it. At its best, theatre has a lasting impact on us.

ASIDE   An anecdote will illuminate and validate the lasting impact of theatre. When I (Tom) was artistic director for a professional theatre company in Richmond, Virginia, the patrons held an elegant dinner party before each opening performance. It was a formal affair with tuxedos and long dresses.

I was seated across the table from a pleasant man in his mid-forties who told me he had not been "to this damned theatre in over a decade!" Putting on my gentlest manner and most diplomatic voice, I inquired why. He told me it was because of "that damned play." I wasn't running the theatre at the time he had been offended, so I tried to learn what play had set him off—for ten long years. He couldn't remember the title. Nor who had written it. Nor who had acted in it. Nor what it was about.

I tried to learn what the play was by getting him to tell me what it looked like, what visual images it had left in his memory. "Well, it was about a clown," he recalled. I racked my brain for plays about clowns. "And there were a lot of them and they all looked alike," he added. "Did they all talk strangely and in fragmented sentences?" I asked. "Yes! That's the one! That damned play drove me out of the theatre!" I realized that the play was a very challenging and fiercely intellectual avant-garde play called *Kaspar,* written by the highly respected Austrian playwright Peter Handke.

Over coffee and dessert, the gentleman told me he was an architect who designed large office buildings. I saw my opening. "Did you ever wish you could design a building that people would talk about when they walked past it? One that people would remember?" He said that had always been his dream. He lamented the fact that people walked past his buildings without noticing them and never remembered them. I suggested that being ignored must be tough for any creative person, and I sympathized with his frustration. He saw where I was heading. He saw that a work of art that has a lasting impact is something every artist hopes to create—every Virginia architect and every Austrian playwright. And, when pressed, he admitted that anything that could make him feel deeply ten years after he had experienced it must have been an important piece of art.

WHY WE VALUE THEATRE

In addition to entertaining you, theatre involves you in a search for your humanity, for what it truly means to be human. Theatre provides you with wonderful examples of how people behave in moments of celebration or stress and how they behave in relationship to their families, their societies, their governments, their deities. From these examples, you might learn to understand why others behave the way they do and how you might behave. We can learn respect for people of different ethnic backgrounds, for example, from Luis Valdez's *Zoot Suit* (Color Plate 2); we can learn how women travel the road to self-fulfillment from classics such as Henrik Ibsen's *A Doll's House* (Figure 1.6);

Figure 1.6 The recent New York revival of Henrik Ibsen's *A Doll's House* revealed that the theme of a woman's journey to self-fulfillment has a powerful impact on contemporary audiences.

Figure 1.7 Archibald MacLeish's powerful play *J.B.* tells the biblical story of Job in a modern setting and explores the relationship of Man, God, and the Devil.

we can learn about our relationship to our deity from plays like Archibald MacLeish's American classic *J.B.* (Figure 1.7).

How will studying theatre increase your knowledge and expand your thinking? It will teach you new ways to analyze your experiences and equip you to apply your new analytical skills to the many challenges you encounter in other academic courses and throughout your life. Studying theatre will increase your knowledge of your culture's history, the society you live in, and the behavior of your fellow humans. It will increase your enjoyment of an art form that has enriched human experience for more than two thousand years and will widen your appreciation of, and compassion for, the human condition.

Whatever else theatre is, it's more than a diverting entertainment. The great American playwright Arthur Miller said it this way: "The arts are a highway to the soul of the people. After the cannons have stopped firing and the great victories of finance are reduced to mere surmise and are long forgotten, it is the art of the people that confronts future generations." Today we know the names of Sophocles and Shakespeare but not of the generals who led the armies or the businessmen who made great fortunes. Will future generations remember Edward Albee and August Wilson and forget Colin Powell and Donald Trump?

If these reasons are not enough to entice you to study theatre, keep in mind that theatre may be a good place to meet a friend. Look what it did for Tom and me.

EXERCISES

1. Find a funny story about theatre that you can tell to the class, and then explain the concept the story illustrates. You might ask some theatre students for a good anecdote, or you might look in books such as Gyles Brandreth's *Great Theatrical Disasters,* Peter Hay's *Theatrical Anecdotes,* and Diana Rigg's *No Turn Unstoned.*

2. Gather a small number of students from your class and watch the DVD or video of the Broadway production of *Sunday in the Park with George.* Afterward, discuss the process of making a work of art. Try to define the creative process based on the ideas presented in this entertaining example of American musical theatre.

3. Turn on your TV to a courtroom drama or sitcom. Hit the mute button on your remote. Now try to follow the story, limiting yourself to what you see. After about ten minutes, turn the sound back on but put a cover over the picture. Discover for yourself that when you exclude your other four senses your experience is not as complete as it is in live theatre.

4. Find your college's mission statement. It may be in the course catalogue or class schedule. Read its justification for requiring courses in the arts, and bring it to class. Ask your instructor to analyze the mission statement and to discuss why he or she feels the study of theatre is valuable.

2

Aristotle's Guide to Pleasure

Modern guidebooks tell us where to find pleasure. We use a guidebook to locate good restaurants, nightclubs, and beaches. Whatever kind of pleasure we seek, our guidebook points us in the right direction. Guidebooks are nothing new, of course, and when Aristotle wrote the first guidebook about theatre, he understood that people seek pleasure. So Aristotle's *The Poetics* not only describes theatre but also tells us how and why theatre gives us pleasure.

EXPOSITION

Aristotle was an ancient Greek philosopher who was born in Athens in 384 B.C.E. and died in 322 B.C.E., at the age of sixty-two. He was a student of the equally famous Greek philosopher Plato, and he wrote essays on so many subjects that modern scholars call him "the greatest thinker of antiquity." Aristotle's works were lost to Europe when the Roman Empire collapsed, and from approximately 400 C.E. to about 1000 C.E. his wisdom was kept alive by Arab scholars in Syria and Spain. When Europeans climbed out of the Dark Ages and rediscovered Aristotle, the Renaissance began. The great poet Dante called Aristotle "the master of those who know." Aristotle wrote about astronomy, physics, rhetoric, ethics, politics, metaphysics, biology, botany, and poetics (the study of literary expression).

Aristotle's *The Poetics* is an important essay that is still taught and studied today. It explains the primary purpose of theatre, provides a methodology for analyzing the form of theatre, and defines the six elements that make up theatre.

Aristotle believed that the primary purpose of all human activity is to provide pleasure. However, Aristotle wasn't talking about "the pleasure prin-

Figure 2.1   Aristotle used *Oedipus the King* to illustrate his idea of an excellent plot in *The Poetics.*

ciple"; he didn't write about back rubs and aromatherapy. On the contrary, he believed that nothing gives more pleasure than learning the *truth*. He knew that we love to learn about ourselves, and he recognized that theatre provides us with an exceptional vehicle to study human behavior and to learn the truth about human nature. He recognized that while we're watching the characters in a drama, we're observing case studies of human behavior that we can learn from. He knew that theatre, at its optimum, is a vitally important experience that can help us understand the truth, and he believed that knowledge of the truth gives us pleasure.

Aristotle believed that the primary purpose of theatre is to provide pleasure and that the greatest pleasure comes from learning the greatest truth.

Aristotle studied the Greek dramas known to him, and he used as his primary example of excellence Sophocles' play *Oedipus the King* (SOFF-o-kleez, ED-i-puss) (Figure 2.1). This great play remains important today, in part because Aristotle held it up as a paradigm.

THE THREE UNITIES OF THEATRE

Aristotle's study led him to believe that plays give an audience the greatest pleasure when their form observes three organizing traits that we have come to call the **three unities: the unity of action, the unity of time,** and the **unity of place.** Aristotle provided us with a methodology for learning about a play by analyzing its formal organization.

FORESHADOWING

The Three Unities

1. The unity of action
2. The unity of time
3. The unity of place

The Unity of Action

A play should have only one simple **plot,** Aristotle argued, so that the audience can learn from its clear example and not be confused by secondary plots. That's why he praised *Oedipus the King,* which has a single direct story to tell. Aristotle discerned that the plot of a play has "a beginning, a middle, and an end," and he argued that the most pleasing plays have plots that occur in that order. Playwrights have invented new forms of plots in the centuries since Aristotle, and today we enjoy plays in which the ending of the story is at the beginning of the play, with the rest of the plot presented as a **flashback.** Further, we like Shakespeare's plays because their plots are **multiple** and **complex.** Still, many of the finest plays written today have a single plot that presents its beginning, middle, and end in that order.

> **ASIDE**   Modern plays like *The Glass Menagerie* and *Death of a Salesman* have plots that Aristotle never imagined. You'll have a chance to examine the intricacies and varieties of these plots in chapter 6.

The Unity of Time

Aristotle believed that we get the greatest pleasure from plays in which the action occurs in one passage of consecutive time. He praised *Oedipus the King,* in which the action takes place in a single day. But how long is a day? Over the centuries, critics have sometimes interpreted Aristotle's notion of the unity of time to mean one twenty-four-hour day, or one twelve-hour day from dawn to sunset, or even that the duration of the fictional action on stage should exactly match the real time the audience lives through. In the last case, if the story unfolds over the course of two hours, then the play that is telling that story should take two hours to perform.

Marsha Norman's powerful *'night, Mother* is an example of a play in which the characters and the audience live through exactly the same amount of time (indeed, a clock on the wall of the stage set shows the exact passage of time), but today we have a more tolerant attitude toward the playwright's use of time than Aristotle did. Harold Pinter's bitterly ironic *Betrayal* reverses the chronological order of its scenes so the audience first learns the

Figure 2.2   Real-life husband and wife James and Rose Pickering played the roles of husband and wife in Harold Pinter's *Betrayal* at the Milwaukee Repertory Theatre.

end of the story and then watches as the scenes that lead to that ending unfold (Figure 2.2). While Pinter's play confuses some audiences, it excites audiences that recognize how he has inverted the traditional sequence of the plot. Despite innovations like Pinter's, many fine modern plays, such as Lanford Wilson's Pulitzer Prize–winning *Talley's Folly*, have plots that takes place in one day.

The Unity of Place

Aristotle believed that we get the greatest pleasure from plays that set their action in one place, the way Sophocles' *Oedipus the King* is set entirely in the public square in front of the palace of Thebes. Today, the popularity of dramatic structures with the flexibility of movie scripts reflects our enjoyment of plays that jump about from one place to another. Yet some of the greatest modern plays are set in a single location and have a unity of place.

To Unify or Not to Unify?

When you read a play or attend the theatre today, you will encounter excellent plays that conform to Aristotle's guidelines and other, equally fine plays that disregard the three unities altogether. Successful plays like Tony Kushner's *Angels in America* (Color Plate 3) pay no attention to the three unities, and failures like the notorious Broadway flop *Moose Murders* observe them rigorously. Now that you understand the unities, you have a first tool for analyzing a play, a first way to talk about the play with friends or to write about it for a class assignment.

THE SIX ELEMENTS OF THEATRE

Aristotle's analysis of theatre led him to conclude that there are **six elements of theatre.** It is amazing that Aristotle was able to sum up theatre in a way that no one has been able to improve on, considering that in Aristotle's time scientists believed that the physical universe consisted of only four elements whereas the periodic table today contains 109 elements. In the twenty-five hundred years since Aristotle wrote *The Poetics,* no one has identified a seventh element of theatre. That is one of the many reasons why his seminal essay has remained a major influence.

● FORESHADOWING

The Six Elements of Theatre

1. Plot
2. Character
3. Thought
4. Diction
5. Music
6. Spectacle

Plot

The word "plot" comes from the ancient tradition of posting the order of a play's scenes backstage as a tool to help the actors remember what comes next.

Aristotle described plot as "the life and soul of the drama." He meant that plot was the most important of the six elements, the one element without which the drama could not exist. Until a plot unfolds, there is no play. When you tell people a story to entertain them, to provide an example, or to make a point in an argument, you tell the events that happen. In a drama, these events make up the plot.

Plots can be organized in many different ways. Aristotle knew only about plots that put the beginning in the beginning and the ending at the end, and he elaborated on his definition by saying that plot is "the arrangement of the incidents." That is, the plot is the totality of those incidents in a story that the playwright has selected to include in the play, and those incidents are arranged in a logical sequence. The drama that Aristotle studied in preparation for writing *The Poetics* was not as varied as the drama you will see in the theatre today, but except for a few modern plays that have an unusual structure, every play has a plot that gives it a life and a soul.

ASIDE   Movies and TV shows have plots that are arranged in many different ways. In Chapter 6 we will explore the three main ways the plots of plays are arranged: with **linear, cinematic,** and **contextual** structures. We'll also explain how a plot works and introduce the concepts **exposition, foreshadowing, reversal,** and **resolution.** Aristotle introduced these ideas in *The Poetics*—but let's not get ahead of ourselves.

Character

Aristotle described **character** as "the agent for the action." Character is the element that makes the action possible. When you attend the theatre, you watch what the characters do. When you try to describe a play, you describe what the characters did. The play unfolds when the characters enact the incidents of the plot. The characters cannot exist independent of what they do, because they achieve their being through the actions they perform, and the all-important plot can't unfold without characters who perform the actions. The two elements are inextricably bound together. Aristotle recognized character as the second most important element of theatre.

Thought

Thought is the meaning of the play, sometimes called the "message." The plot tells the audience a particular story, and the meaning is the universal idea that the audience draws from it.

A play's meaning can be stated by distilling the plot to a single sentence and then extrapolating a generalization from it—a universal truth. The meaning, or thought, of a play can only be communicated through the plot, and the plot can only be presented through the characters. Aristotle teaches us that the six elements are interconnected and have an order of importance in which the element of thought stands third.

ASIDE   Some scholars use the Greek word **dianoia** (dee-a-NOY-a), the word Aristotle wrote in *The Poetics*, to describe this element. Our dictionary defines "dianoia" as "the process of thought." Erudite scholars like to use the Greek word, but the word "thought" is a satisfactory description of this third element.

Diction

Aristotle's fourth element is **diction.** The term describes both the vocabulary the playwright uses and the order in which the words are placed. No two people speak in the same way. You might leave for class and say "Peace be with you" as you go out the door, while your friend might call out "Have a good one." The meaning of both phrases is the same, but the vocabulary is different, as is the order the words come in. That is, the diction is different. In creating a character's diction, the playwright makes that character unique. Imagine this exchange:

A   I wonder, my compatriot, if thou and I art kindred after all?

B   Shucks, I don't know, no how.

The diction of the first character uses a large vocabulary (e.g., "kindred") and a complicated word order that is grammatically correct. The second character's diction uses a smaller vocabulary and the ungrammatical word order of an uneducated person.

> **ASIDE**   We regularly misuse the word "diction" as a synonym for "articulation." Articulation describes the muscular activity through which we separate consonants from vowels so that we can shape sounds into recognizable words. A person with lazy or sloppy speech is guilty of poor articulation. Diction, in contrast, describes the playwright's vocabulary and the sequence in which the words are arranged.

A panhandler was rebuffed by an elegant English actor who said rather smugly, "'neither a borrower nor a lender be,' William Shakespeare." The panhandler replied "'Stick it in your ear,' David Mamet."

Just as each character's diction can be unique, so can each playwright's. Shakespeare's poetic diction in *Romeo and Juliet* is different from David Auburn's vulgar diction in *Proof.* Each playwright's diction establishes the play's level of seriousness and level of realism. A serious, real-life play such as *Proof* has a different diction from that of Neil Simon's silly comedy *The Sunshine Boys* (Figure 2.3). A realistic play like Lorraine Hansberry's *A Raisin in the Sun* uses slang and everyday language that imitates real life, a diction very different from the unreal diction of Shakespeare's lofty verse. No real person ever spoke like the characters in *Hamlet,* and the diction helps us understand that the play is not trying to imitate real life.

Aristotle formed his judgment of a play's diction from studying the ancient verse tragedies of Sophocles. Aristotle believed that the diction of the best plays has the proper amount of ornamentation and elegance. He highly valued plays that were written in verse and that used elaborate images, because he believed their diction gave an audience the greatest pleasure.

> **ASIDE**   One thing that makes Shakespeare difficult for us to read today is his diction. Shakespeare uses a larger vocabulary than we do, and the order in which he arranges words is frequently quite different from the order we're familiar with. People who grow skilled at reading Shakespeare find that they admire his diction and prefer his plays to those of many modern writers. 'Tis truth, forsooth!

Figure 2.3   The characters in David Auburn's *Proof* (left) use strong language. Some audiences find the language of plays like *Proof* and TV shows like *The Sopranos* and *Sex and the City* objectionable. Other audiences recognize that it accurately imitates real life. The diction in the vaudeville sketch in Neil Simon's *The Sunshine Boys* (right) is a rapid flow of one-line jokes.

> NURSE: *(She coughs)* Excuse me, I think I have a chest cold.
> DOCTOR: Looks more like an epidemic to me.

Music

For Aristotle, the element of **music** included everything we hear in a performance, such as the sound effects, the musical accompaniment, and the sounds of the actors' voices when they speak, chant, and sing their lines. Aristotle believed that the more the actors used their voices to embellish the playwright's words, the more deeply the audience would feel the characters' emotions. He recognized that the playwright's poetry can't be expressed by flat, dull speech and thus was particularly attentive to the variety of sounds the human voice can make. He admired actors' ability to manipulate the volume, tempo, and pitch of their speech, for he recognized that they could express emotion through the music of their voices. That explains why actors performing Greek plays—and plays by Shakespeare, Molière, and other playwrights who wrote in a "heightened" or "elevated" diction—sometimes speak differently from the way we speak everyday. The actors are providing pleasure through the sounds of their voices as well as through the intellectual content of their speeches. Just as priests chant to lend added emotion to a religious service and just as characters in a musical comedy burst into song when they're happy, so do actors in classical plays sometimes speak their lines in a melodious manner.

In today's theatre, an audience hears the performance in ways Aristotle never imagined. We have electronic music, amplified human speech, and pre-recorded sound effects. Even though technology has increased the kinds of sounds we experience in today's theatre, Aristotle's original analysis of the elements of theatre remains essentially unchanged. Music remains a less important element than plot, character, thought, and diction because it is not essential to the plot. Music enriches our experience but does not help us learn the truth, and knowledge of the truth is what gives us pleasure.

Spectacle

Aristotle's analysis of theatre led him to believe that what the audience sees is the least important of the six elements. Indeed, he might well have believed that a blind person could satisfactorily experience theatre.

EXPOSITION
• • • • • • • • • • •

Radio drama is a form of theatrical performance in which the entirety of the experience is communicated aurally. There is no spectacle. In the 1930s and 1940s, weekly radio dramas such as *The Shadow* and *The Mercury Theatre of the Air* were as popular as television programs such as *The Sopranos* and *Everybody Loves Raymond* are today. Drama can be experienced without Aristotle's sixth element.

• •

The tragedies and comedies of ancient Greece presented much less visual stimulation than does contemporary theatre. Unlike the scenery in our Broadway musicals, which is almost constantly in motion, the scenery in ancient Greek theatres was stationary. The principal actors didn't move about much, and because they wore masks their facial expressions never changed. Moreover, in Aristotle's time, there were never more than three major characters on the stage at any time. Compare that to Shakespeare's plays, in which large crowds fill the stage (Figure 2.4). Because the theatre that Aristotle analyzed was far more dependent on what the audience heard than on what it saw, he argued that **spectacle** was the sixth and least important element of the theatre.

EXPOSITION
• • • • • • • • • • •

Some examples of theatre today contain spectacle but no music. Samuel Beckett wrote a short play titled *Act Without Words*. The play has no dialogue, and the actors do not make any sounds. No music is played, and there are no sound effects. Watching it is a little like watching a silent movie, yet the play

Figure 2.4 Battle scenes in Shakespeare's history plays involve many actors and complicated patterns of movement, unlike the minimal spectacle of ancient Greek theatre.

is highly entertaining. Audiences laugh at funny bits of stage business and are profoundly moved by the plot.

Today, theatre communicates to us visually so much more than it did in the past that many theatre artists and critics think that Aristotle was wrong and the element of spectacle should be ranked higher than sixth. Theatre has become very complex visually because theatre audiences' ability to absorb visual information has been shaped by television, a medium in which visual change is a vital device for telling the story.

Reviewing the Six Elements

Aristotle's six elements provide excellent tools for analyzing and evaluating a play. You can discuss the plot by observing how it unfolds, evaluating where it is clear or confusing, and imagining what would happen if the scenes of the plot came in a different order. You can discuss the characters by evaluating how believable you found them and how they helped make the plot clear. You can analyze the meaning or thought of the play by considering how it is revealed through the plot and evaluating the relevance of the meaning to the world you live in. You can analyze the diction of the play by considering why it did or did not imitate the way we speak in everyday conversation and evaluating the appropriateness of the dialogue for the characters as well as for the overall tone of the play. You can analyze the music of the play by considering the sounds of the playwright's language and the actors' voices, the sound effects, and the songs and underscoring, and by evaluating the influence of the music on the audience. You can analyze the spectacle of the play by assessing how the scenery, costumes, and lighting contributed to or detracted from your experience. You have six new tools for analyzing a play. The next chapter will give you even more, but you can be thankful to Aristotle for giving you such a good start in *The Poetics*.

EXERCISES

1. After you have been to the theatre, form groups of three to five students and analyze the play using Aristotle's six elements. Discuss these questions:

    a. Which of the three unities did the play observe? How would the play have been different if it had observed all three unities? How would it have been different if it had observed none of them?

    b. What is the plot of the play? As a group, try to summarize it in a single sentence. (You will probably need to formulate a compound-complex sentence.)

    c. Which characters did you feel were the principal agents for the action? Support your choice with a description of how the plot was told through these characters.

    d. Did you find the music or the spectacle to be the more important of the six elements? Why?

    e. How did the diction of the play enrich your experience? Did the characters' dialogue make them believable? Did the diction relate to the meaning of the play?

2. To realize how habituated you are to visual stimulation, sit in front of your TV set, turn on any dramatic program, and mark on a piece of blank paper every time the image changes. Every time the camera cuts to a different angle or the scene changes to another location, make a mark with your pencil. You will discover that the image changes every few seconds and that you see hundreds of different pictures in a short time. If this exercise engages you, repeat it for a commercial and then for a music video. You may be astounded by how many changes your eye is habituated to seeing. Think about how different such visual complexity is from what you see in live theatre.

Dramatic Genres

A teenager fears that she hasn't been invited to a big party. "It's a *tragedy!*" she wails. Her mother says, "Oh, stop being so *melodramatic!*" From the other room, her father calls out, "The whole thing is a *farce!*" You see, you already know the important words in this chapter, but if you're anything like us, you use these words very casually and imprecisely. This chapter defines six words as they are used in analyzing a play. After you've understood and assimilated these definitions, you'll have more tools to use when you talk to your friends or write assignments for a class. You'll be better equipped to analyze and evaluate theatre.

Plays are categorized into **genres** (ZHON-ras). Each genre has different traits and evokes a different emotional response. When you are able to recognize what genre a play belongs in, you will understand what emotional response the playwright wanted you to have, and you will be able to describe to your friends how the playwright wanted you to feel and the difference between that feeling and what you actually felt.

Scholars use a whole slate of names to define the emotional reactions that various kinds of plays evoke. We will look at the six most common genres and the emotions and feelings that correspond to each.

● FORESHADOWING

Six Common Dramatic Genres

1. Comedy
2. Farce
3. Drama
4. Tragedy
5. Melodrama
6. Tragicomedy

Figure 3.1 The twinkle in Falstaff's eyes tells the audience that *The Merry Wives of Windsor* is an example of the comedy genre (John Tillotson as Falstaff for the Colorado Shakespeare Festival).

COMEDY

If the play made you laugh a lot and made you feel good because the story ended the way you wanted it to, with all the right people paired up and the world restored to order, then the play was a **comedy** (Figure 3.1). Comedy is the genre of play makes you laugh, has plots that end happily, and reaffirms the values you hold to be important.

Some people like to distinguish between **high comedy, domestic comedy,** and **low comedy.** A high comedy, sometimes called a **comedy of manners,** is filled with elegant, rich characters who are very concerned with how they behave. It gets most of its laughs from the clever things the characters say. Examples of high comedy include the classic plays of Molière (*Tartuffe* and *The Misanthrope*), the witty English comedies of Oscar Wilde and George Bernard Shaw (*The Importance of Being Earnest* and *Man and Superman*), and the elegant plays of American playwright A. R. Gurney, Jr. (*The Dining Room*). A domestic comedy is usually about middle-class people, and much of the laughter results from the awkward and embarrassing situations the characters are put in by the crafty playwright.

Figure 3.2   Larry Shue's *The Nerd* is an example of low comedy that never fails to make audiences laugh.

The situation comedies you see on TV, from *Will and Grace* to *Everybody Loves Raymond,* belong in this category. A low comedy is about characters we laugh at more because of what they do than because of what they say. Examples include the movies *Dumb and Dumber* and *Jackass* and Larry Shue's play *The Nerd* (Figure 3.2). High comedy, domestic comedy, and low comedy are three variations on the genre of comedy because all three make you laugh, have plots that end happily, and reaffirm values you hold to be important.

FARCE

A play that makes you laugh a lot and lets you feel liberated by the wildly anarchic and improbable things that happen is called a **farce.** If you've ever laughed at a Road Runner cartoon, you've experienced farce. Farces are peopled with eccentric and/or stereotypic characters (like the waiter who always drops his tray of glasses) who speak in a very simple dialogue. Farce has a very fast tempo, with characters running in and out of doors and meeting the very characters they shouldn't (Color Plate 4). While you may see a fair

The word "farce" is derived from the verb "to stuff" ("to force feed"), perhaps because the plays were "stuffed" full of physical comedy.

amount of violence in a farce, it doesn't have any serious impact. Characters get hit on the head, but their skulls don't crack open. A farce is similar to a low comedy, but there's a good way to tell them apart: in a farce the improbable happens, and when we see it we feel joyously liberated because the constraints we live with are abandoned and mayhem prevails. We all want to escape the limits of our real world, and farce lets us do so for a brief time in the imaginary world of theatre.

Great farces have been written in all ages. Many consider Michael Frayn's *Noises Off* the finest farce written in recent years. Perhaps the greatest farce playwright of all was the early twentieth-century Frenchman Georges Feydeau (zhorzhe fay-doe); his *A Flea in Her Ear* and *The Lady from Maxim's* are regularly produced. In Renaissance Italy, traveling troupes of actors performed farces, partly scripted and partly improvised, that were known as *commedia dell'arte* (ko-MAY-dee-a del AR-tay); *The Servant of Two Masters*, based on the *commedia* tradition, is often performed today.

EXPOSITION
. . . .

Slapstick is a term you've probably used to describe farce. A slapstick was a prop used in the *commedia dell'arte,* made from two boards fastened together at one end and loose at the other so it made a loud noise when an actor was hit by it and the two boards slapped together. Harlequin is a comic character who gets beaten with a slapstick in many *commedia* performances (Figure 3.3).

. . . .

Some of the finest farces were written over two thousand years ago by Aristophanes (air-iz-TOFF-a-neez). *The Birds, The Clouds,* and *Lysistrata* (Liss-i-STRAT-a) remain in our repertoire today, and Nathan Lane starred in a howlingly funny Broadway revival of *The Frogs* in 2004 that included new songs by Stephen Sondheim. After you have seen several farces, you will recognize this genre easily and will look forward to seeing many more such plays.

DRAMA

When you leave a performance of a serious play that makes you feel sad because the characters have been defeated, you have encountered a **drama.**

EXPOSITION
. . . .

Some words have several meanings. "Theatre" can refer to a building, a profession, or an entire field of intellectual study. A "play" can be the script that a playwright has written, a performance you attend, or even a planned move that a football team makes when it breaks out of a huddle. The word "drama"

Figure 3.3 The multicolor costume of Harlequin is as familiar as his slapstick. The patterning is called "pied," as in the children's story *The Pied Piper of Hamlin.*

also has many meanings. In a discussion of dramatic genres, no universally adopted word describes a serious play that is not a tragedy. Some people use the term "bourgeois drama," others call this kind of play a "serious drama," the eighteenth-century French scholar Denis Diderot called it a "drame," and many people today call it simply a "drama." Since "drama" is the term we've heard used most often by academics and professionals alike, we'll use it too.

• •

The central character in a drama struggles for something you believe is worth desiring, and you root for the character to get it. When he or she fails, it's almost the same as your not achieving the goal, and you feel sad. The character's defeat reminds you that the world is not the way you wish it to be—the good die young, the sick don't recover, the boy doesn't get the girl, and nobody lives happily ever after (Figure 3.4). You are reminded of some truths that you know but have managed to ignore. But the strange fact is that audiences *enjoy* dramas. We tell ourselves that we only want to watch comedies, which make us happy and take us away from our everyday problems, but dramas give us a different sort of pleasure. They let us feel our deepest emotions without being

Figure 3.4   Henrik Ibsen's *Ghosts* tells the story of a mother whose son is dying from an inherited disease. This sad play is an example of the drama genre.

Figure 3.5 *Fences* is the most popular play by African American playwright August Wilson. Following a successful Broadway production starring James Earl Jones, the play was performed in theatres across America. This photo is from the Milwaukee Repertory Theatre production, in which Lawrence James played the central role of Troy.

personally involved. We know that the outcomes of the play will not directly affect our own lives. Tennessee Williams's *The Glass Menagerie,* August Wilson's *Fences* (Figure 3.5), and Nilo Cruz's Pulitzer Prize–winning *Anna in the Tropics* (Color Plate 5) are excellent examples of the genre we call "drama."

TRAGEDY

"Tragedy" is the most misused term you'll come upon in discussions of theatre. One reason for the misuse is that most of us have never experienced a tragedy—not in the theatre and not in our lives. We regularly apply the term "tragedy" to anything sad, but a play that tries to make you feel sad is a drama, not a tragedy. A **tragedy** is a serious play that tries to make you feel exhilarated because the hero's experience teaches you some profound truth about your life. Far from making you feel sad, a tragedy guides you toward feeling a sort of calm affirmation that your worst expectations about life are true. You feel wiser for reaching this certainty.

EXPOSITION
• • • • • • • • • • • •

The word "tragedy" comes from the ancient Greek and means "Goat Song." The Greeks wrote and performed plays as part of religious festivals, just as many Americans today celebrate the holidays of Christmas and Passover

Figure 3.6   The noble-hearted labor organizer Joe Hill waits in a prison cell for the executioner's squad while his close friend mourns for him. Barrie Stavis's modern tragedy *The Man Who Never Died* was produced by the National Theatre of Cyprus.

with theatrical pageants. The Greeks honored the god Dionysus (DIE-o-NICE-us), the god of wine, ecstasy, fertility, and theatre. Dionysus was associated with the goat, an important source of milk and food in early Greek culture, and was sometimes depicted in art and literature as having the attributes of a goat. In early Greek religious festivals, people sang choral odes to Dionysus, and those "goat songs" slowly evolved into dramas that are among the greatest tragedies ever written: *Antigone, Electra, Oedipus the King.*

Unlike a drama, a tragedy touches you directly. In a true tragedy, you feel awe for the central character, who, despite knowing that the goal can be attained only at the cost of his or her own destruction, brings ruin down on all concerned by continuing to seek the goal because doing so is the only way to be true to his or her own self (Figure 3.6). A tragedy makes you feel proud that such characters exist, but at the same time you feel pity for what happens to them. You admire characters, like Othello, who defend their integrity even when it requires them to kill both their loved ones and themselves (Color Plate 6). You come away from a tragedy knowing something more about yourself. You know how to live your life differently, and that knowledge exhilarates you.

MELODRAMA

The plays we encounter most often and respond to most enthusiastically are the plays that touch us least profoundly. Called **melodramas,** these plays

Figure 3.7 Plays about courtroom trials, such as *Inherit the Wind,* typically are melodramas in which the plots are more important than the characters and good triumphs over evil.

provide entertainment that has the appearance of being serious but ends with the protagonist being victorious. You know that the plots and characters in the *Star Wars* and *Indiana Jones* movies are not serious, but you get caught up in the stories. Melodramas focus more on their complicated plots than on their two-dimensional characters (Figure 3.7). A melodrama provides a story with many exciting twists that are intensified by the thrilling music used to underscore the action. Melodramas teach a very simple moral—usually that good conquers evil—and you don't take melodramas seriously because you know they don't reflect the truth of life. Instead, they reflect the way you wish life could be. You wish the cops would catch the drug pushers, but you know that this rarely happens. Melodrama reinforces the view of life you wish were true, and it does so with a terrifically exciting story and with psychologically straightforward characters who nevertheless overcome physical challenges no real person could conquer. Melodrama provides a diversion from life's real problems. While it may be true that tragedy is more sublime because it affects the way we truly live, melodrama gives us pleasure of a different sort.

The nineteenth century had a popular kind of theatre that was called "10-20-30 melodrama" because the price of admission was as little as ten cents. Today's equivalent is a low-budget action movie.

ASIDE   The word "melodrama" combines "melody" and "drama." Before the invention of movies, nonmusical plays were accompanied by a small orchestra that played melodies to help the audience feel the emotions of the story. When the music encouraged emotional responses that were excessively sentimental or overly excited, the drama became debased. That is why we often use the word "melodramatic" pejoratively to describe something excessive. Today, such underscoring commonly is used to increase the emotional response to daytime soap operas and adventure films.

TRAGICOMEDY

If you leave the theatre feeling agitated, frustrated, and anxious, you have seen a **tragicomedy.** The composite word "tragicomedy" gives you some clue that these plays are made up partly of the serious subject matter of tragedy and partly of the laugh-inducing stuff of comedy. You laugh at the serious things, you cry at the funny things, and you feel disoriented and discombobulated. This genre developed in the twentieth century in an era philosophers call the "Age of Anxiety," which continues today. The human condition seems more uncertain than ever. The bomb could drop at any moment. A terrorist could blow up your church. Our sense of safety is slipping, and the old comforts of religion and political authority don't hold as much assurance for us as they once did. Tragicomedies reflect this truth of the human condition and try to make us feel anxious.

EXPOSITION
• • • • • • • • • • •

The avant-garde plays of the mid- to late twentieth century were almost all tragicomedies and are usually described as examples of the **theatre of the absurd.** Plays such as Eugene Ionesco's *The Bald Soprano,* Edward Albee's *The American Dream,* and Samuel Beckett's *Waiting for Godot* are funny-sad-frightening plays that examine the absurdities of the human condition (Color Plate 7).

• •

REVIEWING THE SIX GENRES

Now that you are familiar with the six most common genres and understand what kind of emotional response each genre tries to evoke, you can figure out whether the playwright has succeeded. For example, you might be tempted to say, like the architect in Virginia, "I didn't like that damned play" when what you really mean is "The play was a success because I felt uncomfortable." Knowing that discomfort is precisely the emotion a tragicomedy *intends* to elicit will help you understand why you felt the way you did.

In Chapter 2 you learned about *The Poetics,* and particularly about Aristotle's description of the six elements of theatre. In this chapter, you have learned to define six categories of dramatic genre. This additional knowledge will help you understand how and why one play makes an audience laugh and another play makes an audience cry. Of course, if a play is poorly performed, you might laugh at something intended to make you cry. If that happens, you'll know how to identify the emotional response the play *should* have evoked, and you'll be ready to evaluate why it failed. To add to the tools in your toolbox, in the next chapter Tom and I will introduce you to the subject of theatrical styles.

EXERCISES

1. Choose two students from your class, so that together you form a group of three. Have each of you independently videotape one TV show (or check it out of a library or rental store) that you believe is an example of domestic comedy and another that is an example of a farce. Make a list of the traits of the genre that you find in the TV shows you have chosen. Meet to discuss your choices, using the tapes as illustration. Be prepared to defend your choice and to challenge the choices made by the other two members of your group.

2. After all students in the class have attended the same play, each student should mark a "ballot" provided by the instructor to select the genre of the play. In class, tabulate the ballots to discover what genre the majority has chosen. In groups of ten to twelve students, discuss the play in terms of the traits of the two genres that received the most votes. The goal is to discover whether a unanimous agreement can be reached among the students.

Theatrical Styles

When you see a play with scenery that looks like a real room, costumes that look like real clothes, and characters that talk and behave like people you know, you are seeing the theatrical **style** called **Realism.** Realism is what you see on TV and in the movies most of the time. Realism imitates the world in a way that is familiar to us. We like plays that seem true to life.

What about theatre that is obviously different from real life—musicals like *Cats,* for example, in which the scenery is a prettily painted junkyard, the costumes are colorful and exaggerated, and the characters are cats that sing and dance around like no cats you've ever seen (and with more skill than most people you know)? It is obvious that musicals imitate the world in a different way from Realism.

All theatre imitates reality. In this chapter, you'll learn about six different ways theatre does this, that is, six different **theatrical styles.** "Style" is the word we use to describe *how* an artist imitates reality. The six styles divide naturally into three related pairs. The first pair expresses the view of playwrights who imitate **objective reality** and show us the world through a scientist's eye; their plays invite us to evaluate things by what they look like and how familiar they sound. The second pair expresses the view of playwrights who imitate **subjective reality;** their plays show us how the artist *feels* about reality, how his or her feelings influence the way things look, and how sounds and dialogue can be unfamiliar. The third pair expresses the view of playwrights who imitate an **idealized reality** in which the world is perfect; their plays show us how the artist *wishes* the world looked. In idealized reality, people speak in beautiful poetry or break into song and young lovers live happily ever after (even young cats).

The names for the six styles are borrowed from literature, painting, and music, so they might be familiar to you. Linda has created six line drawings of the same house for this chapter to illustrate the different ways each of the six styles imitates reality. The house she used as a model is shown in the photograph in Figure 4.1.

Each of the six styles has traits you can recognize. We describe them in this chapter to help you understand why a production looks the way it does. The traits result from the fact that each style is based on an understanding of the world that was popular at the time it was created. Realism, for example,

We sometimes think of Realism as the one true style and all the others as unreal, clumping the other five together and calling them"stylized." But Realism is merely the most familiar of the six styles. No single style is better or truer than another. All are equally valuable ways to help us see and understand the truth of our world.

Figure 4.1 Realism on stage would require a convincing imitation of this real house.

was a brand new style in the late nineteenth century; it became the dominant style for nearly a hundred years and remains the most familiar style today. Each of the six styles illustrates a different way reality can be shown and a different way truth can be understood.

FORESHADOWING

The Six Theatrical Styles

Two styles of imitating *objective* reality:

- Realism
- Theatricalism

Two styles of imitating *subjective* reality:

- Expressionism
- Surrealism

Two styles of imitating *idealized* reality:

- Classicism
- Romanticism

Most of the examples and illustrations in this chapter are from Tennessee Williams's *The Glass Menagerie* and Samuel Beckett's *Waiting for Godot*. *The Glass Menagerie* was first produced in 1944, about a decade before *Waiting for Godot*. Both plays were bold experiments in theatrical style that have had a profound influence on the way plays have been written and produced in the subsequent fifty years. Some of you may know these famous plays, and others can take this opportunity to read or see them. To speed your learning about theatrical style, we give a brief plot synopsis and description of both plays here.

EXPOSITION

• • • • • • • • • • •

Two productions of *The Glass Menagerie* and four productions of *Waiting for Godot* are available on DVD or videotape. Your college library should have some of these, and you can find information about all of them in the videography on the text Web site.

• •

The Glass Menagerie takes place in a tenement apartment in St. Louis. A fire escape leads up from an alley to a landing that serves as a porch, and a door leads into the front room. A dining room is visible upstage, while a kitchenette and two bedrooms are mentioned but not seen. The sparsely and shabbily furnished apartment includes a sofa bed, an old-fashioned wind-up Victrola, an end table, a dining room table and chairs, and a what-not shelf with a collection of tiny glass animals on it. A window with lace curtains looks out on the alley (Color Plate 8).

There are four characters in the play: the three members of the Wingfield family and a "gentleman caller" named Jim O'Connor. Tom Wingfield, the central character and also the narrator, speaks directly to the audience and then steps into the scenes to play the part he lived several years earlier, when he was in his early twenties in the late 1930s. His sister, Laura, is two years older. She is extremely shy and has a slight limp. Their mother, Amanda, is an aging but flirtatious and flamboyant Southern belle who married a man who worked for the telephone company and later abandoned his family (Figure 4.2).

The story is simple. Tom hates his dreary $65-a-month job in the warehouse, and he longs to run away to join the merchant marines and become a poet. He is torn between accepting responsibility as the breadwinner for his family and fulfilling his desire to run off to a life of his own. He cares greatly for his fragile sister but is oppressed by his overbearing mother. Amanda wants Tom to invite a friend home for dinner, because she believes the best future possible for Laura is through marriage. Tom recognizes that his sister not only is slightly crippled and very shy but also lives much of the time in a dreamworld populated by her glass animals.

ASIDE   As a student actor, I played the role of Tom in *The Glass Menagerie.* There's a furious family quarrel in which Tom yells at his mother, "You ugly—babbling old—*witch!*" My tongue slipped in one performance, and I blurted "You ugly—wabbling old—*bitch!*" Later, the actress playing Amanda winked at me and asked, "What does wabbling mean?"

Figure 4.2 The Cleveland Play House's production of *The Glass Menagerie* featured African American actors. The cast (clockwise from left): Leon Addison Brown as Tom, David Toney as Jim, Josephine Premise as Amanda, and Shawn Judge as Laura.

Tom invites Jim O'Connor to dinner, but Laura is so shy she can't sit at the table. Though Jim doesn't know it, Laura had a crush on him when they were both in high school, five years earlier (Figure 4.3). In what may be the play's most famous scene, Jim encourages Laura to value herself. However, when he reveals that he is engaged to be married, the news crushes Laura's hopes. At the end of the play, Tom, now a merchant marine who has traveled far from his mother and sister, tells the audience how the memory of his sister is always with him.

Williams described *The Glass Menagerie* as a "memory play," and we meet the characters and experience the events of the story as they are filtered through Tom's remembrance. In this chapter you will learn that seeing a play through the eyes of the central character is a trait of the style called **Expressionism;** however, *The Glass Menagerie* does not fit a narrow, academic definition of that style. Williams used the term more loosely. He wrote the play at a time when many experiments in theatrical style challenged the Realism that prevailed on the American stage. In his production notes, Williams says that the aim of Expressionism and all other "unconventional techniques" is to find a penetrating and vivid way to express reality. Accordingly, he allows producers the freedom to present the play in whatever way they desire.

When you read *The Glass Menagerie,* you will discover that Williams included stage directions that call for the projection of written captions of the

Figure 4.3 Amanda and Laura look at Jim O'Connor's picture in Laura's high school annual. Laura's glass animals are on the table in the foreground in this photo from the Milwaukee Repertory Theatre production.

kind we call supertitles in opera or see on the bottom of our TV screens, as well as the projection of visual images that are poetic expressions of the mood in certain scenes (Figures 4.4 and 4.5 and Color Plate 9). The original production of *The Glass Menagerie* did not follow Williams's stage directions because director Eddie Dowling and designer Donald Oenslager felt that the "legends" (as Williams called them) would detract from the audience's emotional response (Figure 4.6). Most productions follow the original Broadway production, but there have been enough varied productions of *Menagerie* to provide us with useful illustrations for our discussion of theatrical styles.

Waiting for Godot was written by Samuel Beckett, an Irishman who lived in Paris and wrote in French. A strange and avant-garde play when it first appeared in 1953, in only a few decades *Waiting for Godot* has become a classic that many people describe as the most important play written in the twentieth century. The play takes place on a country road. The stage directions don't specify which country, where the road leads, what the climate is, or the time of day. The only distinguishing things the audience can see are a rock big enough to sit on and a tree. The ground is flat and the sky clear. The setting is a barren wilderness that could be almost anywhere, as you can see in Color Plate 7.

There are five characters in the play. They all dress in old-fashioned clothes that suggest the years around the turn of the twentieth century, but their derby hats are dusty and their suits worn and wrinkled. Their clothes

Figure 4.4   Scene designer Beate Czogalla used soft hanging muslin for the sail-shaped "walls" of the Wingfield's apartment in her production at Georgia College & State University, and the words and images in Williams's script were projected on the cloths by lighting designer Jared Moore. The cloths were suspended in midair with strapping. Director Walter Bilderback explained that "I [used] most of Williams's suggestions for slides, which undercuts the sentimentality in a highly ironic and sometimes campy fashion." This picture shows Laura (Mandy Butler) clutching her glass animals as Tom (Ben Davis) and Amanda (Diane Sullivan) quarrel upstage of a cloth "wall." In keeping with the Theatricalist style of this production, the audience saw only their silhouettes. The projection of Williams's legend echoes Tom's line of dialogue: "You think I'm in love with Continental Shoemakers?"

Godot is pronounced go-DOUGH by Americans and by French speakers, but the English stress the first syllable: GOD-oh.

make them look like bums or like the comic characters of old silent movies that were portrayed by actors such as Charlie Chaplin, Buster Keaton, or Stan Laurel and Oliver Hardy.

The two main characters are Vladimir (known by his nickname, Didi) and Estragon (Gogo). These roles have been played by great comic actors, including Bert Lahr, Steve Martin, and Robin Williams (Figure 4.7). Didi is intellectual and analytical. He continually tries to figure out where he is, what he is doing, and what things mean. He speaks in long, complex sentences and sometimes grows morose and despondent. In contrast, his companion, Gogo, is optimistic yet very emotional and immature. He responds excitedly to whatever happens around him, and he speaks in short phrases.

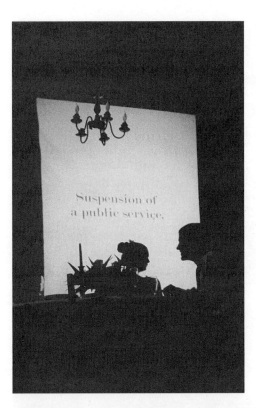

Figure 4.5 "Suspension of a public service" is the legend for the scene in Act Two when the lights go out because Tom has not paid the electric bill. Williams's ironic comment might suggest that the "public service" of bringing a gentleman caller home for Laura soon will also be suspended.

Figure 4.6 The scenery for the original Broadway production of *The Glass Menagerie* included a scrim painted with bricks to suggest the exterior wall of the apartment building. When there was light upstage of the scrim, the audience could see through it to the interior of the Wingfield's apartment as Tom remembers the events that happened there. Here, Eddie Dowling talks to the audience while Laurette Taylor helps Julie Hayden prepare for the arrival of the Gentleman Caller.

Figure 4.7   The roles of Gogo and Didi have always attracted great comedians and famous actors. Bert Lahr is best remembered as the Cowardly Lion in the movie *The Wizard of Oz,* but he was also a Broadway star. He played Gogo in the first American production of *Waiting for Godot* (top). E. G. Marshall played Didi. Do you recognize Marshall from films and television? Robin Williams played Gogo and Steve Martin was Didi in a New York revival of *Waiting for Godot* in the 1990s (bottom).

The two men appear to have known each other for a long time. They are waiting for another man, named Godot. They have a vague recollection that they are supposed to meet him, but they are not confident that they're in the right place, nor do they know when Godot said he would arrive or what he looks like. While they are waiting for Godot to arrive, they pass the time by playing games, discussing their religious beliefs, remembering events from their past, looking for food, doing exercises, telling jokes, and quarreling about who Godot is and whether they should continue to wait for him. None of their activities brings positive results. Nothing they do leads to Godot's

Figure 4.8 The four main characters in *Waiting for Godot* in the Virginia Museum Theatre's production. Front row: William Denis as Gogo and Jerry Matz as Didi; back row: William Preston as Lucky and Robert Foley as Pozzo. Note the rope in Pozzo's hand and the noose around Lucky's neck.

arrival, and they never understand why they are waiting for him or who he is. Yet they go on waiting.

Two other men arrive. One, named Pozzo (POT-zo), carries a whip, speaks in stern commands, and thinks he is important. He is preceded by a very, very old man named Lucky. Lucky carries an armful of luggage, including a picnic basket, and he staggers under the weight of his burden. He has a noose around his neck, as shown in Figure 4.8, and the end of the rope is held by Pozzo as if it were a leash and Lucky his dog. When these two strange men arrive, Didi and Gogo at first think Pozzo might be Godot. After they learn he is not, they question him about a number of things. But Pozzo has no answers that make sense to them. To pass the time, they ask Pozzo to have Lucky perform for them. Lucky begins a bizarre dance and then is given the command "Speak." He launches into a very long speech that sounds like gibberish. Though there are phrases we can understand and he seems to be giving a lecture on philosophy, his ramblings have no apparent logic. When he is finished, Pozzo and Lucky continue their journey. They don't know where they are headed any more than they know where they have come from. They know only that they must stagger on.

Pozzo and Lucky leave, and Didi and Gogo are alone again. They grow sad. The day is ending, and Godot has not come. What should they do? Where should they go? Suddenly a young boy arrives with a message. Mr. Godot won't arrive today, but surely he'll come tomorrow (Figure 4.9). The boy leaves as night falls and the moon rises. Didi and Gogo, having nothing

A three-minute cartoon version of Waiting for Godot *can be seen at www.musearts.com/ cartoons/pigs/godot.html.*

Figure 4.9 Boy tells Gogo that Godot surely will come tomorrow.

Figure 4.10 At the end of the play, Didi and Gogo sit to wait for Godot.

else to do, talk about leaving but instead just sit on the ground to wait. That's the end of Act One.

Act Two, though quite a bit shorter, follows much the same pattern. Didi and Gogo are still waiting for Godot. They engage in pastimes that alternately entertain and depress them. Pozzo and Lucky return, but this time Pozzo is blind and Lucky can no longer speak. They stay for a much shorter time and then stagger off, leaving Didi and Gogo alone again, morose and dejected. The boy arrives with a similar message. Godot won't come today, but surely he'll come tomorrow. Didi and Gogo are alone as night falls. What should they do? They consider hanging themselves from the tree but discover they can't. They agree to leave but don't. At the end of the play, they are where they were at the beginning—alone in the wilderness, waiting for Godot (Figure 4.10).

Much of *Waiting for Godot* is very funny. Some of it is sad. All of it stirs scholars and critics to ponder its mysteries and meaning, and in the theatre it has fascinated and entertained audiences for half a century. Because both *Waiting for Godot* and *The Glass Menagerie* have been produced in a variety of styles, they provide examples that will help you understand the six styles of theatre.

OBJECTIVE REALITY

Realism

Realism, the dominant theatrical style of the past century, is based on the philosophy called **Determinism** that was popular in the third quarter of the nineteenth century. As scientists increased their knowledge of human biology and social scientists learned about the socioeconomic pressures that influence our behavior, their combined knowledge led to the belief that people are "determined" by forces beyond our control and are the product of our environment and our genetic inheritance. Our bodies and our intelligence are determined by the genes of our natural parents, and our behavior is determined by the socioeconomic circumstances in which we were raised. Determinism celebrates logic and science and discards two ideas that had been believed for centuries: the idea that we are preordained by God and he has determined our nature, and the idea that we have free will and can make ourselves into whatever we wish. Determinism sees us instead as the victims of both natural and social forces beyond our control.

Playwrights accepted Determinism as describing the truth of human nature, and audiences believed that they could learn the truth by studying how characters behave in a play. Like the scientist who looks at an insect under a microscope, an audience looks at an imitation of human behavior through the intensifying frame surrounding a stage. By imitating apparent reality, theatre presents examples of reality for us to study. We analyze the characters' behavior to learn *why* they behave as they do, and this helps us understand why *we* behave as we do. Scenery and costumes imitate the rooms and clothes we see about us because these are the environmental influences that shape us. Dialogue imitates the speech of real people who have been shaped by their genetic inheritance. Realism imitates apparent reality in order to show us the truth.

EXPOSITION
• • • • • • • • • • • •

You will also hear the term **"Naturalism."** Realism and Naturalism are used interchangeably today, though a century ago they had slightly different meanings. Some scholars continue to insist that there is a difference between the two styles, claiming that Naturalism imitates apparent reality in absolute detail and focuses on the ugly, unpleasant, and commonplace in our lives, while Realism imitates apparent reality selectively and may focus on the pleasant aspects of life as well as on the dreary. For the purposes of this introductory book, both words are correct. Most people today use the term "Realism" more frequently.

Almost all the dramas we see in the movies and on television are realistic and imitate the world we see around us. We can imagine ourselves talking with the characters, driving in the cars, and living in a house that looks like the drawing in Figure 4.11. But Realism is not limited to imitating the world we live in. It can also imitate the world of an earlier time (Figure 4.12) or of an exotic land, such as the China of Henry David Hwang's *M. Butterfly*, where people wear clothes that are different from ours (Figure 4.13). As long as we believe that what we are seeing exists now or existed once or exists somewhere, the style is Realism (Figures 4.14 and 4.15).

REVIEW

Reality Check of the Three Traits by Which Realism Can Be Identified

1. Does it look like a world you know or one you believe existed at some earlier time or in some exotic land?
2. Do the characters speak in a language you believe people speak now or spoke at some earlier time or in some exotic land?
3. Do things happen for reasons you can understand, and is there a logic to why things happen the way they do?

Figure 4.11   This line drawing of the house shown in Figure 4.1 is an artist's rendition of the style of Realism.

Figure 4.12 Note the realistic detail of the set and costumes for this production of Dickens's *A Christmas Carol*. This example of Realism is set during the mid-nineteenth century.

Figure 4.13 Henry David Hwang's *M. Butterfly* is set in twentieth-century China and includes scenes performed in the exotic and unfamiliar conventions of Chinese opera. Even though this looks "unreal" to us, it is an example of Realism because it accurately imitates what the real world looks like.

Figure 4.14 The style of most films is Realism. This photo from the movie version of *The Glass Menagerie* shows the objective reality of the play's world in accurate and complete detail.

Figure 4.15 This production of *Waiting for Godot* was made for television as part of the *Beckett on Film* series. Though it was shot in a sound studio, the absolute detail of set and costumes illustrates the style of Realism.

Theatricalism

Theatricalism is based on the belief that, as Shakespeare wrote, "all the world's a stage and all the men and women merely players." Theatricalism

Figure 4.16   The style of Theatricalism is illustrated in this self-referential photo in which Tom performs the role of "Tom" taking a photo of Linda performing the role of "Linda" taking a photo of Tom. Note that we both are wearing modern clothes but are reflected in a mirror with an ornate rococo frame not unlike the frame of a decorative proscenium arch (see Figure 13.3).

shows us the truth of our world by imitating our objective imitations of it; that is, Theatricalism imitates the way theatre imitates life. Theatricalism recognizes that we are self-conscious creatures who perceive our own actions as part of a performance. We know that we're acting in our everyday lives, as illustrated by the self-conscious photo in Figure 4.16. Theatricalism shows us the truth of the self-conscious performance we call "living."

Theatricalism became a popular style in the mid-twentieth century. A famous example of this style is Thornton Wilder's play *Our Town,* in which a character named the Stage Manager talks directly to the audience and tells them who the characters are and where the action is taking place. The audience sees the objective reality of an empty stage but is asked to imagine the kitchens and drugstore that the Stage Manager describes in words, while the actors walk about on the stage, pantomiming doors, newspapers, and ice cream sodas. The objective reality is a theatre, and the performance imitates the way theatre imitates life (Figure 4.17).

At one level, the performance is about theatre, and Theatricalism displays how theatre creates the illusion of objective reality (Figure 14.18). The scene design for productions in the style of Theatricalism boldly reminds the audience that they are attending a play and sometimes shows the audience a reflection of themselves (Figure 4.19). The philosophical truth that Theatricalism shows us is that separating illusion from reality is as difficult as distinguishing between a real event and a theatrical imitation of it. To make this point clear, Theatricalism shows us how theatre creates its illusions: scenery

Our Town won the Pulitzer Prize for drama in 1938. Paul Newman starred in the 2003 Broadway revival that later was videotaped on stage, was broadcast nationally in 2004, and soon will be available on video and DVD.

Figure 4.17 *Our Town* takes place in the present moment, but the character of the Stage Manager tells us to imagine that the action is taking place long ago. In this scene, George Gibbs and Emily Webb sit at a "soda fountain," which we can see is only a wooden plank set on the back of two chairs, while they watch the Stage Manager play the role of the "drugstore owner" pretending to make ice cream sodas. The actors' precise pantomime helps the audience imagine a real drugstore counter and sodas, and we delight in participating in the imitation of the way theatre imitates real life.

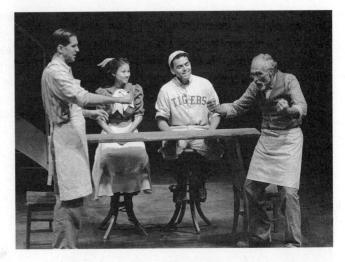

Figure 4.18 The real house shown in Figure 4.1 is drawn here in the style of Theatricalism. Notice how the house announces that it is a house.

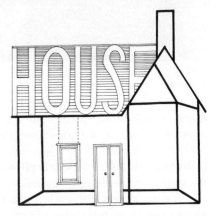

is changed before our eyes, actors put on their costumes as we watch, and characters speak directly to us, explaining when they are "inside" the play and when they are "outside" it (Figure 4.20).

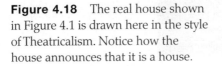
REVIEW

Reality Check of the Four Traits by Which Theatricalism Can Be Identified

1. Is the action set in a theatre?
2. Do the characters play roles in a play within a play?
3. Does the production show you how the theatre works, for example, how scenery moves and how actors assume their characters?
4. Does the play demonstrate how hard it is to distinguish between illusion and reality?

Figure 4.19   Josef Svoboda (SVO-bud-a), a very influential twentieth-century scene designer, created the scenery for this production of *Waiting for Godot* in the style of Theatricalism. The action was set in a theatre. The stage design repeated the architectural box seating areas of the auditorium, and the upstage wall was a multipaneled mirror that reflected the actors, the tree in the center of the stage, the auditorium of the theatre, and the audience. The audience watched itself watch the actors acting their roles in the play.

Figure 4.20   Tom Wingfield sits "inside" his own memory in this production of *The Glass Menagerie.* Compare this picture to Figure 4.6, in which Tom is "outside" the place and time of his memory, separated by a scrim painted to suggest the exterior of the apartment building. Here Tom is simultaneously talking to the audience in the present moment and sitting in the apartment he lived in in the past. The conventions of Theatricalism invite us to keep in mind that we are participating in the creation of the play.

Figure 4.21

How to Look at Modern Art

Lamp on a table

The form of a lamp from one point of view

The form of a lamp from two points of view

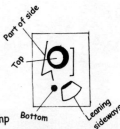

The form of a lamp from many points of view

SUBJECTIVE REALITY

Expressionism and Surrealism both imitate *subjective* reality. In order to explain these styles, we first need to describe the intellectual and historical context in which they evolved. The same curiosity that led some scientists to seek truth by studying our objective experience led others to seek it by studying our subjective experience. In the final decade of the nineteenth century, not too long after Realism became the dominant theatrical style, doctors such as Sigmund Freud began to study the way dreams reveal the truth of human experience and how our conscious actions are influenced by our subconscious desires. At about the same time, playwrights such as Sweden's August Strindberg began to write strange new dramas called "dream plays." A few decades later, these scientific and theatrical innovations combined to inspire German playwrights to develop Expressionism and French playwrights to develop Surrealism. These playwrights were part of what is called the Modernist Movement, a development in literature, music, and the visual arts that dominated the first half of the twentieth century. **Modern Art** rebelled against the representation of objective reality. The artists chose instead to express the unconscious, the primitive, and the irrational truth of the human condition through abstraction (Figure 4.21).

Why was Modern Art dissatisfied with the truth of objective reality? Artists rejected Realism because they wanted to show the deeper truth hidden by outward appearances. Both Expressionism and Surrealism show us how the artist *feels* about the essential truth of the world, instead of what the artist *thinks* about the objective appearance of the world. These styles show us a visually distorted picture of the world and express the profound truth known to the artist—the truth that we may never have recognized or have tried to ignore.

EXPOSITION
• • • • • • • • • •

The difference between objective and subjective reality is the subject of *The Picture of Dorian Gray,* a wonderful story by Oscar Wilde that has been made

Figure 4.22   Hurd Hatfield played the title role in the film version of *The Picture of Dorian Gray*. His appearance remains unchanged until the end of the film, but the painting in Figure 4.23 shows what the interior truth of his character had become.

Figure 4.23   Ivan Albright's "The Picture of Dorian Gray" (1943–1944) is in the style of Expressionism and shows the interior truth of Dorian Gray's corrupt, diseased character.

into a fine movie. Dorian Gray is a handsome and honorable young man who has his portrait painted (Figure 4.22). When he sees how admirable he looks in the painting, he wishes that he could keep his looks forever and that the painting instead would change as he ages. He gets his wish. To everyone's astonishment, Dorian's appearance never changes. But as he becomes more debauched and evil, the *painting* changes. It shows his inward truth, which is very different from his outward appearance (Figure 4.23). Dorian hides the painting so no one else can see it, and at the end of the story he stabs it. The painting reverts to showing the handsome and pure young man, but Dorian himself turns into the grotesque, worm-eaten, bloody monster that he is in truth. Only then is his subjective reality seen by others. They are no longer deceived by the misleading appearance of his objective reality.

• •

Expressionism

Expressionism is a style that developed in early-twentieth-century Germany after doctors theorized that we can learn the truth about ourselves by analyzing

Figure 4.24 The real house shown in Figure 4.1 is drawn here in the style of Expressionism. The distorted shape and severe angles suggest the artist's emotional reaction to the house.

the images in our dreams. Expressionism is based on the belief that dreams reveal the truth we hide from ourselves in our waking state, that the wildly distorted images that we see when we dream are what we truly feel (Figure 4.24). According to Expressionism, dream images are our honest perception of reality. When we are able to analyze and understand the distorted images of our dreams, we learn the truth.

Expressionism depicts violent and extreme emotions because it developed at a time when artists felt frightened by the way big government and big industry were exploiting people. The average human was being turned into a cog in a big machine that produced money but oppressed individuality. The Expressionists were angry, and they created theatre that expressed their rage at the way humankind was losing its freedom. As a result, Expressionistic theatre has an angry tone and a shocking appearance and expresses itself in violent language. It shows the world as a terrifying nightmare, as you can see in the photo from the classic Expressionistic film *The Cabinet of Dr. Caligari* (Figure 4.25). Expressionists feared that a conflict between capitalist businesses would lead to war and that war would crush the average person. When World War I broke out in 1914, they saw their nightmares come true.

Expressionism was born when theatre developed the techniques for showing subjective reality in objective form. The first technique of Expressionism is to show the world through the eyes of the central character. Because Expressionists believed that people (and therefore their characters) were the victims of an oppressive industrial society, their central characters see a world that threatens them. This view led to scenery, costume, and makeup designs that made use of highly contrasting or extremely intense and garish colors (reds and oranges and blacks) or that had sharp angles that seemed about to stab at the characters, as seen in Figure 4.26. A second trait

Figure 4.25   The 1919 film *The Cabinet of Dr. Caligari* is an excellent example of Expressionism. Note the sharp angles in the design, the high contrast in the black-and-white composition, and the actors' exaggerated makeup. This picture shows the moment in the story when the dummy is discovered in the box. See the text's Web site for a description and plot synopsis of *The Cabinet of Dr. Caligari.*

is that only the central character is psychologically complex, with all the others seen through the main character's eyes and exhibiting only a single symbolic trait. Their names describe their jobs (the Doctor, the Policeman) or their relationship to the central character (the Friend, the Seducer). A third trait is that the dialogue, rather than imitating real speech, is instead filled with angry descriptions of violence and frequently is compressed so that it sounds like a message you'd find on a Post-it note: *"DOWNER NEWS! MALL! BACK 7! DINNER OUT!"* You can reconstruct the full message from the fragments: "I have received some very distressing news, and I have gone to the mall. I will be home around seven o'clock. Why don't we plan to have dinner at a restaurant instead of eating at home?" In Expressionism, a character's emotion often is so extreme that he or she is unable to speak in grammatically complete sentences.

Expressionism is no longer the startling theatrical innovation it was ninety years ago, so if your local college revives an Expressionistic play such as *The Adding Machine* (Figure 4.27), take advantage of the opportunity to see it. You may be excited to discover how this fascinating style affects you. You can see an Expressionistic sequence in the film *Casino Real,* a spoof of the James Bond movies. Also, some violent video games are Expressionistic; in them you see the world subjectively, and when the villain comes to get you the garish colors, sharp angles, distorted proportions, and violent sounds of the game's world are nightmarish.

Figure 4.26 This Expressionistic scene design for *Waiting for Godot* (top) has sharp angles and stark contrasts. It creates a world that presses dangerously on the place where Didi and Gogo wait. Another world is seen through Tom Wingfield's eyes in this Expressionistic scene design for *The Glass Menagerie* (bottom). The floor and furniture are askew, and the surrounding buildings lean in threateningly.

The Glass Menagerie

L. Sarver

R E V I E W

Reality Check of the Four Traits by Which Expressionism Can Be Identified

1. Do you experience the story through the eyes of the central character, and is that character a tormented victim of society, business, or war?

Figure 4.27   Elmer Rice's *The Adding Machine* was written in the style of Expressionism. The revival shown here was directed by Jerry B. Cleveland at Wayne State University in Detroit. Actors Abe Dahlallah and Sarah Garza played Mr. Zero and Daisy, and the scenery was designed by Nick Rupard. Note the strangely angled furniture and the cogs of a big machine that illustrate the abstract world as seen through Mr. Zero's tormented vision.

2. Are the scenery, costumes, and makeup distorted, and do the designs use intense color and sharp angles?
3. Do the characters speak in short, fragmented dialogue?
4. Do most of the characters have names that describe what they do rather than individualized names?

Surrealism

Surrealism, which developed in France in the peaceful years following World War I, is based on the belief that the images in our subconscious reveal the truth and that the truth can be beautiful, lyrical, and sometimes very funny. Instead of rendering the dark nightmares of Expressionism, Surrealism puts on stage the fantastical and whimsical images from our subconscious (Figure 4.28).

ASIDE   Alfred Hitchcock directed a suspense film with Gregory Peck and Ingrid Bergman called *Spellbound* (not to be confused with the 2003

(continued)

Figure 4.28   The real house shown in Figure 4.1 is drawn here in the style of Surrealism. The artist has shown a dreamlike and playful attitude. The chimney becomes a human form, the window winks at you, and the stairs have turned into a long tongue.

film of the same title that is about a national spelling competition). In the middle of Hitchcock's *Spellbound* is a dream sequence that was designed by Salvador Dalí, a famous Surrealist painter. Dalí's visual rendering of the dream complements a doctor's explanation of how a psychoanalyst helps a patient understand the meaning of a dream. As the doctor describes the character's dreams, we are shown how the dreamer turned a ski slope into the roof of a house and how a revolver became a wagon wheel. We learn how the psychoanalyst's analysis of the dream images helps the dreamer understand the truth of his experiences in the same way an analysis of the clues at a crime scene helps a detective find a murderer. We urge you to watch *Spellbound*.

The term "Surrealism" was coined in 1918 by the French author Apollinaire. Englishman Christopher Logue wrote a short poem honoring Apollinaire that captures the whimsical spirit of Surrealism:

> *Come to the edge.*
> *We might fall.*
> *Come to the edge.*
> *It's too high!*
> *COME TO THE*
>   *EDGE!*
> *And they came*
> *and he pushed*
> *and they flew.*

The Surrealists did not seek subjective truth exclusively in dreams. They also believed that they could release the images in their subconscious when they were awake if they could find a way to keep their conscious minds from intervening or from censoring the creative process. Surrealists sought ways to put themselves into a trance so they could express their subconscious directly. Some tried hallucinogenic drugs, some tried fasting, and others tried staying awake until their minds lost their rational controls. While in these states of heightened sensitivity, many Surrealists tried "automatic writing," that is, writing down on paper whatever came directly from their subconscious. Painters put images directly on canvas without any preconception of what they would be, so the images seem jumbled and strangely juxtaposed. These efforts produced some of the most exciting art of the twentieth century. Figure 4.29 shows a production of *Waiting for Godot* that was conceived in the Surrealist style.

Surrealism has five recognizable traits. First, Surrealism's dream images are drawn in curves, not angry angles, and are usually seen in pretty pastel

Figure 4.29 Note the curved lines, uncluttered space, and whimsical mood of this Surrealistic design for *Waiting for Godot.* The unrealistic costumes and scenery are painted to intensify the Surrealistic style.

colors. Second, the pressure of space and time is relaxed, and things happen more slowly and seem to have more space around them than they do in Realism. Thus, Surrealism's dream images are usually cheery and unthreatening (Figure 4.30). Third, images change into other images right before our eyes, just as in a dream—a beast can turn into a handsome prince. There is a playfulness to the metamorphosis of objects in a Surrealist's dream (Figure 4.31).

A fourth trait of Surrealism is the transformation of words into pictures, usually in a whimsical way. The saying "time hangs heavy" can be visually

Figure 4.30 The audience saw Tom Wingfield's remembrance of the apartment he lived in with his mother and sister through the lens of Tom's hazy memory in this production at the Yale School of Drama which was influenced by the style of Surrealism. All the walls and furniture were painted "unrealistically" in unthreateningly subtle shades of off-white, and the soft off-white fabrics for the costumes were chosen to create the impression of Tom's fond feelings for the past.

Figure 4.31 We laughed when we saw this Surrealistic bronze wingback chair in a public square in Guadalajara, Mexico. A man has been playfully metamorphosed into a chair. His face is molded into the back of the chair, his hands and feet become the chair's legs, and his enlarged ears become the wings of the chair. We see Surrealistic metamorphoses like this more often in cartoons than in sculpture, but it is liberatingly delightful wherever we encounter it.

rendered as a clock hanging heavily off the edge of a table. Salvador Dalí painted many pictures exploiting this verbal-visual joke. On the Internet, search Dalí's painting *The Persistence of Memory*.

ASIDE   One day Linda was working in her studio and the sun was streaming in the window. She asked me to draw the blind. Instead of pulling the cord, I scribbled something on a piece of paper and handed it to her. I had transformed her words into pictures. Figure 4.32 shows how I had "drawn the blind."

Figure 4.32   Tom's "drawing of the blind."

The fifth and final trait of Surrealism is that its logic is associative as opposed to causal. "Logic" is the word we use to describe the relationship of ideas or events. **Causal logic** describes a relationship in which one thing *causes* something else to happen: you fail a test because you did not attend class or read the assignments. **Associative logic,** in contrast, describes how your mind moves from one idea to another through the *associations* between the two ideas instead of through direct causation: you think of the state of Utah, and you associate Utah with Mormons, and you associate Mormons with Brigham Young, and Young with children, and children with toys, and toys with games, and games with sports, and sports with television, and television with commercials, and commercials with beer. Whoa! How did you get from thinking about the Mormons in Utah to thinking about beer? By associative logic. Associative logic is the way a creative mind works, and causal logic is the way an analytic mind works. The sequence of events in a Surrealistic play may puzzle you at first because one event is not caused by another. Instead, one event is associated with another, and that association leads to a plot that is very much like the sequence of events in a dream. To understand the plot of a Surrealistic play, you have to analyze the play as a whole the same way a psychoanalyst must consider a dream as a whole. The dreamer is the key to the meaning of the symbols in a dream, and the playwright is the key to the meaning of the symbols in a Surrealistic play.

You are not likely to see any pure examples of Surrealism in the theatre today, but you'll see it in other arts. Surrealism may no longer be the startling theatrical innovation it was seventy years ago, but you'll see it almost every day in music videos, TV movies such as *Alice in Wonderland*, and even magazine ads.

REVIEW

Reality Check of the Five Traits by Which Surrealism Can Be Identified

1. Are the scenery, costumes, and makeup distended into curved, swirling images that have unusual proportions, and is there a lot of open space in what you see?

2. Do people or objects change their appearance before your eyes and turn into other images?

3. Is the tone of the play whimsical, and are you amused by the visual jokes?

4. Does the play offer an altered sense of time, with some events happening more quickly or more slowly than they do in real life?

5. Does the logic of the sequence of events seem very difficult to follow?

EXPOSITION

Postmodernism describes the innovations in artistic expression in the years since Modern Art became unfashionable. Scholars and theorists offer extensive and complex definitions of Postmodernism that advanced students will find intriguing and challenging. For this introductory book, it's sufficient to say that, in the theatre, Postmodernism is a development that blends some of the characteristics of Theatricalism and Surrealism and that has three recognizable traits. The first of these traits is that the scenery is designed in an abstract manner, similar to Surrealism, called **imagistic design.** The second trait is that the costumes are an eclectic mixture of historical eras and national dress that is reminiscent of Theatricalism because these costumes could co-exist only in the theatre. The third trait is that the performance distorts our sense of time and creates a self-consciousness that keeps us aware that we are seeing a performance and should not suspend our disbelief. We'll elaborate on each of these three traits here so you can recognize Postmodern theatre when you encounter it.

For those American theatregoers who are middle-aged and grew up with Realism, the scenery of Postmodern theatre seems weird and confusing. For theatregoers who grew up viewing MTV, it should be very familiar. Imagistic design is easiest to use on film and video, but it can be used on the stage as well (Color Plate 10).

The second trait of Postmodernism is that the costumes are a jumble from many historical eras and from many different cultures. A king from medieval England stands beside a diplomat in a modern business suit and a soldier in a camouflage uniform, while characters in Elizabethan costume listen to their conversation. This jumble creates a visual world that never existed, a world that exists only now, in the theatre (Figure 4.33).

The third trait of Postmodernism is that time unfolds more slowly or more quickly than it does in "real" life. One character might move in slow motion while others move at a normal pace. The tension between their tempos makes the audience aware that actions can be experienced in different ways simultaneously.

ASIDE   Here's a description of a production of Henrik Ibsen's *Hedda Gabler* that Tom directed and for which Linda designed the costumes and Joseph Varga designed the scenery. The play traditionally is pro-

Figure 4.33   These costumes from a variety of historical periods were designed for a Postmodern production of *Macbeth*.

duced as an example of Realism, with a box set representing a sitting room in Norway in 1890 and with the characters wearing the appropriate clothes of the period, speaking in everyday language, and behaving normally. Figure 4.34 shows that the setting for our production had a raked floor with sparse furniture and no walls. Surrounding the floor was a sepia-toned painting of a city, but there were doors in it. The setting included a ten-foot-tall statue of General Gabler instead of the painting of Hedda's father that the script describes and that traditional productions have hanging on a wall. Although the statue was referred to as General Gabler, many in the audience recognized that it was a sculpture of the playwright Ibsen. While all the other characters ignored the statue, Hedda saw it as the same huge object that the audience did. At certain moments, while other characters were speaking normally, Hedda would move toward the statue in slow motion as though she were living at a different tempo. This action altered the audience's perception of time. Although most of the dialogue was spoken in a traditional manner, sometimes a short sequence of lines was spoken over again, as though there had been a time warp. This disrupted the audience's sense of time. At selected moments in the production, the characters, instead of speaking to one another, continued their dialogue while speaking directly to the audience. The characters were lit in eerie green spotlights that took them out of the world of the play and into their own minds, while at the same time the dialogue continued as though the audience was not seeing what it knew it was

(continued)

Figure 4.34 Joseph Varga's imagistic scene design for *Hedda Gabler.* The floor of the room seems to swirl out of the oversize statue of playwright Henrik Ibsen, and the painted cityscape surrounding the room reinforces the dreamlike quality of the production.

seeing. The audience experienced several actions simultaneously. To further disrupt and alter the audience's perceptions and to move the audience from an intellectual to an emotional experience of the play's dramatic action, the characters were costumed in an eclectic manner: some were dressed as though the action was taking place in 1890, and others as though the year was 1990; one character wore a suit from the 1920s with running shoes from the 1990s.

Postmodern productions are much like Surrealism and also much like Theatricalism. Only time will tell whether Postmodernism will join the ranks of the other six theatrical styles.

IDEALIZED REALITY

Before Expressionism and Surrealism, and even before the advent of Realism in the latter part of the nineteenth century, artists showed us the truth of idealized reality. The two styles that prevailed from ancient Greek times to the mid-nineteenth century were Classicism and Romanticism.

Classicism

Classicism is based on the belief that we can learn the truth if we use our powers of reason to create an ideal world. A first step in that path is to adhere

Figure 4.35 The real house shown in Figure 4.1 is drawn here in the style of Classicism. Note the exact symmetry and the formal use of columns, triangular pediments, and perfectly proportioned rectangles.

to the motto of the ancient Greeks: moderation in all things. Classicism rejects excess, whether in human emotions or in architectural design, and it celebrates the control we can assert by using our reason. Classicism approves of balance and proportion in all things, including architecture, human behavior, and forms of government. Items that are proportionate and in balance are good, while items that are out of proportion or balance are not. Classicism believes that the truth of an idealized reality can be known when we use our willpower to create an ideal world and that the first step in doing that is to achieve perfect moderation and balance. Take a look at Linda's drawing in Figure 4.35 for an illustration of Classicism.

Classicism leads painters and sculptors to display the ideally proportioned human form. All the statues from ancient Greece that we see in museums were sculpted to show idealized humans whose heads are exactly one-eighth the height of the total figure. Although the sculptors knew that humans aren't perfectly proportioned, they made art that showed the ideal we aspire to. Classicism also leads architects to use mathematically precise proportions in designing their buildings, citizens to form a government that resists the centralization of power, and playwrights to demonstrate how disaster befalls characters who are guilty of extreme behavior. Excessive pride is wrong, the Greeks believed. The Greek word for excessive pride is **hubris** (HEW-bris), a word you'll encounter often in reading about ancient Greek tragedy. The central characters of Classical drama struggle to maintain rational control over their natural impulses, and Classical plays teach a moral: moderation is the path to happiness.

In design, Classicism is a formal, austere style that evokes the essence of ancient Greece. Classicism's scenery employs the vertical columns and horizontal steps associated with ancient Greek architecture, and the purest Classical design has perfectly symmetrical balance. Color Plate 11 shows Classical costumes that evoke the long lines and draped garments worn in ancient Greece. Even new plays done in the style of Classicism make us think of ancient Greece.

The language of Classical drama is elevated in tone and form. Instead of imitating the everyday speech of Realism, the characters speak in formally

Figure 4.36 Classically inspired architecture proposes an idealized reality in which reason and order prevail. Classicism is often seen in state government buildings and university administration buildings, as in this example.

structured sentences that demonstrate how people *ought* to speak. If our will directs our minds, we will speak in an idealized manner and engage in philosophical debates. Classical dialogue frequently takes the form of an intellectual debate between two characters who express opposing ideas, and the ideal is the moderate point between their positions.

Classicism originated in the fifth century B.C.E. Although we associate it with the art and thought of ancient Athens, Classicism has remained a popular style through the centuries and has risen in prominence whenever people have believed they could improve on nature by shaping the world to their own vision of moderation and balance. In seventeenth-century France, playwrights wrote plays of perfect balance about characters from Greek mythology. Nineteenth-century American architects returned to Classicism, and many university administration buildings are designed in the Classical style (Figure 4.36).

REVIEW

Reality Check of the Four Traits by Which Classicism Can Be Identified

1. Do the scenery and costumes remind you of ancient Greece or Rome? Are they formal? Do they approach symmetrical balance?
2. Do the characters speak in formal language, and do they engage in intellectual debates?
3. Does the central character assert his or her will in an effort to control basic impulses?
4. Is the tone of the play austere and intellectual?

Romanticism

During the Renaissance, people began to think that the willful constraints of Classicism opposed the natural freedom of the individual, and they began to suspect that Classicism was not the only vision that could reveal the truth. Classicism's quest for an idealized reality was challenged in the eighteenth century when the concept of the unique individual captured the imagination of Western European culture. The unique individual is free to pursue his or her natural self and is not constrained by reason. People began to believe that truth could be found by throwing off the intellectual straitjacket of Classicism and celebrating the ecstasy of the *quest* for perfection. That quest figures prominently in **Romanticism.**

Romanticism is based on the belief that truth is discovered through feeling the emotions of our idealized image of perfection. The truth that we experience in everyday life and the truth that rational Classicism offers are the result of *thought* and are very different from the image of perfection that we *feel* is true. We feel that people should be beautiful and happy, that we should all speak elegantly, and that our houses and our clothes should be beautiful. Like Classicism, Romanticism shows us an idealized reality, but it's an image of perfection based on our emotions, not on our reason.

Romanticism sets its stories "long ago and far away," in bygone historical eras or in mythical times and magical locales where things are the way we would want them to be. Romantic stories take place in the long-ago time of the Three Musketeers or in the imagined future of Luke Skywalker, in King Arthur's mythical court or in the magical world of *The Lord of the Rings*. The objective reality of our own world is disappointing, so we escape to the idealized truth of a better time and place.

Because we feel that the average human is a compromiser and thus not as admirable as a hero who seeks perfection, Romantic playwrights create characters who are exceptional. Romantic heroes never compromise their ideals, even when reason says they'll fail. We're swept up in their adventures. Romantic heroes act to "do good" for society and for others and are not interested in personal gain. When Romantic heroes suffer, we admire them and wish we had their courage.

ASIDE   Some Romantic heroes are based on historical people, but the myth overshadows the biographical details and we know them only through their legend. The real Roman slave named Spartacus may have kicked his dog for all we know, but the Romantic hero that Kirk Douglas plays in the movie *Spartacus* lives and dies for the noble cause of freeing the Roman slaves.

Romantic heroes seek to be unique, to be true to themselves no matter the cost. A good example of a Romantic hero is Don Quixote in the musical *The Man of La Mancha* (Figure 4.37). We admire his quest for perfection even when we know he cannot attain his goal. The effort to achieve the ideal embodies the truth of Romanticism: the image of perfection is the most valuable truth we have.

In Romantic tragedies, we admire the effort of the heroes who fail to attain the ideal. In Romantic comedies, we identify with the heroes who achieve what they strive for even though we know that in the real world they could not succeed. Indiana Jones finds the Holy Grail only in a Romantic story; we know that in reality he would be killed. Luke Skywalker can kill the embodiment of evil only in a Romantic tale.

The supporting characters in Romantic drama are perfect in their own way. Some are perfectly heroic, so they are handsome; others are perfectly evil, so they are grotesque; still others are the villain's perfect victims, so they are entirely vulnerable. The supporting characters in Romantic drama are closer to stereotypes than to individuals because they show us the idealized reality by which we can quickly know the truth they portray.

These idealized characters speak in idealized dialogue. The language of Romanticism is the opposite of the vulgar language of Realism. It is "elevated" over the everyday prose you and I speak because it includes beautiful

Figure 4.37 Don Quixote is the title character in *The Man of La Mancha*. When he sings "To dream the impossible dream," he gives voice to the central message of Romanticism.

visual images and artfully balanced diction. Sometimes it is delivered in formal poetry. Some of the greatest professions of love are those that Cyrano speaks to Roxanne in *Cyrano de Bergerac,* a glorious example of Romanticism.

Instead of the formal, mathematically precise architecture of Classicism, the architecture of Romanticism is built from curved lines that swirl toward heaven, like the spire atop the drawing of the house in Figure 4.38. Instead of being written according to rational guidelines, Romantic plays are thrilling adventures that jump from one location to another, have several subplots,

Figure 4.38   The real house shown in Figure 4.1 is drawn here in the style of Romanticism. Note the ornate decoration and the swirling spire that reaches toward heaven in this artist's notion of an idealized house.

and flip-flop between happy and sad scenes, ultimately soaring to great emotional heights. These sprawling and swirling plays show us that truth is found through a quest for the ideal.

REVIEW

Reality Check of the Four Traits by Which Romanticism Can Be Identified

1. Is the action set in an exotic and distant historical era or in a mythical time and magical locale?
2. Do the characters speak in "elevated" language?
3. Is the central character striving toward an ideal that he or she could never achieve in real life?
4. Are you swept up in the adventures of the plot and the thrilling emotions of the story?

IDENTIFYING THEATRICAL STYLE

Recognizing the various styles will help you understand how the playwright sees the world and why a play has affected you the way it has. Begin your analysis by asking yourself if the play is an example of Realism or if it was intentionally stylized. If it was stylized, think through the various styles to decide which best describes the play. Use the reality checks we've provided throughout this chapter. Figure 4.39 may also be helpful. Keep in mind that very few plays are done exclusively in one style. Theatre mixes styles the way a chef mixes the ingredients of a salad.

Realism

Theatricalism

Expressionism

Figure 4.39 Realism on stage would require a convincing imitation of the real house in the photo. The line drawings surrounding the photo illustrate each of the six theatrical styles.

Romanticism

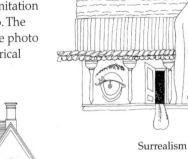

Surrealism

Classicism

No one of the six artistic styles is any better than the others. Rather, each is a distinct way in which artists present their vision of the truth. Some artists imitate objective reality and create works in the styles of Realism and Theatricalism. Some imitate subjective reality and create in the styles of Expressionism and Surrealism. Some imitate idealized reality and create in the styles of Classicism and Romanticism. Still other artists create plays in more than one style.

The more you know about the varying styles, the more you can open yourself to the unfamiliar and potentially exciting truths of the performance unfolding before you. Analyzing a play's theatrical style will help you understand why you liked or disliked the production you attended. When you add this third major analytic tool to your analysis of the six elements and three unities first introduced by Aristotle and to your analysis of the play's genre, you will discover that you understand the play more completely than you realized. These three analytic approaches provide you with sufficient knowledge to write about theatre—which is what we'll help you prepare for in the final chapter in Act 1.

EXERCISE

After your class has attended a production, bring a copy of the theatrical program to class. Highlight the title of the play and the names of the playwright, director, scene designer, costume designer, lighting designer, sound designer, dramaturg, composer, musical director, and choreographer so that you can refer to their names when you discuss the play in class.

In class, write on a sheet of paper the style you believe the play demonstrated, listing three traits of that style and giving specific examples of each trait you recognized in the production.

Next, tally the number of students who chose each style. Then form groups of five to eight students to discuss the two styles that were chosen most frequently. Discover whether your group can reach a unanimous decision about the style and discuss how the style influenced your collective response.

CHAPTER 5

Writing about Theatre

Whether you write an essay for a class, a review for your college newspaper, or an e-mail message to a friend, you will probably write about theatre sometime soon. This chapter aims to help you clarify three categories of writing about theatre and then to help you prepare, organize, and refine what you write. On our Web site, you'll find examples of each of the three categories—examples written by journalists, scholars, and students like yourself. These three examples illustrate the points made in this chapter and provide you with models for your own writing.

◖ F O R E S H A D O W I N G

Three Types of Writers about Theatre

1. Reviewers and Critics
2. Scholars
3. Students

REVIEWERS AND CRITICS

You probably use the words "reviewer" and "critic" interchangeably. Most of us do. Tom will ask, "Have you read a review of the new play?" and Linda will answer, "The critic loved it." This topic would be clearer if people distinguished between reviewers and critics, but they don't, and we know that nothing we write is likely to change people's habits.

   "Reviewer" ideally should refer to reporters who write about plays for a daily newspaper and who stick to the five "Ws" of journalism by answering the same Who, What, Where, When, and Why questions that shape other reporters' stories about politics, sports, or train wrecks. It would be nice if reviewers' reporting of facts took precedence over the voicing of their opinions and if their desire to entertain with clever writing took a back seat to their writing clear and lean prose. However, people who read newspapers want reviews to be a "consumer's guide," and they want the journalist's opin-

Figure 5.1   An actor's view of the critics.

ion to help them decide whether they should see the play being reviewed. Unhappily, too many reviewers write their opinions without explaining their standards or providing examples of what they liked and disliked. Too many fail in their effort to use witty prose to entertain their readers (Figure 5.1). We've posted a sampling of reviews on this book's Web site; also most newspapers can be accessed on-line, so you can read a variety of reviews at your convenience. In addition to theatre reviews in your college and hometown newspapers, we encourage you to read reviews from the *San Francisco Chronicle,* the *Chicago Tribune,* and, most importantly, the *New York Times.* Discover for yourself how reviewers try to balance factual reporting with opinion and whether they write entertaining reviews.

The reviewer who wrote that an actor has "delusions of adequacy" may have coined a memorable phrase but was guilty of being clever at the expense of reporting facts.

ASIDE   John Simon writes reviews for *New York Magazine.* His readers greatly admire his knowledge, intelligence, and taste and the muscular clarity of his prose. However, many actors hate Simon because he writes cruel attacks on actors' physical appearance. One actor became so angry at Simon that when she encountered him in a fashionable restaurant she dumped his dinner plate in his lap!

Some years ago, Simon gave a public lecture in Philadelphia, and Tom was invited to introduce him. Simon's brilliant speech was a justification for his approach to reviewing. He argued convincingly that because the audience sees the actor's face and body, the audience can't suspend its disbelief unless the actor's looks are appropriate to the character. He argued, for example, that an African American actor could not be believable as a medieval English king and that an overweight actress could not effectively play roles like Laura in *The Glass*

(continued)

Menagerie. Simon is a very good public speaker, and he successfully persuaded his audience.

At the small dinner party after the lecture, however, Simon revealed that he *enjoys* writing cruel remarks and isn't always altruistic. He admitted that he writes particularly abrasive reviews whenever he is renegotiating his contract with *New York Magazine.* Apparently, his publishers use the quantity of mail they receive about his column as a measure of his value—the more mail, the more readers; and the more readers, the higher salary he merits. It doesn't matter whether the letters praise or damn Simon; only the quantity counts. In that respect, one of the dinner guests observed, Simon is like an actor on a soap opera. If a lot of mail comes in about a character, the actor may get a raise; if very little mail comes in, the actor may lose the job. Simon's virulent reviews appear to be a way for him to increase the quantity of mail when he's seeking a salary raise. If this is true, is he writing honest reviews?

"Critic" ideally should refer to essayists who write critiques for weekly or monthly publications like the *Sunday New York Times* or the *Hudson Review* and who, unlike the daily reporter, have sufficient time to write carefully revised essays that analyze and interpret plays. We believe that critics should have a theoretical context for their critiques and a historical perspective for their observations, and that they should link their topics to contemporary cultural concerns.

Of course, we can't have things the way we'd like them. Some reviewers who write for daily newspapers offer little more than their unsubstantiated opinions ("Two thumbs up!"), and others who write for monthly magazines do little more than report the bare facts. While we can't get the world to use the definitions we'd like, we can tell you what we believe reviewers and critics *ought* to do. After you've read our wishes, you can read the examples on the Web site and measure them against your newly informed expectations.

We believe a well-written review should offer a thumbnail synopsis of the play's plot and a clear statement of the major themes explored by the playwright. It should identify any prominent actors, directors, or designers connected with the production. It should include a brief description of the director's interpretation, as well as the actors' performances, the designers' work, and (most important) the audience's response. Skilled reviewers should compare the play to others they've written about. Also, reviewers should write so that their readers will know whether the reviewer thought the play was a *successful* production, *why* the reviewer thought that, and whether the *reader* might wish to see it. Reviewing is difficult to do well, we believe, because a lot of information must be organized and condensed into a brief and concise report.

A critique is very different from a review. A critique should reveal that the writer is well educated in artistic and cultural history, knows the many theoretical schools of criticism, and can analyze a play using a variety of the established tools of criticism. A critique ought to explore a central idea at significant length and use one or more plays to illustrate its points, and it should be interesting to read even if the reader never expects to see the plays it discusses.

EXPOSITION
• • • • • • • • • • •

Look up "critique" in your dictionary. You'll find that it means to examine, not to find fault. Criticism is finding fault, but writing a critique is examining a work of art or piece of literature so the reader can analyze it, interpret it, and explain it.

• •

The topics of a few critiques we've read recently will give you a feel for what a critique can be: the sociological implication of older female characters paired with younger male characters in the romantic relationships of new American plays; the effectiveness of plays that do *not* conform to the three unities suggested by Aristotle; the significance of current trends in casting persons of color in roles traditionally played by white actors; the success of comedies that raise serious political issues; the reasons why tragicomedies are unpopular with audiences in smaller cities; the reasons why American culture encourages directors to impose the style of Postmodernism on Shakespeare's plays. Whatever idea a critic examines, you should be stimulated to think further about it after you've read the critique.

SCHOLARS

Scholars do historical, analytical, and theoretical research and then make contributions to our knowledge of theatre by writing about it. As you study certain aspects of theatre in depth or do research for an assignment, you will probably read scholars' books or the articles they write for publications such as *Journal of Dramatic Theory and Criticism.* You may read a biography of a famous actor or an essay describing the reconstruction of a theatre from the Baroque era. You might read an analytical book or article that interprets Shakespeare's plays or those of a contemporary author such as Henry David Hwang. You might read theoretical writings such as a manifesto for a particular theory of drama or a philosophical explanation of the theatrical experience. Scholarly writing demonstrates the vitality of intellectual inquiry in the field of theatre, and professors at leading universities regularly publish the results of their research in articles and books. We'd guess that there are book-length studies of every topic you're reading about in *Another Opening, Another Show.*

STUDENTS

As a student in an introductory course, you're a would-be reviewer, a critic-in-training, or a scholar-in-the-making. Whether you write a review of a production you've seen or a critique of some play you've read, you'll be writing an essay. Unless your instructor has assigned a particular topic, you must decide whether you want to review the whole production, pretending you're writing for a newspaper, or instead want to review only one narrow topic you've learned about in class. In the first instance, you can reread our description of what ought to be included in a well-written review and use the examples on the text's Web site as your models. If you choose to discuss a narrow topic—for example, the relevance of the play's political meaning in America today—the organization we describe in "What Is an Essay?" will help you present your argument.

EXPOSITION   *What Is an Essay?*
● ● ● ● ● ● ● ● ● ●

An essay is a short, forceful, and well-organized presentation of an idea that aspires to persuade the reader to agree with the writer's thesis. The length of an essay will depend on its topic. Some topics are appropriate for the 500-word essay assigned by many instructors; other topics are appropriate for longer essays. The first step in writing a successful essay is choosing an appropriate topic, as Robert Cohen points out in his appendix to *Theatre:*

> Be careful to limit it to what you can realistically cover in the time allotted and what you can, in all good conscience, write about in the paper.*

As an example, consider the topic of this essay you are reading: the answer to the question "What is an essay?" One thousand words will be needed to write about a topic with this scope, because several types of evidence and argument will be needed to prove the thesis.

In order to convince the reader of your thesis, your essay must be well organized. An essay has three parts: an introduction, which states the thesis succinctly; the main body of the essay, called the "development," which supports the thesis with evidence and arguments; and a conclusion, which restates the thesis. The introduction must have a thesis statement that presents the author's point and prepares the reader to understand the arguments that follow. The sentence stating the thesis may be complex, but it must be written clearly. Successful writers revise and sharpen their thesis statement until it is as clear as they can make it, because the success of their argument depends on a clearly understood thesis statement. As an example, look at the clear thesis statement of this essay: "An essay is a short, forceful, and well-organized presentation of an idea that aspires to persuade the reader to agree with the author's thesis."

―――――――
*Robert Cohen. *Theatre,* 5th ed. Mountain View, Calif.: Mayfield Publishing Co., 2000, p. A-4.

After setting forth the thesis statement in the introduction, successful writers develop their argument by using a variety of types of evidence. Each paragraph of the development must support, expand, or illustrate the thesis. Unrelated ideas, no matter how interesting, only confuse the reader and do not belong in a well-written essay. Each paragraph of the development must begin with a topic sentence that states the idea to be explored in the paragraph and connects that idea to the essay's thesis. Topic sentences are very much like an essay's thesis statement, because they state clearly the point to be made in the paragraph. Topic sentences differ from the thesis statement in that they are not independent ideas but instead serve the thesis they support. The paragraphs that make up the development portion of an essay are commonly referred to as the "body" of the writer's argument.

The essay's development provides the writer with an opportunity to persuade the reader by presenting evidence that takes the form of authority, example, or logic. Authority commonly involves statistical data or an expert witness. Example generally denotes the use of a particular instance that illustrates the point being made. Logic refers to the deductive process that leads from one idea to another until the sequence of ideas and deductions leads inexorably to a conclusion. A well-written essay will include at least three paragraphs of development, and in many cases writers will use all three kinds of evidence. After developing their thesis through evidence, authors conclude with a short restatement of the thesis they have proved.

As an example of a well-written essay, consider the one you are reading. Its topic is clear from its title, and its thesis statement is set forth in the very first sentence of the introduction. Next, the thesis is advanced through three paragraphs of development. The first paragraph describes the three parts of an essay and the importance of a thesis statement; the next paragraph describes the concept of development; and the last of the three paragraphs defines the three standard types of evidence. The development portion of this essay uses all three forms of evidence: authority, example, and logic. The authority is Robert Cohen's statement on choosing the proper topic for an essay. An example is provided in the final sentence of the second paragraph, which offers the thesis statement of this essay as an example of a clearly written thesis statement. Logic is applied in the cause-and-effect reasoning of the three developmental paragraphs, leading the reader to agree with the essay's thesis statement. A successful essay has a concluding paragraph that restates its thesis, as this one has done. If you have been persuaded that an essay is a short, forceful, and well-organized presentation of an idea that aspires to persuade the reader to agree with the writer's thesis, then this essay may be judged to have achieved its purpose.

• •

Whether you write a review or a critique, you can put to use the tools you learned in the first four chapters of this book. Assume you've been asked to write a critique of *The Glass Menagerie* and *Waiting for Godot.* You might argue that the episodic plot of Williams's "memory play" serves the play's meaning even though it rejects Aristotle's unity of time, whereas the chrono-logical beginning-middle-and-end plot of *Godot* serves Beckett's meaning by respecting the ideas in Aristotle's *The Poetics*. Alternatively, you might compare the genres of the two plays, arguing that the tragicomedy of *Godot* is off-putting for many audiences because of its cynicism, while the drama of *Menagerie* is more pleasing for the general audience because of its sentimentality. Or you could examine the two plays' styles, comparing the ways in which both make use of the traits of Theatricalism.

The critiques on our Web site will provide you with some helpful examples. With a little practice and effort, you'll find that you can write very clear essays that will offer you new insights into theatre.

ANOTHER SET OF TOOLS

Nearly two hundred years ago, the German playwright, poet, and critic Goethe (GER-ta) wrote an essay in which he described three questions that you can use to organize your thoughts and feelings about a play. Goethe's questions are another set of tools you can use when you write about theatre.

● FORESHADOWING

Goethe's Three Questions

1. What was the artist trying to do?
2. Did the artist succeed in doing it?
3. Was it worth the doing?

To see how Goethe's three questions work, imagine you've just returned home from a production of *The Glass Menagerie* and you want to write an e-mail message to a friend in which you evaluate the performance of the actor playing Laura.

What was the artist trying to do? becomes "What was the actor trying to do?" The actor was trying to create the character of Laura as written by Tennessee Williams. Begin by thinking through the play and deciding what Williams's character is like. What does the dialogue say Laura should look like, sound like, and behave like? (In Chapter 7, you'll learn how an actor creates a character from the information in a playwright's script.)

Did the artist succeed in doing it? becomes "Was the actor so successful in creating Laura's appearance, behavior, voice, and emotional complexity that you suspended your disbelief, forgot the actor, and believed in Laura?" Was her voice believably soft and gentle? Was her limp convincing? Did you believe she was extremely shy and on the edge of losing her sanity when she played her Victrola and touched her glass menagerie? Was she young enough and thin enough to look like Laura? (We agree with John Simon, in theory, but we don't feel the need to be offensive in describing the actor's appearance.) Goethe's second question helps you analyze and describe the actor's work and discover the degree to which the actor succeeded or failed in what she was trying to do.

Was it worth the doing? becomes "Was the actor's effort justified?" If the actor tried to create the playwright's character—tried to create Laura—and if you agree that Williams's character is necessary as an agent to further the action of the plot, truthful as a depiction of human behavior, and vital to your emotional response to *The Glass Menagerie,* then you may find that the actor's effort was worth the doing. What if the actor has been successful in creating a character that is different from what the playwright wrote? What if the actor, for example, portrayed Laura as a manipulative woman who uses her physical disability to get her mother and brother to take care of her? You must decide whether you think the actor's surprising interpretation helped or hindered your understanding and emotional response to the play. If it helped, then what the actor did was worth the doing. If it hindered, then what the actor did was not. Goethe's third question requires you to take a stance as to what you believe is good or bad.

Let's do this exercise a second time, this time to analyze and evaluate the work of a scene designer for a production of *Waiting for Godot.*

What was the artist trying to do? becomes "What kind of reality was the scene designer trying to create?" Use what you learned in Chapter 4 about theatrical styles to answer this question. Did the production intend to present the Surrealism of a subjective reality, the Classicism of an idealized reality, or the Realism of an objective reality?

Did the artist succeed in doing it? becomes "Did the scene designer succeed in creating the style, place, time, and value system of the imaginary world?" If the designer was striving to create a Realistic exterior but the rocks were spongy rubber and sagged when the actors sat on them, the designer failed. If the designer was trying to create an Expressionistic exterior and you felt that the characters were oppressed, the designer succeeded. If you knew where and when the action of the play was taking place and you suspended your disbelief, then the designer succeeded.

Was it worth the doing? This question requires you to judge whether the designer's interpretation was appropriate for the play. Not all designs are, and you must ask yourself if the scene design communicated the meaning and mood of the play in a valuable way. (In Chapter 9 you will learn more about how a design communicates ideas and creates mood.) Review the illustrations of *Godot* and *Menagerie* in Chapter 4 and judge which of the designs you find least appropriate and therefore least worth the doing.

We hope this introduction to writing about theatre will be helpful. We've described three kinds of writing, explained how to organize and develop an essay, and demonstrated how you can use a variety of analytical tools to help you write about theatre. Your efforts will improve the more you write, of course. In the same way a playwright rewrites and revises a play during rehearsals and previews and in the same way Linda and I revised and rewrote this second edition of our book over and over again, you should rewrite and revise your written assignments many times.

ASIDE   Sometimes an old joke makes a point most clearly. Have you heard the one about the tourist who gets lost in New York City on his way to hear a concert? He sees a young man walking down the street, carrying a violin, and asks him how to get to Carnegie Hall. The young man answers, "Practice, practice, practice." What's true for the violinist is true for the writer.

EXERCISES

1. If your instructor has a Ph.D. (Doctor of Philosophy), he or she will have written a **dissertation,** a book-length work of scholarship. If your instructor has an M.F.A. (Master of Fine Arts), his or her graduate education will probably have culminated in a written **thesis** describing the directing, designing, or acting of a role in a play. Ask your instructor to describe the research that went into the dissertation or thesis so you can learn about how intellectual activity is part of both theatre scholarship and a theatre artist's creative work.

2. After you have seen a play, cut out of the newspaper (or print from the Internet) three published reviews and bring them to class. On the board, make a list of what each reviewer reported, noting the differences. By a show of hands, determine which review your class judges to be the most complete and successful. Then discuss why the majority voted that way.

3. Encourage your instructor to invite a professional reviewer to speak to your class. Ask that person what education and training would prepare you for a job with a newspaper, how he or she approaches the job, and what standards he or she applies to evaluating a play.

4. Write an e-mail message to a friend describing what you *dis*liked about a play you saw for the theatre class you're taking.

5. Write a review of a play you've seen, pretending that you're writing for a newspaper. Compare your review with one or more published reviews, noting the differences and assessing the success of your effort.

The Creative Process

The creative process is a mysterious one. Exactly how inspiration happens—how a composer hears a melody, how a painter sees colors, or how a poet feels an image—isn't clear. But we all love the works these artists create.

The Public Broadcasting Service gave a glimpse of the creative process in a recent promotional spot. Perhaps you saw it. A composer is seated at his piano, frustrated at his inability to create. He squirms, tries a few notes, slumps, tears at his hair, and puts his head down in despair. He looks out the window and sees five black telephone wires. Birds start to settle on the wires, and suddenly the composer "hears" the sequence of notes the birds represent on a five-line musical staff. He plays the notes tentatively. Then, in a rush of creative inspiration, his fingers fly through his new composition. Inspiration comes when we least expect it. The creative process moves in mysterious ways.

Theatre is a collaborative art, but in the beginning is the word. The playwright's words are shaped into a story that is interpreted by a director, performed by actors, and given an imaginary physical world by designers. A great deal of work goes into creating a theatrical event before an audience experiences it, and that creative process is what you'll learn about in Act 2.

The first four chapters in *The Creative Process* explore the creative and interpretive work of playwrights, actors, directors, and designers. The final chapter, "Putting It Together," takes its title from the Stephen Sondheim lyric you read in Chapter 1; it describes a real case study of the creative process that led to our production of *Troilus and Cressida* at the Colorado Shakespeare Festival.

CHAPTER 6

The Playwright's Story

Playwrights are storytellers. Whether we're listening around a camp fire, reading in our favorite chair, or watching in a darkened movie house, good stories hold us in thrall. Novelists tell their stories in books, filmmakers through moving images, and playwrights through the unique medium of theatre.

Playwrights are the seminal artists of the theatre. Actors, directors, and designers can't do their work until the playwright has written the script. The performance you enjoy is the result of the collaboration of all these theatre artists, but it is based on the playwright's play. There is genuine creativity in the work of actors, directors, and designers, as you will read in the chapters that follow, but most of their work is interpretive. In the beginning is the word—the playwright's story.

> **ASIDE**   Some of you are asking, "Don't some plays get written without playwrights?" Yes, some do. Those plays are developed out of improvisations that actors do in rehearsals, and some plays are even improvised at the very moment of performance. The tradition of improvisation dates back to the *commedia dell'arte* of the Italian Renaissance, but it is rare in our time. For the purposes of this book, we are limiting our discussion to the mainstream theatre you will most often experience. Your instructor might want to expand on the subject of improvisational theatre.

THE PLAYWRIGHT'S PROCESS

How does a play get written? First, the playwright imagines a story and the characters in it. Then the playwright decides what parts of the story to include in the play. Next, the playwright plans the plot, which is the sequence of scenes. Finally, the playwright writes the dialogue and stage directions for those scenes. It all sounds simple and orderly, doesn't it? DON'T BELIEVE IT! If writing plays were that easy, any one of us could be another Shakespeare. We've teased you by presenting an orderly, rational description of what playwrights do, but playwrights are creative human beings, and the creative mind doesn't work in an orderly, sequential fashion. Quite the contrary—creative endeavors are usually far more unpredictable. Because playwrights are creative, not analytic, they tend to work associatively, not sequentially. (For a fuller explanation of associative logic and sequential logic, refer to the discussion of Surrealism in Chapter 4.)

> **ASIDE**　Nicholas Meyer, a famous screenwriter, was hired to write a screenplay based on Philip Roth's novel *The Human Stain*. Despite his years of experience and his proven skills and talent, Meyer couldn't work out how to write it. After many weeks of failure, his wife told him to give up, and he did. Some weeks later, inspiration struck. "I was sitting there in the bathtub, staring at my toes getting wrinkled, and I was not thinking about this at all—I promise you—when suddenly, out of nowhere, like tumblers clicking successively in place on a safe: Act I, Act II, Act III. Don't know why, don't know where it came from." The creative mind is a terrible thing to waste. If you have one, use it!

The Creative Journey

Where do playwrights work? In their heads. On a piece of paper. At a computer screen. Playwrights can be anyplace when they imagine their characters and stories, and they can invent dialogue at any time of day. One playwright we know talks out loud while driving on the freeway, while another only gets going when she's staring at her computer screen. English playwright Noel Coward wrote *Private Lives* in forty-eight hours while sitting on a hotel bed in Shanghai. Other playwrights spend years writing a play.

English playwright Somerset Maugham told students the way to become a successful playwright was to marry someone rich.

Playwrights frequently begin their work with an image that appears to them out of nowhere and fits somewhere in the middle of the play. Tennessee Williams said that before he began writing *A Streetcar Named Desire*, all he had was an image that came to him of a woman beneath a bare light bulb and wearing a slip (Figure 6.1). Williams started with a visual image. Other playwrights begin with words. A writer imagines snatches of dialogue, impressions of characters, and feelings of outrage or ecstasy in no particular order and forges them into a coherent pattern.

When a reporter asked American playwright Herb Gardner to describe the playwright's profession, he replied, "How do you ask a Kamikaze pilot if his work is going well?"

At some stage of the writing, the associative process gives over to the sequential, and the playwright's intuitive work becomes a coolly rational act. This aspect of the playwright's work *can* be described, and we'll demonstrate how a playwright imposes order on creativity with an examination of *The Glass Menagerie*. First, the story:

> Once upon a time, in the years just before 1920, a young man named Wingfield who worked for the telephone company traveled through a small town in Mississippi. One Sunday afternoon, he fell in love with a flirtatious Southern belle named Amanda, and soon afterward they married. The couple

Figure 6.1 The character of Blanche DuBois in Tennessee Williams's *A Streetcar Named Desire* has an emotional breakdown near the end of the play. This picture from the 1998 revival shows how Williams's seminal image of a woman beneath a bare light bulb was written into his play.

moved to St. Louis and had two children, a daughter named Laura and, two years later, a son named Tom. After some years, Wingfield abandoned his family and continued his travels. He never contacted his family again, except to send a picture postcard saying he'd fallen in love with long distance. Impoverished, the family moved into a shabby tenement apartment. By the late 1930s, Tom was in his early twenties. He supported the family by working in a shoe factory, and Amanda helped out by selling magazine subscriptions over the telephone. Laura tried to go to business college, but she was so emotionally fragile—and so embarrassed because she limped—that she couldn't do it. She spent most of her time walking in the park or sitting at home listening to old records on a windup Victrola and playing with her collection of tiny glass animals. Tom and his mother were both unhappy and fought frequently. Tom dreamed of becoming a poet, and he spent a lot of time escaping to the movies. He also considered following his father's footsteps and running away from his oppressive mother and unstable sister. Amanda believed she must find a husband for Laura because the girl would be unable to care for herself, so she nagged Tom into inviting a "gentleman caller" to dinner. Tom brought home Jim O'Connor, a fellow worker from the shoe factory. Several years earlier O'Connor had gone to high school with Laura, and she had had a crush on him that he didn't know about. Laura was so timid that she couldn't sit at the dinner table, and Jim followed her into the parlor to talk with her. He tried to build up her self-confidence, but when he told her he was engaged to be married, Laura's hopes were crushed. Jim left, and the family was once again alone. Sometime later, Tom ran away to join the merchant marines. No matter where he traveled, the memory of his beloved sister remained with him.

This story could have been told in a novel, a movie, or a play. With all that narrative material available, the playwright had to decide when in the narrative to begin the play and when to end it. Williams wanted his audiences to feel the agony of remorse that Tom feels, so he began his play at the very end of the story—when Tom is a merchant marine traveling from place to place—and ended it only moments later in the story, with Tom alone, thinking back on his life but wishing he could forget his family and escape his remorse. All the scenes in the play are parts of Tom's remembrance. Another playwright might have wanted the audience to feel Jim O'Connor's relief at escaping the marriage trap or Amanda's despair over her daughter's disability and probably would have chosen a different beginning and ending.

After deciding the beginning and ending of the play, the playwright must decide what episodes of the story to include and what characters are needed for those scenes. The playwright's process requires hundreds, perhaps thousands, of choices. Williams chose to exclude scenes of Laura walking in the park or Tom working at the shoe factory. He also excluded scenes with Tom's father. Instead, he chose to limit his play to only a few of the scenes that led up to Tom's running away from St. Louis, and those scenes required only four characters.

Plot Structure

Next, the playwright must decide the plot, the sequence in which the selected scenes unfold. In *The Poetics*, Aristotle describes the plot as "the life and soul of the drama." From his study of Sophocles' *Oedipus the King*, Aristotle determined that the plot is the most important of the six elements of theatre, the one without which there can be no play. The plot is often described as "the order of the incidents," and playwrights can arrange the order of the scenes in their plots in whatever way best tells the story. While stories have a beginning, a middle, and an end, playwrights can structure the events of their plot in a variety of ways. Let's discuss three structures that you should be able to recognize.

FORESHADOWING

Three Common Structures for a Playscript

1. Linear
2. Cinematic
3. Contextual

Linear   The most common structure for a playscript, and the one you'll encounter most often, is a linear one. The incidents of the plot are arranged in a sequential line, hence the adjective "linear" (LIN-ee-er). The incidents are arranged chronologically along the line of time, and the first scene takes place near the beginning of the plot. *Waiting for Godot* is arranged chronologically, as is *Oedipus the King*, the play Aristotle used as his ideal in *The Poetics.*

The linear structure has some variations that you will observe in the plays you see. A bold difference between the two examples we're using is that *The Glass Menagerie* jumps backward in time and excludes events that happen between the episodes Williams chose to include in his plot, whereas *Oedipus the King* goes straight through from start to finish with no gaps in its time line. Both plays are linear, but *The Glass Menagerie* has an **episodic linear plot** and *Oedipus the King* has a **continuous linear plot.**

Linear plots have a second variant in addition to the continuous and episodic arrangements: some plays have a **simple plot** that tells a single story, like *Oedipus the King*, while others have a complex plot that interweaves several stories. A prime example of a complex plot is Shakespeare's *Henry V,* which interweaves three stories: one about King Henry, a second involving his tavern friends, and a third about the French. Sometimes these stories overlap and intersect, but each story remains coherent.

No qualitative distinction can be made between a simple and a complex plot, or between a continuous and an episodic linear plot. While some stories may lend themselves to one or another of these structures, no play is better than another because of its structure.

Cinematic   Ever since movies introduced the idea that a story can be told in flashback, some playwrights have chosen to arrange the incidents in their plots in a nonchronological order in which the structure of the plot is not the same as the order of events in the story. Imagine *Oedipus the King* with a cinematic structure:

> Once upon a time, blind Oedipus wanders away from the city of Thebes. He walks past Mount Cithaeron (ki-TIE-ron), past the spot where he was abandoned as a baby, and he remembers—and we see in a flashback—how the Shepherd rescued him and gave him to the Corinthian Shepherd. Oedipus staggers on his way, and in the next scene he is a youth in Corinth, thinking he's the prince of that land. The next scene flashes forward to Oedipus in

Thebes, listening as the Corinthian Shepherd reveals that Oedipus is the son of the Theban royal family.

The order of the incidents in this version is jumbled and out of chronological sequence. A playwright might choose this structure if the story of Oedipus's coming to terms with the knowledge of his true birth were more important than the story of Oedipus's discovery of that truth.

Another cinematic plot structure allows the playwright to include scenes on more than one level of reality. In Arthur Miller's *Death of a Salesman*, several scenes are presented not as they happen in objective reality but as the title character, Willy, imagines them. The audience encounters the subjective reality inside Willy's head. The clearest example of this is the scene in which Willy is playing cards with his neighbor Charley and imagines that his dead brother, Ben, is in the room with them. Charley can't see or hear Ben, but Willy and the audience can. The plot is advancing on more than one level of reality.

Waiting for Godot has a simple linear plot, even though it is not clear how much time passes between the first and second acts. *Death of a Salesman*, on the other hand, has a cinematic plot that jumps about in time; also, some of the scenes that take place in Willy's memory are presented as he remembers them, which may be different from the way they truly happened. But their reality is not as distorted as the extremely stylized scenes of Expressionistic plays such as *The Adding Machine*.

Contextual   The contextual structure is rather rare. One example is *The Private Life of the Master Race*, written by the twentieth-century German playwright Bertolt Brecht. This play is made up of twenty-seven different short scenes, some twenty minutes long and some only two minutes long. Each scene is independent of the others in the sense that it has its own characters and a complete, self-contained plot. Each scene can stand on its own as a complete work, however short it might be. No cause-and-effect logic leads from one scene to the next, and the play has no traditional plot with a beginning, middle, and end. Instead, the play is a collection of short playlets, similar to a bound collection of short stories or to a CD of hit songs by a popular singer. Productions of *The Private Life of the Master Race* (Figure 6.2) usually include only nine to twelve of the scenes. The director selects which scenes to include and determines the order in which they are to be presented. As a result, the content and experience of any two productions might be significantly different.

What gives this play its artistic coherence is that all the scenes are variations on the same subject. Each scene shows how depressing it was to live in Germany in the 1930s, when the Nazi regime was in power. Each scene relates to the others because all share a common subject, and each scene takes its importance and its meaning from the context in which it is placed, that is, from its relationship to the totality of scenes.

A more common example of a contextual structure is a musical review such as *Side by Side by Sondheim* or *Red, Hot and Cole*. These entertaining theatrical

Figure 6.2 A cabaret song titled "The Ballad of the Jewish Whore" was the entirety of the short playlet that was one of fourteen included in a production of Bertolt Brecht's contextually structured *The Private Life of the Master Race* at Seattle's Playhouse Theatre. The supertitle projection of the playlet's title indicates that this production was done in the style of Theatricalism.

events, sometimes called anthologies, are made up of songs and comic sketches drawn from a wide variety of sources all by the same composer. The composer gives the production its context, and each song belongs in the play only because it was written by that composer.

Contextually structured plays can be difficult for the average theatregoer to enjoy because most of us have a strong experience of plays with a linear plot. We like a story with a beginning, middle, and end and often are confused by plays that do not have a clearly understood linear or cinematic structure.

ASIDE   A novel with a contextual structure was published in 1969. *The Unfortunates*, written by B. S. Johnson, has twenty-seven chapters that are not bound into a traditional book but instead are held in a box. Readers are instructed to begin by reading the chapter titled *First* and to conclude by reading the chapter titled *Last*. The other twenty-five chapters can be read in whatever order the reader chooses. *The Unfortunates* tells the story of a Saturday afternoon in one man's life, and it includes memories of earlier times and descriptions of events on that afternoon. The story takes on different meanings depending on the order in which the chapters are read.

THE PLAYWRIGHT'S TECHNIQUE

After choosing a linear or cinematic structure, a playwright determines the sequence in which the events of the story unfold—the order of the scenes of the plot. Scenes are short portions of the plot during which something happens that changes the course of the narrative. Whether a playwright gives the scenes numbers or names or writes the play so that the scenes flow organically from one to another, the order they come in shapes our response. Think of scenes this way: a scene is to a plot as a brick is to a wall. Scenes are the building blocks playwrights use to construct a plot, to "wright" it.

The early scenes of the plot are called the **introduction.** In the dialogue of the opening scenes, the playwright introduces the main **characters,** provides any necessary exposition, and establishes the **status quo,** the stable situation in the world of the play. The characters, as you learned earlier, are "the agents for the action." Exposition is the information the audience needs in order to understand the characters and the status quo. It includes information about the characters and about events that happened in the story before the plot began. For example, early in *The Glass Menagerie,* Tom tells the audience that his father abandoned the family long ago. The playwright can include additional exposition at any point in the play, usually to relate events that have happened elsewhere or during the time that has passed between scenes.

Playwrights also provide foreshadowing in the early scenes, planting information in the dialogue that prepares you to understand events that will happen later in the plot. For example, the characters in *Waiting for Godot* say very early in the dialogue that they must stay where they are to wait for Godot. When they remain in the same place at the end of the play, you are prepared to understand why. The playwright can include additional foreshadowing when necessary to prepare you for things that are soon to happen.

Aristotle describes a play as "an imitation of an action." In playwriting terms, an **action** is any event that changes the status quo. If a door is open and somebody closes it, that's a physical action. The status quo has been changed. If a character has a change of mind, that's an intellectual action. The status quo has been changed as completely as if a physical action had occurred.

A play imitates many small actions as it unfolds. To create a scene, a playwright uses the raw materials of **dialogue, description,** character, and action. (We'll describe these raw materials in the next section of this chapter.) A scene is the small segment of an entire play in which one conflict is introduced and resolved, the building block for making a play. It is one brick that when placed with other bricks makes up the whole building. A scene imitates a small action, and the totality of scenes imitates a major action. The plot is the sequence of the totality of scenes; it takes you on a journey from the status quo at the beginning of the play to the changed circumstances at the end.

ASIDE   The correct name for someone who creates a playscript is "playwright." A playwright "wrights" (constructs) a play in much the same way a shipwright "wrights" (constructs) a ship. The literary activity of writing a playscript is called "playwriting" because it involves writing words. The word "playwrite" does not exist. When you understand that creating a play is an act or construction as much as a literary endeavor, you will understand what a playwright does.

One way to increase your understanding and appreciation of a play is to analyze its plot. Whether a play has a linear structure that is continuous or episodic, simple or complex—or even a cinematic structure—the plot includes an important question that is asked fairly early in the play. This question is called the **dramatic question** (Figure 6.3). The audience (or the reader) may not immediately recognize the dramatic question, but the search for its answer is what provides the play with its forward motion. We want to learn the answer, to find out what will happen. Will Tom Wingfield leave home? Will Godot arrive? The moment when the dramatic question is asked is what most theatre people call the **inciting event.** It marks the end of the introduction and the beginning of what is often called the **rising action,** the sequence of scenes in which events complicate the plot and heighten our suspense.

ASIDE   A play that has a *contextual* structure and therefore is made up of a number of short scenes, like Brecht's *The Private Life of the Master Race* or A. R. Gurney Jr.'s *Scenes from American Life,* has a dramatic question in each short scene, but no one dramatic question that governs the structure of the whole play.

About three-quarters of the way through most plays comes a moment we call the **crisis** or the **turning point.** Some people use one term, some the other—the terms are synonymous. At this critical moment, an event happens that changes the course of the story and leads inevitably to the answer to the dramatic question. Frequently, the event is a decision made by the central character. The scenes that follow the crisis are often called the **falling action,** because during these scenes the plot "falls" toward its ending.

When, very late in the play, the dramatic question is answered, the play has reached its resolution. You learn whether or not Tom leaves home; you learn whether or not Godot arrives. In the **conclusion,** the brief part of the play that follows the resolution, any lesser questions that were raised during the play are resolved and a new status quo is established.

You now understand that the arrangement of the incidents of the plot is carefully wrought by the playwright. Creating a play is an act of construction every bit as much as it is a literary act of writing.

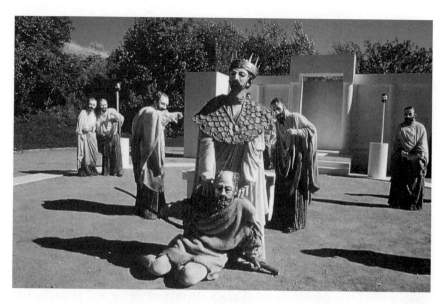

Figure 6.3 Aristotle used *Oedipus the King* as the exemplary play in *The Poetics*. Here Oedipus interrogates an old servant as he seeks the answer to the dramatic question, Will Oedipus learn who killed King Laius?

THE PLAYWRIGHT'S TOOLS

A playwright is an author who tells a story in which an inciting event disrupts the status quo by asking a question that sets in motion a sequence of events that conclude only when the question is answered and a new status quo is established.

FORESHADOWING

The Playwright's Four Tools

1. Dialogue
2. Stage directions
3. Characters
4. Actions

Dialogue

Dialogue describes the speeches that the characters say and is the playwright's primary tool. Most of the words a playwright writes are dialogue, and the dialogue is the entirety of the words that the audience hears spoken from the stage. Here's a sample bit of dialogue:

HE   I want to leave the room.

SHE   If you do, I won't sleep with you.

HE   I'll be back in three minutes.

SHE   If you leave, that's it.

HE   The five thousand dollars out there is very important to me.

SHE   You don't want me.

HE   I want the five thousand dollars more.

SHE   Come back in here.

Without any of the additional tools the playwright uses, it is very difficult to know how this dialogue would be spoken or by whom or what the dialogue means. While you were reading this sample conversation, you probably formed an initial sense of the meaning. Hold onto that impression while we discuss how the playwright's other tools clarify the dialogue and make the meaning more precise.

Stage Directions

Some of a character's actions are *implicit* in the dialogue. In the eight lines of sample dialogue, the actor playing HE must exit in order for SHE's last line to make any sense. Playwrights also write *explicit* **stage directions.** These descriptions tell the actors what their characters do or feel at particular moments. Although the audience never hears these descriptions, the stage directions are used by the playwright to shape what the audience experiences in a performance. Let's add some stage directions to these same eight lines, just the way a playwright might:

HE   I want to leave the room.

SHE   *(crying)* If you do, I won't sleep with you.

HE   *(disgusted)* I'll be back in three minutes.

SHE   If you leave, that's it.

HE   *(getting up)* The five thousand dollars out there is very important to me.

SHE   You don't want me.

HE   I want the five thousand dollars more.

       (HE exits.)

SHE   Come back in here.

Now the meaning of the dialogue is much less ambiguous. By including these stage directions, the playwright has ensured that the actors will perform the roles in a particular manner and that the audience not only will hear the dialogue but also will hear it spoken in a particular way and will see the characters do particular things. Has your first impression of the dialogue remained the same, or has it changed? Let's see what happens if the final stage direction is altered:

HE   I want the five thousand dollars more.

       (HE starts to leave. SHE pours a drink over his head. HE hits her with a pillow, they roll about on the bed, and they kiss. HE exits and she calls after him, laughing.)

SHE   Come back in here.

Now the dialogue ends happily instead of angrily. Altering this single stage direction has changed the meaning of the dialogue and more precisely defined the characters. Stage directions added to dialogue go a long way toward making a play come alive.

ASIDE   Some plays have no dialogue at all and are made up entirely of descriptions and stage directions. Samuel Beckett's *Act Without Words* is an excellent example of this unusual kind of play. The entirety of the audience's experience is formed from watching the actors doing the actions described by playwright Beckett.

Characters

Aristotle defines a character as "the agent for the action." Without a character, there'd be no way for the audience to hear the dialogue or see an action happen, because the character is the agent that speaks the dialogue and enacts the stage directions. Characters give body and coherence to the dialogue and the descriptions.

Let's return to our eight lines of dialogue. Did you imagine that the characters were your age? If so, the meaning of the action is quite clear: it's a lovers' quarrel. But what if the characters are a young mother and her five-year-old son? Read the initial dialogue again, without the stage directions, and imagine it spoken by these two new characters.

This time, HE wants to continue playing his game, and SHE wants him to take a nap. The line "I won't sleep with you" no longer is a euphemism but is now a simple declarative sentence. Also, the references to five thousand dollars lose their reality and their urgency, don't they? Indeed, you can probably imagine the lilting melody in the mother's voice that conveys a gentle warning as SHE says the last line, "Come back in here."

By using the raw materials of dialogue and description, the playwright reveals the characters' actions, but until you know who the characters are, you can't understand what's going on. You will learn in Chapter 7 that actors get information about their characters from four sources in the playscript: what the playwright says about the characters in stage directions, what characters say about themselves, what characters say about other characters, and what characters do. In these same four ways, the playwright shapes the characters. The playwright writes descriptions of particular emotional attitudes and specific activities; writes the characters' own dialogue, in which they describe themselves; writes the other characters' dialogue, in which they describe each other; and, most important, creates the characters' actions—both the physical actions and the intellectual choices that define each character. Using these four devices, the playwright creates the characters who make it possible for the plot to unfold.

Figure 6.4 Amanda achieves her goal in *The Glass Menagerie* when Laura meets the Gentleman Caller her brother Jim has brought home to dinner. (Milwaukee Repertory Theatre)

Actions

You saw a simple definition of "action" earlier in the chapter. Let's look at an example of action from *The Glass Menagerie* (Figure 6.4). Amanda wants to find a husband for Laura; that's her goal. Her obstacle is that no young men are interested in Laura. Amanda overcomes this obstacle by pressuring Tom to bring home an eligible young man who works with him at the shoe factory. Tom consents and brings Jim O'Connor home for dinner. Amanda has completed her action—she has changed the status quo and produced a result.

THE PLAYSCRIPT'S THEMES AND MEANING

A playwright might include many stimulating **themes** in a play. "Theme" is the term used by many teachers, reviewers, and critics to describe an abstract idea that exists outside the play as well as within it, an idea that can be discussed or written about. For example, a theme in *Waiting for Godot* might be expressed by the question: Has God abandoned Man? One of the compelling themes in *The Glass Menagerie* is that the love between siblings is more lasting than a mother's love.

The playwright's *major* concern, the idea the writer is keenest to communicate to the audience (or reader), is the idea that is expressed through the plot of the play. That idea is the play's **meaning.**

There is a simple way that you can figure out the meaning of a play, and it works whether the play is profound, like *Oedipus the King,* or frivolous, like a TV situation comedy. First, tell yourself the plot of the play. Next, condense the plot to one simple sentence; your sentence should begin, "This is the story of . . . ." Finally, make a generalization from that sentence—something that applies universally.

Here's an example, using Sophocles' *Oedipus the King:* "This is the story of Oedipus, who tries to escape the fate that the oracle of Apollo tells him but who discovers to his horror that he has fulfilled it by killing his father and marrying his mother." The generalization based on that synopsis might suggest the meaning "People are the victims of their fate."

Near the beginning of this chapter, we wrote that in the beginning is the word, the playwright's story. As you will learn in the next three chapters, actors, directors, and designers build upon the playwright's invention to shape the production that you experience when you go to the theatre. Your experience of that production is shaped by both the creative and the interpretive work of the collaborating artists, all of which is based on what the playwright has wrought.

EXERCISES

1. Read either *The Glass Menagerie* or *Waiting for Godot* and then, at home, write a synopsis of the plot in a single declarative sentence that begins "This is the story of . . . ." Next, write down the meaning of the play, the generalization about human experience that you can extrapolate from your statement of the plot. Bring your written work to class so that you can discuss what you and other students found the meaning to be. You will probably discover areas of agreement or disagreement that the play prompted.

2. Identify two themes in the play you read and think of other novels, movies, or plays that explore the same themes. Compare how the different writers feel about these themes.

3. After your class has attended a performance of a play, describe a moment in the play when the story was advanced by an action *not* expressed in dialogue.

4. Describe a moment in a play your class has seen when the story was advanced by an action that was expressed *only* in dialogue.

5. Describe the basic structure the playwright used for a play your class has seen, and discuss how the meaning of the play would have been different if it had been given a different structure.

CHAPTER 7

Actors and Characters

Actors start their work by reading the playwright's script. They analyze and interpret the playscript, and then they create their characters. When you go to the theatre, you see two actions simultaneously: what the actor does and what the character does. There's a profound difference between the actor and the character. In this chapter, we describe that difference so you can learn to appreciate the actor as much as you enjoy the character. After you have grasped this difference, we will describe some ways actors create a character and the nature of the characters they create. Then we will offer some insight into the rigorous reality of an actor's professional life.

An actor is a real human being who lives in our world. A character is a fictional being.

Ian McKellan is a real person. Gandalph was a character that McKellan played. Actors use the playwright's words, the designer's costumes, and their own talent and skills to create the characters we see on stage or screen. We *always* see the actors, but we pretend to ourselves that we are seeing the characters. If actors are successful, we *believe* in the characters they play, and the two blend into one. We frequently even mistake one for the other. When you describe the movie *Casablanca* to a friend, you might say, "And then Humphrey Bogart shoots the Nazi officer." But Bogart never shot anyone. Bogart fired a blank pistol and another actor fell down, pretending that his character was dead. Bogart didn't do the shooting; he did the acting. His character shot the other character.

> **ASIDE**   Linda asked me to tell this real-life anecdote that illustrates the way people can confuse the actor with the character. I was performing the role of Jerry in Edward Albee's funny and powerful play *Zoo Story*. Jerry is an intense, alienated, and disturbed young man who meets a stuffy businessman on a bench in New York's Central Park. Jerry talks to the businessman for a long time and finally tricks the man into holding a knife so Jerry can run onto it and commit suicide. The play was quite new when I did it, and the violent ending was considered startling. Some friends rode with me in a cab to the theatre, but when we met up after the performance, one person in the group held back. She had known me casually before she saw the play and had

seen me shortly before the performance began, but apparently the character of Jerry was so unsettling for her that afterward she was frightened to get in a cab with him—that is, with me. She couldn't separate the actor from the character.

Separating the character from the actor is more difficult when we're talking about movie and television actors. On stage, the character dominates the actor, and after we leave the theatre we remember what the character did. Hamlet died at the end of *Hamlet,* Eliza came back to Henry Higgins at the end of *My Fair Lady,* and Walter Lee told the white man to keep his money in the climactic scene of *A Raisin in the Sun.* On movie and television screens, however, the actor dominates the character, and we remember what the actor did. Humphrey Bogart shot the Nazi, Whoopi Goldberg led the choir of nuns, and Jimmy Smits solved the crime. Why does the actor dominate the character in film and television? First, the size of the actors on the screen overpowers you. On the big screen, actors' faces are 20 feet tall; they seem more important than you are—and more important than their characters. On television, actors' faces in close-up fill the whole screen; they too seem more important than their characters. Second, on TV and in the movies, actors look pretty much the same every time you see them. You grow familiar with them and expect to recognize them from film to film. Denzel Washington in *Training Day* for example, looks pretty much the same as Denzel Washington in *The Preacher's Wife.* The cult of personality dominates TV and movies, and we tend to experience film and television through the personalities of familiar actors.

On stage, the actors' faces seem rather small. You see their entire bodies at a distance, and you see them in the context of the scenery and in the company of other actors. Also, stage actors delight in transforming themselves so that they seem like different characters in each role (Figure 7.1). The great actor Laurence Olivier took pride in altering his appearance, his voice, and his posture, and in doing so he astonished audiences with his versatility. Olivier was able to perform these alterations in film as well as on stage. Watch the videos of his performances as the king in *Richard III,* as Heathcliff in *Wuthering Heights,* as Archie Rice in *The Entertainer,* and in the title role in *Othello.*

ASIDE   Some actors take great delight in fooling an audience. When a male actor wants to remain unknown to the audience, he will list himself in the program under the alias George Spelvin. This practice is widespread. A friend of ours once played two roles in the same play, using his own name for one role and the name George Spelvin for the other role. He received wonderful reviews as George Spelvin but was panned in his own name.

Figure 7.1 Actor Sam Sandoe created such different appearances, postures, and voices for his two roles as King Priam (left) and Calchus (right) in Shakespeare's *Troilus and Cressida* that the audience discovered the same actor had played both roles only when they read the program.

The distinction between the actor and the character is a difficult one to remember. Sometimes we are dominated by the actor and forget the character. Do you remember that Nicole Kidman's character in *Moulin Rouge!* was named Satine? In this case, Kidman's name, not the character's, is what we remember. At other times we are dominated by the character and forget the actor. Do you remember that the character James Bond was played by Sean Connery, Roger Moore, Timothy Dalton, George Lazenby, and Pierce Brosnan? Here the character is what we remember, and we don't pay much attention to the actor's name. (How many of you honestly remember George Lazenby?) The distinction between actor and character will become clearer once you understand how an actor creates a character.

WHAT ACTORS WORK WITH

An actor is a craftsperson who has learned a particular set of skills, in much the same way carpenters and computer programmers have learned their sets of skills. Some actors have learned their skills better than others, and some have more natural aptitude. That's why some actors are better than others.

In practicing their craft, actors work with the text, the self, and the context. The **text** is the playwright's written words that make up the playscript. The **self** is the actor's voice, body, imagination, and discipline. The **context** is the circumstances in which the actor works—the time, the space, the other people, the physical circumstances of the setting and costumes, and the audience. Let's look at each of these raw materials more closely.

⬤ *F O R E S H A D O W I N G*

The Actor's Three Raw Materials

1. Text
2. Self
3. Context

Text

The text, or playscript, is that seminal creative work that the playwright wrote. It provides the actors with much of the raw material for their performances. The playscript gives clues about the character the actor must create, and one skill an actor must master is how to analyze a playscript in order to discover the character. A playscript offers four sources of information that the actor must examine. Let's take a look at these sources.

⬤ *F O R E S H A D O W I N G*

Four Sources of Character Information

1. What the playwright says about the characters in stage directions
2. What characters say about themselves
3. What characters say about other characters
4. What characters do

Stage Directions   The first source of information is what the playwright says about the characters in stage directions that are outside the dialogue. Some playwrights provide lengthy and detailed descriptions of their characters, and actors must read these descriptions with great care, noting all pertinent information. English playwright George Bernard Shaw was famous for writing very complete descriptions in which he told the actor what the character looked like and sounded like as well as the character's beliefs and motivations. Few playwrights write as extensively as Shaw did, but most provide what they believe will be helpful information. Some playwrights place descriptions of a character at the front of the playscript, some include descriptions at the place in the script where a character first appears, and others sprinkle the information throughout the script, interspersed with the dialogue. Actors can trust the playwrights' directions and must use them in creating their characters. Of course, not all playwrights provide descriptions. Indeed, the practice is relatively recent; only in the past 150 years have playwrights included descriptions of the sort that Shaw provided. Shakespeare and other playwrights who wrote in earlier eras expected the actors to extricate information about their characters from the dialogue. Also, the playwrights expected to be on hand during rehearsals to explain the characters to the actors. Some modern playwrights, like Tennessee Williams, provide helpful stage directions. Others, like Samuel Beckett, write very few stage directions.

What Characters Say about Themselves   Characters frequently describe themselves through their dialogue and tell others (and you) what they look like, what they sound like, what they believe, and what they know. Much of this information is accurate, but actors have to be careful. Characters can lie, or they can be wrong or deluded. A character may describe himself as very handsome, and he might be—or he might be lying or he might think he's handsome when all the other characters describe him as grotesque. Actors need to be cautious and not take their characters' self-descriptions as accurate unless those descriptions are corroborated elsewhere in the playscript. The dialogue does, however, provide information that actors can use in creating their characters.

What Characters Say about Other Characters   A character might say, "Here comes Mary and she looks angry" or "Mary is the tallest woman I know" or "Mary can be depended on to tell us the truth; she never lies." The actor preparing the role of Mary must take note of all these descriptions but must also be cautious about taking them at face value. Is the character who describes Mary's anger saying it honestly or in jest? Is the character who describes Mary as a tall woman telling the truth? Is the character who describes Mary's integrity speaking ironically? The actor must sort out these bits of information and integrate them into her understanding of the character Mary.

Consider the character Iago in Shakespeare's tragedy *Othello* (Figure 7.2). Iago is one of the greatest villains ever written, and by the end of the play he's described as a "damnèd villain" and a "demi-devil." Early in the play, all the characters like and respect Iago, and he's described as "a man of honesty and trust." If the actor portrays Iago as the oily villain the audience knows him to be, the other characters will seem stupid and the play won't make much sense. The information that the actor finds in the dialogue by and about Iago should guide him to create a character who appears to be attractive, modest-spoken, and stalwart.

What Characters Do   The first three sources of information actors find in the playscript are valuable, but not as important as the fourth: what the characters *do*. Characters are delineated more by actions than by words. Iago, for example, extorts money from Roderigo, lies to Othello, beats his wife, and stabs Cassio. Despite what Iago says about himself and despite how much the other characters' lines describe Iago as "honest," it is what Iago does that makes his character clear to the actor playing the role.

Man is the sum total of his actions.
    —JEAN-PAUL SARTRE

A good way to discuss this concept of character is by reference to Existentialism, the dominant philosophy of the twentieth century. Existentialism was best explained by the French philosopher and playwright Jean-Paul Sartre, who observed that we are the sum total of our actions. Whatever we

Figure 7.2   The character Iago must seem trustworthy and honest in the early scenes of *Othello.* Here Iago swears an oath to serve Othello faithfully. Scene designer Eric Fielding's split-faced stone mask in the background suggests to the audience that faces can be deceiving and that Othello may be foolish to trust Iago. (Colorado Shakespeare Festival)

say we are and whatever others think we are, we are truly defined by what we *do*. Consider this example. Your neighbor is a good family man. He provides well for his wife and children, goes to church regularly, pays his taxes, and maintains his house and yard attractively. He volunteers time to coach the Little League team, is a careful driver, and is well liked where he works and where he lives. One day he comes home from work and murders his wife and children with a shotgun. No matter how favorably his neighbors and the members of his church describe him in terms of the good things he did before that fateful day, the world will forever describe him as a murderer. No matter what justifications, motivations, and rationalizations he offers, he is a murderer. He is what he did. He did some good deeds. He killed his wife and children. He is the sum total of his actions.

For the first three sources of information about a character, actors write down all the pertinent information and then sort out what is true. They end up with a list of physical descriptions, vocal qualities, and personality traits that will help them create the character. For the fourth source—what the character does—actors have to work harder. They are helped in this work by a system of character analysis that was developed nearly a century ago by Russian actor, director, and teacher Constantine Stanislavsky. The **Stanislavsky System** is the dominant system of character analysis used by actors today, and it has a particular vocabulary.

EXPOSITION
. . . .

We won't have a chance in this introductory book to describe many of the fascinating alternative approaches to acting, so you might ask your instructor to tell you about the Polish teacher Jerzy Grotowski, the Japanese Tadashi Suzuki, or the American Ann Bogart or about the ways Asian and African theatrical traditions are reshaping American acting. Because Stanislavsky-based acting is still dominant in American theatre, we'll limit our discussion to this approach.

. . . .

If you understand the basics of an actor's work, you will appreciate how an actor goes about creating a character and will be more qualified to judge and describe an actor's performance. Here's a short version of a Stanislavskian actor's vocabulary:

Objective: What do I want?
Obstacle: What's in my way?
Action: What do I do to get what I want?

An actor analyzing Oedipus's first scene will determine that Oedipus's **objective** is "to comfort the citizens of Thebes." His **obstacle** is the fact that Creon has not yet returned with advice from the Oracle at Delphi. His **action** is "promising to follow the oracle's advice." Note that the objective is phrased as an infinitive: "to comfort." The obstacle is phrased as a statement: "the fact." The action is phrased as a gerund: "promising." The actor's analysis prepares him for the scene and gives him something active to do. "Promising" is doing something; it is an action that the character Oedipus does.

> **ASIDE**   A role is the entirety of a character's part in a play. It is called a "role" because in earlier times actors received their lines written on a roll of paper. (The words "role" and "roll" once meant the same thing.)

In Stanislavsky's system of analysis, a character has one overriding desire in a play, a **super objective.** This super objective answers the question "What do I want?" throughout the character's **role.** A character's complete role is constructed from a large number of **units.** Each unit begins when the character wants something new, and it continues for the duration of the character's quest for that objective. Units are the building blocks with which a character's total role is built. The objective for each of the character's units must relate to the super objective. Oedipus's super objective is to find out who killed King Laius. In the unit with the blind prophet, Tiresias, Oedipus's smaller objective is to learn what Tiresias knows, because that knowledge might help Oedipus discover the murderer.

A conscientious actor uses the Stanislavsky System to analyze every unit of the role. Actors spend a lot of time on this task before rehearsals begin and they continue their work throughout the rehearsal process so that they may perform the role believably. Actors add what they learn about a character from this rigorous analysis of actions to what they learn about the character's appearance, voice, and behavior from a close reading of the playscript. Actors use all this information to understand the character they are creating.

EXPOSITION
• • • • • • • • • • •

Actors trained in the Stanislavsky System use the word **"beat"** to describe a segment of a role that is even briefer than a unit—a segment with a tiny objective (to speak to a friend on the phone) and a small obstacle (the friend hasn't answered yet) that guides the actor to a small action (listening to the rings). The word "beat" came into use when American students studied with a Russian actress who would talk of a tiny "bit" of action. Her accented English made the word "bit" sound like "beat," and that word became part of actors' vocabulary.

• •

Self

Actors' only instrument is their own self. Actors can grow extremely jealous of painters who use a brush and of musicians who use a violin, because those artists' instruments are separate from themselves. The better the violin, the better the music it can produce. Because the actors' instrument is the self, there can be no separation between artist and instrument. Actors must use their own body, their own voice, their own imagination, and their own discipline. Actors apply each of these four aspects of the self to create the character that the playwright imagined in the script and that they have discovered through their analysis. Through the use of these four aspects of the self, actors interpret the playwright's character and create a performance.

▶ FORESHADOWING

The Four Aspects of the Self

1. Body
2. Voice
3. Imagination
4. Discipline

Figure 7.3   Actor Kim Pereira was born in India but he wears the European costume of Lucky in *Waiting for Godot.* (The Laboratory Theatre, Florida)

Body   The actor must use his or her body to look like the character. By analyzing the script, the actor can learn the character's age, size, posture, and carriage. Is the character young or old, tall or heavy, ramrod erect or bent with illness? Does the character move gracefully or with a notable limp? During the performance, we in the audience will hear the same information in the dialogue that the actor reads in the script, and the actor's physical characterization must conform to what we hear. Frequently, the script is not specific, and the actor's own appearance can represent that of the character (Figure 7.3). Many stage actors enjoy developing their characters' unique look and frequently alter their own appearance in the service of their craft. For example, if the character is described as blond, the actor might dye his hair or wear a wig. Of course, there are limits to the degree that actors can disguise their own bodies and appearance, but some amazing physical characterizations can be achieved with the help of costumes and makeup. Figure 7.4 shows how effectively a woman can play the male role of Falstaff in Shakespeare's *The Merry Wives of Windsor.* A close analysis of the script also guides the actor to the mannerisms of the character. Is the character calm or fidgety? Does she wet her lips or comb her hair repeatedly?

This first and most obvious step in creating a character is achieved by making certain that the actor's body conforms to the dictates of the script. The talented and imaginative actor goes beyond the barest necessities and invents details of the character's physical being that make the character unique and interesting. If her character is confident, the actor may determine that she moves slowly. If his character is timid, the actor may determine that he rarely looks another character in the eye. Talented actors work to make their characters as individualized and complex as a real person.

Figure 7.4   Pat Carroll played Falstaff in Shakespeare's *The Merry Wives of Windsor* at the Shakespeare Theatre in Washington, D.C. The character is male but the actor is female. The actor has disguised her own body and appearance in order to look like the character described in the play.

Voice   The actor must use his or her voice to sound like the character. Many scripts require a character to have an accent or a regional dialect. If the character's first language is Russian or if the character is from Texas, the actor must be skilled enough to affect the correct speech so as to create a believable character. Similarly, the actor must determine the character's vocal quality. Is the voice high pitched or low? Does the character speak in a nasal whine or with a full-throated and honeyed voice? Does the character have a lisp or a whiskey rattle? Further, the actor must find the character's tempo and rhythm. Does the character speak quickly or slowly, evenly or haltingly? Some of this information is found in the script, but much of it will come from the actor's imaginative choices. As long as those choices do not conflict with what the playscript requires, the actor may choose to speak in a way that makes that character unique.

Each person has such a singular manner of speaking that we easily recognize our friends and family on the phone. The actor's job is to create the character's particular way of speaking. For example, if her character is methodical and well educated, the actor might decide to articulate her consonants precisely. If his character is hard of hearing, the actor might choose to speak just a little too loudly. The actor's creativity builds on the interpretive use of the playwright's creations.

Imagination   We all have particular talents. An actor's talent is merely a different kind of talent from that of an athlete or a mathematician. Actors have a talent for "feeling" themselves into their characters by using their **imagination.** Actors, poets, and other artists often have an ability to feel more broadly more and more deeply than the average person. They also have a talent for communicating this feeling to others. This talent is called "empathy." It is different from sympathy. When we *sympathize* with someone's sadness, we have an intellectual understanding of it but remain apart from it; we "share" their sadness. When we *empathize* with that sadness, we feel it in our bodies; we "participate" in it.

Because actors must convince the audience to suspend its disbelief and to pretend that the actors' characters are real, this talent for empathizing with someone else is essential, but actors need more than native talent. Actors must achieve an empathetic identification with their character in *every performance* and can't depend on inspiration alone. They must have a technique for reproducing the emotion *on demand*. Stanislavsky discovered a way for actors to reproduce emotion: a process he called **emotional recall.** Stanislavsky taught actors to recall moments from their own life experience when they felt an emotion very similar to the one the character experiences and to use their own emotion as a substitute for the character's. Here's an example from Tennessee Williams's *The Glass Menagerie.* The script says that Laura is extremely shy when the Gentleman Caller comes to her home, so the actress has to experience extreme shyness at the moment she sees the actor playing Jim O'Connor. To do this, the actor needs to recall that emotion from her own life by concentrating very hard on remembering the physical sensations she experienced when she felt extremely shy—what she saw at that time, what she heard, and what she smelled, tasted, touched, and felt. Through this concentrated act of remembrance, the actor can reexperience her own true emotion. After she has repeated this exercise frequently, she can quite readily recall how it feels to be shy. Then, during rehearsals, she can recall the emotion every time she speaks the character's lines. After many repetitions of this effort, a sort of magical transference brings about a fusion of the character's lines and the actor's emotion. The result of all this hard work is a truthful performance that the audience believes (Color Plate 12).

In the process of creating a character, actors must use their skill at imagining with as concentrated a rigor as they use their skill at imitating physical and vocal behavior. An actor's ability to imagine emotion can be increased through training and experience, but a natural talent for empathy is essential. A long role requires an actor to create a large number of the character's emotions, and self-discipline is needed to create truthful emotions that an audience will find believable throughout a performance.

ASIDE   One result of the technique of emotional recall is that the audience is regularly tricked into believing that the actor has turned into the character. An actor went to see a film starring Marlon Brando, and the great actor's sister went with him. Brando is celebrated as one of the finest modern actors because of his extraordinary ability to use emotional recall to create believable emotions for his characters. As they sat in the darkened theatre, Jocelyn Brando kept up a running commentary on Marlon's performance with observations like "That's Marlon being mad at Dad," "Now he's using the time he got a puppy," "That's when he got a bad report card." The character's emotions were persuasive, and the actor's substitutions were invisible to everyone but his sister.

Discipline   The fourth aspect of the actor's self that must be applied in the preparation of a performance is **discipline.** In order to achieve a careful analysis of the text, the rigorous physical and vocal delineation of the character, and the imaginative creation of the character's emotions, the actor must be as disciplined as a research chemist, a concert pianist, or a professional athlete. Acting is hard work, and the actor must use willpower to ensure that the necessary discipline is observed.

ASIDE   In preparing the role of Othello, Laurence Olivier worked on his voice for six months before rehearsals began and managed to lower his speaking range from a light baritone to a bass-baritone. He also pumped iron to build up his body so that he would look more like the mighty warrior Othello is described as in the playscript (Figure 7.5). One reason why Olivier is revered as one of the greatest actors of the twentieth century is because he disciplined himself rigorously in the practice of his craft.

Context

Acting is not a solitary art. The fellow artists and the physical circumstances in which the actor works contribute to the context in which a performance is created. Context includes the amount of time in which the work must be done, the space where the production is rehearsed, the other people the actor works with, the particular circumstances of the production (the setting and costumes), and the audience.

Time is part of the actor's context. Having just read about the extensive work actors do in preparing a role, you may wonder when they do it. Typically, actors are hired only a few weeks before the first rehearsal. They have a very short time in which to analyze the script and to begin recalling true emotions that they can substitute for their characters' feelings during the rehearsal period. When rehearsals begin, actors work an eight-hour day six days a week. In addition, they spend whatever time they can at home learning lines, continuing their analysis, and recalling their own emotions.

Figure 7.5 Laurence Olivier played the role of Othello only after he had spent months building up his physique through rigorous physical exercises and lowering the pitch of his speaking voice through rigorous vocal exercises.

Conscientious actors spend forty-eight hours a week in rehearsal and another twenty-four hours a week working on their role at home. With a typical rehearsal period in American theatres today of less than four weeks, time is an important part of an actor's context.

The space the actor works in is another part of the actor's context. Most plays in America are rehearsed in empty rooms that are inadequate and inappropriate. Rehearsal halls are rarely as large as the stage, and many have obstructing pillars, flickering fluorescent lights, or dirty bathrooms. Unfortunately, the actor's typical work space is not conducive to the pursuit of excellence.

People are the third part of an actor's context. Actors work very closely with other actors, not all of whom they like or respect. Yet actors must collaborate with one another so that their characters' objectives can meld smoothly and so that the performance can be safe and effective (Figure 7.6). Actors also must work with directors, choreographers, musical directors, fight directors, musicians, costume designers, and stage managers. An actor's performance is shaped to a very significant degree by the work of the other people involved in the production.

It is common for a production to be designed before rehearsals begin, so actors must accommodate their work to the stage setting and the costumes that have been planned by others. Design is another part of the actor's context.

Finally, of course, the actor works with the audience. Each performance of a play is different because each audience is different. Sometimes the theatre

Figure 7.6   Even if actors dislike each other, they must collaborate to ensure that they don't get hurt and that the audience can suspend its disbelief. The actors' rehearsals for this fight in Robert Potter's *Queen Margaret* involved the director, the fight choreographer, the costume designer, the scene designer, the weapons master, the property master, the lighting designer, and the stage manager. Other people are an important part of the actor's context. (Colorado Shakespeare Festival)

is filled with enthusiastic people who laugh and applaud. Other times the theatre is half empty, and the audience rattles candy wrappers and talks out loud. The audience significantly influences the actors' work.

During a performance, actors are very aware of the audience, and they think on three levels at once. They don't *become* the character, because that would mean they would stop being themselves—that they would be insane. Instead, they think "as their character" and at the same time continue to think "as themselves." As their character, they think about what their character wants, feel their character's emotions, and react to what the other characters say and do. As themselves, they monitor how they're acting and how the audience is reacting: is the pace fast enough? is my voice loud enough? how can I make the audience look at me and not at that kid playing with the dog upstage?

The third level has nothing to do with their acting and everything to do with their real lives: did I put the butter in the refrigerator? when will my divorce be final? When the second or third level distracts the actor from the first level, trouble arises. That's when actors don't hear their cues and forget their lines. Their awareness of the audience's part in the context is vital, but it mustn't become distracting.

ASIDE   Actors are wary of sharing the stage with children and dogs because audiences smile and go "ahhhh" instead of paying attention to the adults and the plot. The sophisticated English actor and playwright Noel Coward took a friend's young son to the theatre. Mid-performance, the audience started giggling at some dogs belonging to the characters in the crowd at the side of the stage. The boy asked what the dogs were doing, and Coward told him that the one in front was blind and the very kind dog behind was trying to push the other one off the stage.

WHERE ACTORS GET TRAINING

For centuries, young actors learned their craft by joining a permanent company of actors and working their way up from nonspeaking **walk-on** to major player, or by apprenticing to an accomplished actor who gave them private instruction. Today, most young actors get formal **training** at college, pursuing a course of instruction in much the same way as pre-med students. Students who major in theatre learn how to analyze plays, study the history of theatre and drama, and begin to learn their craft. They take classes in skills such as voice production, stage combat, foreign dialects, historic dances, and circus technique—and they take many courses in acting. A sequence of acting classes usually starts with exercises in relaxation and concentration and progresses through observation and imitation to improvisation and emotional recall, then to "scene study" in which students act short scenes from contemporary plays, and finally to acting scenes from dramas that challenge the actor's language skills and physical control. "Period Styles" is the name commonly given to acting classes in which students prepare scenes from plays written in earlier centuries, when the conventions of performance were different from today's: ancient Greek tragedies, sixteenth-century Italian farces of the *commedia dell'arte*, eighteenth-century English comedies of manners, and twentieth-century tragicomedies of the theatre of the absurd, among others. A year-long course in acting Shakespeare is often the final class.

Along with their formal instruction, students act in plays. They learn by doing, in front of an audience. The plays produced by a college are, in part, a laboratory in which students develop their craft (Figure 7.7).

Many students continue their studies beyond college. They attend professional schools in New York like The Neighborhood Playhouse or The Juilliard School, or they embark on a university's three-year degree program, comparable to programs offered by medical and business schools that lead to the M.D. and M.B.A. degrees. Actors earn a Master of Fine Arts (M.F.A.). Four of the most respected graduate schools for actors are Yale, Delaware, New York University, and the University of California at San Diego.

Figure 7.7 Young actors develop their skills and practice their craft in college productions such as Marquette University's *Something's Afoot,* shown here, a musical parody of Agatha Christie's murder mysteries. (Costumes by Linda Sarver)

In whatever way actors get their early training, their learning doesn't stop when their formal schooling ends. Actors continue to study throughout their careers. Even the most famous can be found in scene-study classes at respected places like The Actors' Studio, where master teachers help them hone their skills, practice their craft, and develop their talents.

ASIDE   Actors sometimes take their work too seriously. A student actor was rehearsing to play the title role in the powerful drama *The Diary of Anne Frank.* Overwhelmed by the challenge, she worried that she would be a failure in the role. She was particularly afraid of disappointing her fellow actors. After two weeks of rehearsals in New York City, she had to drive three hours upstate to the summer theatre where she'd be performing. Alone in her car, she grew more and more agitated. It started to rain. Her windshield wipers were dirty, and she was having trouble seeing the road. All she could think about was how humiliated she would be when the audience jeered at her. She started crying. She was concentrating so completely on how badly she would play the role of Anne Frank that she didn't realize she had slowed to 15 miles an hour—creeping along in the fast lane of the expressway.

(continued)

Drivers behind her honked, swerved around her on the right, and cursed at her. She didn't see any of this but instead just hunched over the driver's wheel, crying, wailing to herself about how terrible she would be in the role of Anne. She was isolated in her obsession. Finally, in her rear-view mirror, she saw the flashing blue light of a police car. She came out of her reverie just enough to slowly inch her way to the right lane and then pull onto the shoulder. She was crying hysterically by this time and tears were streaming down her face. As the officer walked up to her car, she rolled down the window. His face tense with rage, the policeman yelled, *"DO YOU KNOW WHAT YOU'RE DOING?"* Through her sobs she answered, "I'm doing Anne Frank, and I'm going to be terrible."

In the same way that athletes cry when they lose an important game and doctors are thrilled when they save a patient, actors need to succeed. It's the most important thing in the world for them. Acting is more than a job. It's a vocation, a life-consuming calling in much the same way that a member of the clergy feels a calling to serve. Old actors will tell youngsters, "You don't choose theatre, theatre chooses you." Sure, theatre is playful, and we call acting "playing," but theatre matters vitally to the people who create it and it has a lasting impact on the audience, and that is why theatre is vitally important to *you*.

HOW ACTORS GET WORK

Actors don't answer ads in newspapers or go to employment agencies, and nobody comes to their campus on Career Day to recruit them. Actors **audition.** Everyone agrees that the process of auditioning is imperfect, but nobody has ever come up with a better way to match actors to roles (Figure 7.8). In Hollywood they may call it a **screen test,** but it all comes down to actors performing a short selection from the script and the director choosing the actor for the job. If you want to see auditions in progress, watch *A Chorus Line,* the movie based on the hit Broadway musical.

ASIDE   Many prominent actors auditioned to replace Nathan Lane in the hit musical *The Producers*, and English star Henry Goodman was chosen. A few weeks later, box office receipts began to fall off. Goodman was fired, and Lane's understudy was put into the role. Auditions are an imperfect way to choose actors, but Goodman fared just fine. His contract guaranteed him a full year's employment; and he earned $13,000 a week for *not* acting.

Figure 7.8

*"Don't get tense, it's just an audition.
Now, the character is an unemployed actress
who always whines about not getting jobs because
the girls that get hired are younger and sexier.
Can you relate to that?"*

Here's how actors get work in the profession, whether the job is on Broadway or at a regional theatre far from New York. The commercial **producer** or the regional theatre's **artistic director** needs an actor to play Laura in *The Glass Menagerie.* He (Linda has agreed we can use the male pronoun in this example even though many producers and artistic directors are women) doesn't have the money to travel all around the country holding auditions, and he doesn't have the time to audition every actor who'd like to be heard. So the producer hires a **casting director,** who makes a living by providing a service—selecting the actors that will audition. The casting director prepares a **breakdown** and sends it to every actors' **agent** in New York. A breakdown is a very short description of the roles to be cast (age, gender, ethnicity, physical type, musical or dance skills), and it provides some basic information about the production (title of the play, dates of the job, salary range, where the play will be produced, who will direct it). Agents "represent" actors— they help their clients get jobs, negotiate contracts for them, and advise on their careers. Agents make a living by taking 10 percent of an actor's salary. When the agent's clients work, she makes a living; when they don't, she doesn't (Tom has agreed we should describe the agent as a female). The agent goes through her files and chooses which of her clients she thinks might have a chance of getting the job described on the breakdown. She submits the actors' **photo/resumés** to the casting director. A photo/resumé is an 8×10

NOEL TRUE
SAG-AFTRA-AEA

Height:	5'5"	Eyes:	Brown
Weight:	125	Hair:	Brown

Film

Bianca	*Heaven Aint Hard to Find*	Hodgepodge Productions	Richard Hodge, Dir.
Corinne (Lead)	*Me and My Mom*	NYU Grad Film	Mark E. Johnson

Television

Tina Brookstone	*Law & Order: SVU*	Wolf Films/Studios USA	
Ashley (recurring)	*All My Children*	ABC-TV	
Nurse	*The Guiding Light*	Procter & Gamble	
Lauren	*Bell Atlantic Industrial*	Circle Interactive, Inc.	

was a regular on Sesame Street, ages 5-8

Off-Broadway

Woman, Young W. (US)	*St. Lucy's Eyes*	Cherry Lane Theatre	Billie Allen

Off-Off Broadway

Mary	*Whoa-Jack!*	Worth St. Theater Co.	Jeff Cohen
Joy, Woman, Grandma	*Snapshots 2000*	Worth St. Theater Co.	Jeff Cohen
Natasha	*The Three Sisters*	Mud/Bone Collective	Giovanna Sardelli
Lis	*First You're Born*	NYU Director's Lab	Torben Brooks

Regional

Gina	*Ghosts*	The Shakespeare Theatre	Ed Sherin
Julia	*The Rivals*	The Shakespeare Theatre	Keith Baxter
Hermia	*A Midsummer Night's Dream*	The Shakespeare Theatre	Mark Lamos
Nina	*The Seagull*	Shakespeare Santa Cruz	Risa Brainin
Hero	*Much Ado About Nothing*	Berkeley Rep.	Brian Kulick
Viola (US)	*Twelfth Night*	The Guthrie Theater	Joe Dowling
Haydee	*The Count of Monte Cristo*	Pioneer Theater Co.	Chuck Morey
Olivia	*Twelfth Night*	Hudson Valley Shakes.	Terrence O'Brien
Anne Page	*Merry Wives of Windsor*	Shakespeare Santa Cruz	Sari Ketter
Juliet	*Romeo and Juliet*	Colorado Shakes. Fest.	Henry Godinez
Helen of Troy	*Troilus and Cressida*	Colorado Shakes. Fest.	Tom Markus
Helene	*Strangers in Their Own Land*	Horizons Theater	Leslie Jacobson

Training

Acting	MFA, New York University's Graduate Acting Program
Dance	Advanced ballet, tap, jazz, clogging, modern, ballroom
Voice	Mezzo/Alto (belt)

NOEL TRUE

Figure 7.9 This 8×10 glossy photo (left) shows the casting director what this actor truly looks like. The resumé (right) of early-career actor Noel True tells casting directors what roles she's played, where, who directed the plays, and where she was trained.

black-and-white photo of the actor with some information about the actor on the reverse (Figure 7.9). A photo/resumé is for an actor what a business card is for other professionals. For each role to be cast, the casting director receives one or more submissions from many different agents. The casting director then screens these to select who will be invited to audition.

Have you figured out that the actor is not necessarily aware of what's going on? The actor may not know auditions will be held for the Arizona Theatre Company's forthcoming production of *The Glass Menagerie.* Her agent may not have submitted her photo/resumé to the casting director. The casting director may not have selected her to audition. Actors, particularly young actors, are rarely in control of their careers (Figure 7.10).

Let's assume our actor *is* going to audition. What happens? Her agent phones her a couple of days in advance and tells her when and where the audition will be held. She is told what scene from the play she will be asked to read. Even if the audition is for a well-known play, the casting director will have **sides** available in her office.

ASIDE   Before plays were protected by copyright laws, the complete script was kept under lock and key so that no competitor could steal it.

Actor   Actor's Agent   Audition   Casting Director   Director

Figure 7.10   The casting process involves many people.

Actors learned their lines from pages that had the final phrase of the previous character's speech written at the top of each page, followed by their own speech. These pages were called "sides," the term still used today.

Our actor prepares as carefully as she can, perhaps even learning the words of the scene. The audition usually is held in a small room in a New York office building. She waits in the hall with the other actors until it's her turn. The casting director admits her and introduces the director, who sits at a table with her photo/resumé in front of him. They may exchange a few pleasantries. Then the actor reads her scene, with a **reader** saying all the other lines. A reader is usually a young actor who's been hired to sit in a chair facing the actor (facing away from the director) and speak all the lines spoken by all the other characters in the auditioner's scene. The director may ask the actor to repeat part of the scene, making an adjustment of some sort: "Try flirting with the Gentleman Caller instead of shrinking from him." The entire audition takes five to ten minutes, and then the actor leaves. She goes home and will probably never hear another word about this job.

If the director wants to consider the actor further, he might have the casting director invite her to a **call-back** audition. The director has the casting director phone the agent, who phones the actor to schedule the call-back. This audition is similar to the first, but the actor may be asked to read an additional scene or to read a scene with another actor who has been called back for the role of Jim O'Connor. When the call-back is over, the actor leaves and will probably never hear another word.

At the end of the audition process, the director chooses the actor he wants to offer the role to. He usually chooses one or more alternatives in case his first choice is not available. Then the casting director phones the agent, who phones the actor with the offer. Presuming our actor wants to play Laura, the agent will negotiate to get her the highest possible salary (and thereby increase her own 10 percent) and will also negotiate a few other items, like travel arrangements, quality of accommodations, or use of a car. Finally the actor accepts or declines the offer. Actors who aren't offered the job learn what happened only indirectly—their agent never calls them with an offer. Actors

Richard Burbage, the actor who first played the role of Hamlet, had the last word about his career. The engraving on his tombstone reads "Exit Burbage."

who are submitted by their agent but not selected by the casting director rarely even know they have been submitted. Actors whose agents don't submit them never know it. That's part of why actors frequently are frustrated with their agents and why lots of angry jokes are told about agents.

> **ASIDE**   An actor comes home from an audition and finds his apartment on fire. He asks what happened, and the fireman tells him that his agent stopped by, assaulted his wife, beat his children, killed his dog, and set the drapes on fire. The actor is shocked into silence and then says, "You mean my agent came to my house to see me?"

WHAT AN ACTOR'S LIFE IS LIKE

Nathan Lane earned $50,000 a week when *The Producers* first opened on Broadway. Most actors don't earn enough in a year to pay for medical insurance. You've seen the fabulous life of jet-setting celebrities on *Entertainment Tonight*, but *People* doesn't write about the thousands of workaday actors who can't afford their monthly rent. Most actors struggle. We're going to provide you with a bit of information that will help you understand what their lives are like. It isn't all greasepaint and glory, as you're about to discover.

Actors belong to national unions just like those for plumbers, musicians, electricians, and university professors. Unions negotiate working conditions for their members: the number of hours you can work each day, the frequency of your rest breaks, the length of your annual paid vacation, your pension plan, your medical insurance, your protection from sexual harassment, and, of course, the minimum salary you can be paid. Actors belong to several unions. Actors Equity Association (usually called just "Equity") oversees all stage actors. The Screen Actors Guild (SAG) is for film actors. The American Federation of Television and Radio Artists (AFTRA) is for actors who work on videotape and for all radio actors. Each union has its own rules and regulations, and most actors belong to all three.

While each union has its own statistics, the profile of one is pretty much like the profile of another. Here are some statistics from Equity's *Annual Report for 2001–02*, the most current numbers available at the time we're writing. Equity had 39,507 members nationwide, and 43.7 percent worked during the year. That means that 56.3 percent did not have a job—22,224 actors did not earn a single penny by acting on the stage during the entire year. Only 14.5 percent of the membership was employed in an average week. That means that 85.5 percent of the total membership was *unemployed each week*. The median income for the year was $6,277. If Nathan Lane was at the top of the field and earned fifty grand a week ($2.6 million for the year) and if the unemployed majority were at the bottom and earned zip, then the median for the *year* was less than one-eighth of what Lane earned in a *week*. Most working actors—we'll put aside the 56.3 percent who don't land a single job—have several short-term jobs during a year. They may act in a play for eight weeks in Atlanta, work for three days on a TV series filmed in New York, narrate a radio commercial for a local station, and still need to augment their income working as a waiter, word processor, or dog walker. As a wise man once said, you can make a killing in the theatre, you just can't make a living.

Since 1990, the three Law and Order *TV series have provided New York actors with more than 36,400 days of work. The minimum daily wage is $655.*

ASIDE   By comparison, the national average yearly income for school teachers in 2001 was $44,367, and the national average for dental hygienists in 1999 was $48,150. When your parents discourage you from becoming an actor, listen to them.

Actors' lives are difficult on an emotional level, as well. Most of you will work at one job for an arc of years, live in one city, and raise a family. Actors go where the work is, live out of a suitcase for as long as it lasts, and continually make and lose new friends. It is a very lonely life much of the time, and actors have a hard time maintaining a stable financial or domestic life. It isn't all greasepaint and glory—not by a long shot (Figure 7.11).

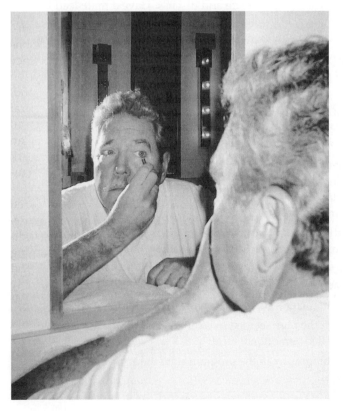

Figure 7.11   Actor Steve Small puts on makeup to play the character Ben in Arthur Miller's *Death of a Salesman.* (New Harmony Theatre)

So why do they do it? The economic rewards may be modest, but acting offers social, spiritual, and personal rewards that actors value. They know that their work contributes to society, that the theatre they create improves the quality of life for their fellow citizens. We actors believe with a nearly religious fervor that our art brings enlightenment to the world and that our spiritual lives are enriched by the experience of making theatre. We actors raise our sense of self-worth when we express ourselves through our art and achieve personal fulfillment. The great Laurence Olivier once told an interviewer that acting is the worst profession in the world with respect to financial reward and emotional suffering, but that an actor has no choice: we can't not do it.

From Olivier down to the absolute beginner, all actors need the playwright's words in order to begin their work. Actors analyze and interpret the script as a first step toward creating their role and then collaborate with the director and designers to create the performance you attend. In the next chapter, we examine the director's impact on your experience.

EXERCISE

After your class has attended a performance, bring the program (playbill) to class so you can refer to it for the names of the actors and characters. Gather in groups of ten to twelve students and select one male actor's and one female actor's performance to analyze and discuss. Have a male lead the discussion of the female actor's character and a female lead that of the male actor's character. Use the following questions to stimulate your discussion.

1. What aspect of the character's appearance did the script require, and what aspect of the character's appearance seemed to be the actor's own creation?

2. What aspect of the character's physical behavior did the script require, and what aspect of the character's physical behavior seemed to be the actor's own creation?

3. What particular physical skills did the script require that the actor must have learned in formal training before rehearsals for this production began, and what did the actor do physically that was not required for the performance and seemed to be the actor's unique contribution?

4. What trait of the actor's vocal characterization was required by the script, and what seemed to be the actor's own creation?

5. Did the character's voice seem to be the actor's voice, or did the actor affect a foreign accent, a regional dialect, or a particular way of speaking?

6. What was the character's super objective?

7. What moment in the play seemed to be an instance of the actor's using the technique called "emotional recall"?

8. Did the actor's biography in the program state the actor's formal training? If so, what was it?

8 CHAPTER

The Director's Impact

The director has the artistic responsibility for the entire production. The playwright's words are the seminal creation; they begin the process that ends in the experience you have when you attend the theatre. Without the written play the director would have nothing to do. With it, the director shapes the performance by communicating his interpretation of the playwright's script to the designers and actors. The director decides where the actors stand when they say their lines, which doors they enter and exit, what gestures they make, what the characters look like, what the scenery looks like, and where the spotlights should focus. The best summary of a director's duties came from our friend's nine-year-old son. "My dad's a director," he said; "in a theatre, he's the one who tells everybody where to go and what to do and what to say and how to say it."

Directors, of course, give directions. The word "direction" describes at least four different functions: *guidance*, or telling how to get someplace (guiding the actors to appropriate entrances and exits); *instruction*, or showing how to do something (instructing the actors how to bow to a king); *explanation*, or telling what something means (explaining to the actor the meaning of a particular line); and *inspiration*, or telling why something is important (exciting the actors about the play's meaning). A good director performs all four of these functions with skill, imagination, and taste.

EVOLUTION OF THE DIRECTOR

The job of the director is relatively new in the theatre. For centuries the theatre got along satisfactorily without directors. Let's look at how directors came into being and how directors' tasks were accomplished before the theatre had directors.

The earliest theatrical era for which we have recorded information is the Golden Age of ancient Athens, from about 450 B.C.E. to 350 B.C.E. Sophocles (SOF-oh-kleez) and other playwrights of ancient Athens supervised rehearsals of their own plays and performed many of the functions of the director. The Athenian theatre was sophisticated in its organization, and the government assigned a rich person to finance the production of a playwright's script. This financier was called a **choregus** (ko-RAY-gus). If the playwright was not available to oversee rehearsals or was not skilled at some of the tasks of the director—coaching the actors or staging the chorus's dances—the choregus would hire a **didaskolos** (die-DAS-ko-lus), a specialist whose job was to help the playwright give direction to the performance. The first part of the word "didaskolos" comes from the same stem as the word "didactic" and suggests our word "teacher." The playwright's contribution was knowing what the lines meant, why the characters did what they did, and what the audience should feel. The ancient Greeks began a theatrical practice of playwright-directors that was to last for centuries.

Two thousand years later, the playwright was still the director—Shakespeare supervised the staging of his own plays. Because Shakespeare was an actor as well as an author and a share-holding partner in the theatre's business, he could tell the other actors how to perform his plays. In *Hamlet* he has the young prince give instructions to a troupe of actors. These famous lines are probably the sort of direction Shakespeare gave his fellow actors:

HAMLET   Speak the speech, I pray you, as I pronounced it to you, trippingly on the tongue: but if you mouth it, as many of your players do, I had as lief the towncrier spoke my lines. Nor do not saw the air too much with your hand, thus, but use all gently . . . suit the action to the word, the word to the action.

TRANSLATION   Say the words, I beg you, just the way I said them, and articulate them clearly: because if you mumble, as some of you actors do, then I'd just as soon have the public announcer say them. And don't flap your hands around, like this, but be selective in your gestures . . . match your actions to what the words tell you to do, and say the words so they make sense with what you're doing.

Even today some playwrights direct their own plays, although it doesn't happen very often. Playwright David Mamet directed his hit *Oleanna,* and Martin Charnin wrote and directed the musical hit *Annie.*

The function of director moved out of the playwright's hands when theatre became a profitable business and decisions on how to do a play started being made on the basis of what would sell tickets rather than on what would serve the playwright's intentions. This change began in Shakespeare's time but didn't become standard practice until the eighteenth century. People who made a living in the theatre learned that audiences would pay to see famous actors, so those players grew in importance until they gained enough power to say how things should be done. Over the years, the function of director shifted from the playwright to the actor. For two hundred years, theatre was directed by actor-managers who ran the business and were its main attraction. These actor-managers told the actors where to go, what to do, what to say, and how to say it. Actor-managers directed the productions to suit their own ego, and playwrights revised their plays to ensure that the actor-manager had the starring role. This practice led to financial rewards but created artistic distortions.

One of the greatest American actor-managers was Edwin Booth, brother of the infamous John Wilkes Booth, the man who assassinated Abraham Lincoln. A modern-day actor-manager was Tony Randall, best known for the role of Felix on the TV series *The Odd Couple*. Randall founded the National Actors Theatre, which produced plays on Broadway.

> **ASIDE**   The last great actor-manager of the English stage was Donald Wolfit, whose career ended in the 1950s. The wonderful play *The Dresser* is about Wolfit. It was made into a film starring Albert Finney and Tom Courtenay.

Toward the end of the nineteenth century, another major change took place. The actor-manager was supplanted by a new worker in the theatre who was neither a playwright nor an actor. This new position, the director, gave shape to the performance. Most theatre historians identify George, Duke of Saxe-Meiningen, as the first director, and most date the beginning of modern directing from the year 1874. Saxe-Meiningen was a small duchy in Germany. As its ruler, Duke George made the laws, collected the taxes, and ran his duchy to suit himself. He also loved theatre. He used his tax revenues to make theatre and hired his citizens to work in his theatre. He alone decided how the plays would be produced. He interpreted the scripts, oversaw the designs, and told the actors where to go, what to do, what to say, and how to say it. He was meticulous in his concern for detail, and everything about his productions was done for the purpose of making a single clear, artistic work. He did not write the scripts, and he did not act in the productions. Instead, he stood in front of the stage and shaped every aspect of the production so that the play had an artistic coherence. In short, he directed.

George, Duke of Saxe-Meiningen, is credited with being the first director in the modern sense of that word.

In 1874, the Duke took his theatrical troupe on tour. In every capital of Europe, the artful and carefully rehearsed productions of the Saxe-Meiningen players amazed audiences and excited theatre artists. No one had seen a production in which everything was arranged to support one theatre artist's point of view. No one had seen a production in which the leading actor stood where that character needed to be in order to tell the story instead of at center stage, or a production in which each minor actor was a believable character who helped tell the story and in which the designs helped tell the story instead of enhancing the star's appearance. Other directors soon began imitating Saxe-Meiningen's way of presenting plays. Two of the most influential were Frenchman André Antoine and Russian Constantine Stanislavsky.

Antoine founded a small theatre in Paris called the Théâtre Libre (tay-AH-tra LEE-bra). The name "Free Theatre" did not mean that admission was free; it meant that the artists were freed from governmental supervision and artistic traditions. The Théâtre Libre became the prototype for small theatre companies across Europe and America and presented artfully rehearsed plays that were carefully directed.

Stanislavsky founded the Moscow Art Theatre, which is still in operation today. It is where Stanislavsky introduced the acting system explained in Chapter 7. The books he wrote describing his work as a director were highly influential. Our sense of what a director does can be traced from Saxe-Meiningen to Stanislavsky to American directors like Elia Kazan, who directed Tennessee Williams's *A Streetcar Named Desire,* to the faculty who direct plays at your college.

Why did the concept of the director develop when it did and not earlier? The process appears to be a logical outgrowth of Determinism, the same philosophy that led to the theatrical style of Realism you read about in Chapter 4. The playwrights who wrote Realistic plays accepted Determinism as the truth of human experience, and directors realized that humans can best be understood when studied in a context that reveals how they are determined. To do that, a single person had to shape a play's production, to direct it. An audience studying a theatrical production through a proscenium arch is like a scientist studying a subject through a microscope. An objective eye is needed to put actions and behavior into perspective and to arrange a coherent world that the audience can study. That's what the director provides.

DUTIES OF THE DIRECTOR

The director's job is a complicated one, and each director does it a bit differently. The duties a director performs, however, can be summarized in a list of ten aspects. Let's look at each of these aspects in detail.

● F O R E S H A D O W I N G

Ten Aspects of a Director's Work

1. Selecting the script
2. Researching the world of the play
3. Analyzing the script
4. Selecting the key collaborators
5. Conceptualizing the production
6. Realizing the conception in sight and sound
7. Casting the roles
8. Rehearsing the production
9. Being the spiritual leader
10. Cashing the check!

Selecting the Script

In American theatre today, directors rarely get to choose the plays they direct. Back when playwrights were their own directors, and later when actor-managers chose the plays, scripts were selected by the same people who would oversee the production. When the director evolved as someone different from the producer, the person who finances and controls the business end, the director became an employee. In America's commercial theatre the producer hires the director, and in not-for-profit theatre the artistic director selects the script and hires the director. In most cases, the director selects the script only indirectly—by deciding whether to accept the job that has been offered.

Directors accept a job offer for the same reasons we all do when we are making a career choice: to pay the rent, advance a career, or maintain the health insurance that comes with a union contract. Directors would *like* to consider if the script is theatrically vital and emotionally and intellectually moving. Will it say something to an audience that the director believes is important? Does the script reveal some truths about human experience that will help make this a better world? Unfortunately, directors rarely make their choices based on the answers to these kinds of questions.

Researching the World of the Play

A director must understand the world the playwright has imagined. That means he must do a lot of research. If you're directing an American play that takes place in a familiar setting like a kitchen and among a family of people who dress in ways you recognize and whose dialogue sounds like people you know—and if you have the playwright around to explain what the script means—then you won't need to do much research. On the other hand, Broadway director Joe Mantello had to research the rules and jargon of baseball, as well as the behavior of sports celebrities, in order to direct Richard Greenberg's 2003 Tony Award–winning play *Take Me Out* (Figure 8.1). If you were hired to direct *Waiting for Godot* or *The Glass Menagerie,* you'd have a lot of research to do.

Most directors begin by reading about the playwright's life to discover if any characters or events in the play might be illuminated by an understand-

We'll let the director be a male in this brief section and a female in the next, OK? And if you'd like to imagine him as an Asian and her as a Latina, that's OK too, because good directors come in all ages, ethnicities, and genders.

Figure 8.1   *Take Me Out,* by Richard Greenberg, won the 2003 Tony Award for Best Play. Frederick Weller, Neal Huff, and Daniel Sunjhata were featured in this play about a gay baseball player's "coming out." It was directed by Joe Mantello.

ing of the writer's real experiences. Next, directors read virtually everything the playwright has written—plays, essays, interviews—as well as any books or articles that have been written about the playwright by critics. They want to learn the ideas that dominate Beckett's thinking or the themes that run through Williams's plays. If the play has been produced before, directors research previous productions to discover how other directors have interpreted the play intellectually and how they have conceptualized it for the stage, as well as what reviewers liked and disliked about earlier productions.

Directors then research the historical era in which the action takes place so they can understand the economic and political world of St. Louis in the late 1930s or of Europe in the years immediately following World War II. They also research any specific references in the plays—Williams's allusion to the German air attack on the Spanish town of Guernica or Beckett's many quotations from the Bible.

Work expands to fill the available time, as the old saying goes, and the amount of research a director does depends on what he needs to learn and how much time and energy he can devote to it. In the same way you have to stop your research and start writing a paper, directors have to stop their research and admit that, although they can never know enough, they must move forward.

Analyzing the Script

Directors analyze a play's genre in order to know the emotional impact it should have on an audience (Chapter 3) and its theatrical style in order to understand the kind of reality the playwright imagined (Chapter 4). A good director works hard to analyze the script's dramatic structure so she knows how it "works," that is how and why the narrative unfolds the way it does. Her analysis reveals the play's exposition and foreshadowing; identifies the inciting event, crisis, and resolution; charts the rising and falling action; and identifies the playwright's various themes as well as the play's ultimate meaning (Chapter 6). Our hard-working director analyzes the characters to ensure that she can help the actors understand their super objective as well as their motivation in each unit of the action. She also studies the playwright's diction: why was the play written in rhymed verse or vulgar slang?

Like research, analysis is a never-ending job. It's common for directors to continue to discover new things about a script throughout the entire rehearsal period, but directors who don't analyze a play before going into rehearsals are not ready to meet with their collaborators, the next step in the process of directing.

Selecting the Key Collaborators

The director is accountable for all the artistic facets of a production. Because few directors are equally skilled in all theatrical crafts, directors need a team of **key collaborators** who will design the scenery, costumes, lighting, and sound; conduct the musicians and coach the singers; choreograph the dances and stage the fights; and provide historical research and analytical materials for the artistic team's use. The director will guide this work, so a compatible team must be chosen, one that shares a common vision and a common way of working. The better the collaborators, of course, the greater the chance for a vital and successful production. One of the sad realities of American theatre today is that directors rarely get to choose their collaborators. Commercial producers hire the designers they want, and so do artistic directors of not-for-profit theatres. The optimal creative team is rarely assembled.

> **ASIDE**   A National Football League coach resigned, complaining that his employers interfered with his work and wouldn't let him hire the players he wanted. "If they want me to cook the dinner," he said, "they've got to let me shop for the ingredients." Theatre directors make the same complaint.

Conceptualizing the Production

Conceptualizing the production is an intellectual and creative process through which the director and the key collaborators determine how the script is to be interpreted and how that interpretation is to be realized on the stage. The director is the single person whose vision gives shape to the work of all the collaborators so that the production has a unity, a focus, and a purpose. The director provides a unique image and gives a central organizing authority to the production. The director keeps things moving toward a single goal. You'll learn more about the process called "conceptualizing the production" in Chapter 10, where we describe our work on Shakespeare's rarely produced *Troilus and Cressida* (TROY-lus and KRES-si-da).

Realizing the Conception in Sight and Sound

After the production has been conceptualized, the director gives the go-ahead to the collaborators, who begin to turn their ideas into actual scenery, costumes, light, sound, and dance. Even after directors begin rehearsing the actors, they must make periodic checks to make certain everyone's staying true to the production concept.

Casting the Roles

If the audience doesn't believe in the characters, the whole show will fail no matter how intriguingly it was conceived, how beautifully it was designed, or how well it was written. The audience experiences the play through the characters, so the director better have a talent for casting. Directors claim that casting is 80 percent of directing. A little luck doesn't hurt, either.

Figure 8.2 Lea Salonga originated the role of Kim in the hit musical *Miss Saigon.* The role demands that the actress be young, beautiful, and Asian and have a gorgeous soprano singing voice.

Particular qualities and skills are needed for each role, and the director must find actors who possess them. The actor playing the title role in Shakespeare's *Hamlet* must speak long speeches in a way that makes their meaning clear and also needs to be trained in stage combat. The actor who plays Walter Lee Younger in *A Raisin in the Sun* must convince us that Walter is frustrated and enraged. The actor who plays Kim, the female lead in the musical *Miss Saigon,* must be Asian, beautiful, and young and must have a gorgeous soprano singing voice (Figure 8.2). In short, the actor must meet the audience's expectations of the character. That explains why typecasting is so common in the theatre. Some plays, fortunately, have characters who can be cast from any age group, any gender, and any ethnic background. Some adventurous directors interpret certain plays nontraditionally, opening up roles for actors who otherwise might not be considered (Color Plate 13).

Casting is also difficult because the director must choose among available actors. The director may want Denzel Washington to play Walter Lee Younger, but if Washington is busy making a film or can't come to terms on salary, then the director must choose another actor. Like politics, theatre is the art of the possible. It is one compromise after another.

Rehearsing the Production

Rehearsing is what most people think of when they picture a director at work. They conjure an image of a person yelling, pleading, and communing with actors who carry their scripts around in a dingy rehearsal hall that has lines drawn on the floor marking out what the setting will be like. This image is not far from the truth. Although you've read that a lot of a director's work is done before the first rehearsal, the rehearsal hall is where the production comes to life. A director performs five different kinds of work during rehearsals.

FORESHADOWING

The Five Parts of the Director's Rehearsal Work

1. Staging
2. Coaching
3. Structuring the dynamics
4. Standing in for the audience
5. Orchestrating the final rehearsals

Staging   **Staging** is usually done in a rehearsal hall. After lines are drawn on the floor to indicate where the walls of the set will be (Figure 8.3), the director begins the process of arranging the actors' movements, a process known as **blocking.** As the actors' movements are blocked out, the director places the actors with an eye to how various "pictures" can help tell the story. Directors follow fundamental practices of visual composition when they block out the staging, and simply looking at a sequence of still pictures of a production should allow you to follow the story.

Figure 8.3   Note the lines taped on the floor of the rehearsal room to help the actors learn what the set will be like.

Figure 8.4 What happens at this moment in *The Glass Menagerie* is spelled out in the script—Laura shows Jim the unicorn in her glass menagerie—but where the menagerie is placed on the stage and how Laura moves to it are part of the director's blocking. (Ellen Lauren as Laura, Milwaukee Repertory Theatre)

Some blocking is formal—the dance choreography of a musical like *Hairspray*, for example (Color Plate 14). Some blocking results from a playwright's specific instructions in the script—Laura's showing Jim the unicorn in her glass menagerie, for example (Figure 8.4). Some blocking is invented by the director in order to tell the story visually.

ASIDE   When Tom directed Shakespeare's *Much Ado about Nothing,* he invented staging for the moment when the wedding of Claudio and Hero is disrupted by the evil Don John, who confirms Claudio's accusations that Hero has been promiscuous, saying that "these things are true." Tom staged a group of monks so that the candles they were carrying formed a cross, adding sparkle and religious symbolism to the stage picture. When Don John announced that the bride was a whore, he strode through the monks, scattering the cross into a chaos of streaking lights. The story was told visually at both a literal and a symbolic level.

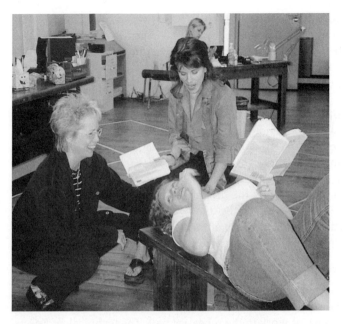

Figure 8.5   Director Jane Page coaches actors Patricia Dalen and Natily Blair during a rehearsal of David Auburn's *Proof* for the theatre company at the Arvada Center for the Arts and Humanities outside of Denver.

Coaching   **Coaching** the actors to perform their roles requires that directors work closely with the cast (Figure 8.5). Because each actor works in a unique way and because directors must work with many actors on each production, directors must have flexible working methods. One actor may respond best to coaxing, another to demonstration, another to intimidation, another to discussion, and yet another to improvisation. Directors must do whatever brings results. Actors need to understand why their characters do certain things—they must understand their characters' motivations. To be helpful, directors must understand the actor's process and the vocabulary that derives from the teachings of Stanislavsky. In addition to being good at conceptualizing a production and understanding how to tell a story visually, a director must be skilled at coaching actors.

ASIDE   Here's an old theatre joke. A veteran director tells a young actor to move to the window and look out while he says his line. The actor takes one step and then asks the director, "What's my motivation?" The impatient director snarls back, "How about your paycheck?"

Structuring the Dynamics   The director must structure the **dynamics** of the performance in very much the same way the conductor of an orchestra structures the dynamics of a symphony during rehearsals. The director must decide when the dialogue should be loud or soft, when the actors should speak fast or slowly, when their movements should be hurried or deliberate, and when the stage picture should be large or small. While there are some guidelines for this craft (at moments of excitement, for example, the performance should get louder and there should be a lot of movement), much of this work is subjective and reflects the director's own sensibilities.

Standing in for the Audience   Directors try to imagine how the audience will see and hear the production. In this sense, the director is the audience's stand-in. Directors must make countless judgments that will anticipate the audience's response. In structuring the dynamics, coaching the actors, and staging the action, directors make thousands of decisions on the assumption that the audience will like what the director likes. One measure of a director's quality is the degree to which the director's tastes are shared by the audience. If the audience finds the pace of the action too slow, doesn't believe in an actor's performance, or is confused by the staging, then the director has failed.

An old saying applies here: "A hit play is well acted, and a flop is badly directed."

Orchestrating the Final Rehearsals   The final phase of the director's work includes the **technical rehearsals** and **dress rehearsals** that take place in the theatre after the weeks of work in the rehearsal hall. The technical and dress rehearsals are when the actors first go onto the set and first wear their costumes, when the lights are focused and all the light and sound cues are rehearsed—when the designers' work is added to the work of the actors. The director's job is to ensure that all the parts and pieces are true to the original vision and that the various elements of the production are coordinated by the stage manager to contribute to the total effect. The fit of the costumes, the speed of the scene shifts, the volume of the actors, the color of the lights, the tempo of the musicians—all these aspects and more must be orchestrated to achieve a coherent production that expresses the director's vision.

The final element that is added is the audience. At **previews,** or preview performances, the director watches both the actors *and* the reaction of the audience to determine if any changes should be made at the next day's rehearsal. The preview audiences' responses help the director shape the production during the final rehearsals before the opening performance.

Being the Spiritual Leader

From the very first meeting through the conceptualizing of the production to the realization of the production on opening night, the director's job is to lead a large group of temperamental artists and artisans. The playwright, actors, designers, stagehands, and box office treasurer have all placed their confidence in the director. They all need the director to show them the way and provide answers. In some instances the director must be the stern parental figure who says "Do it *now,* and do it *right!*" In other instances the director must be the nurturing parental figure who says "You're doing wonderfully, and they're going to love you."

Figure 8.6   Director Michael P. Webb of the Starlight Theatre at Rock Valley College in Illinois has the charisma to generate enthusiasm in all the participants of large-cast productions.

Good directors possess a mixture of skills, experience, talent, and knowledge along with a gift for organization and a sensitivity to the audience. In addition, good directors have so much charisma that people accept their leadership, listen to their advice, and trust their direction (Figure 8.6).

Cashing the Check!

It doesn't matter whether you've done your work brilliantly or poorly, or whether the audience loves your production or ridicules it. You've done the job you were hired to do, and it's time to cash the check! A director's work ends with the first performance, and the stage manager takes over the responsibility of supervising performances and maintaining the quality of the production. Unlike athletic coaches and symphony conductors, who are present at each game and concert, a theatre director's job is done after opening night.

INTERPRETER OR CREATOR?

In the hundred and thirty years since George, Duke of Saxe-Meiningen, staged his carefully directed productions for the artists of Europe and changed forever the way we make theatre, an interesting debate has developed about the nature of the director's work. Is the director an interpretive artist, or a creative artist? That is, does a director merely interpret the creative work of the playwright and put it on a stage, or does a director create a piece of theatre from many raw materials, only one of which is the writer's script?

The interpretive argument is that the director is dependent on the playwright, who has created the plot, the characters, and the dialogue. Theatre got along fine without directors for more than two thousand years. All the director does is facilitate the work of the actors and designers.

The creative argument is that the director is the primary creative force, the singular artist who imagines the production. The director manipulates the actors, supervises the design, and brings the literary script to theatrical life. The script is only a blueprint for a production, whereas the performance is the creation of the director.

There's good evidence and logic on both sides of this debate, and it's unlikely that either view will prevail. Whichever side of the argument you are on—and you're likely to change sides depending on the production you use as an example—one thing is true. Since 1874, the director's impact on how theatre is made has continued to grow, yet the director needs the playwright's script before work can begin. While it's tidy to say that the director "tells everybody where to go and what to do and what to say and how to say it," we should remind ourselves that Shakespeare spoke for all playwrights when he wrote "The play's the thing."

EXERCISE

After your class has attended a performance, gather in groups of ten to twelve students and select one student to lead the discussion. Use the following questions to stimulate your discussion.

1. Why do you think the director chose to direct this play?

2. Did the director choose his or her key collaborators (designers, choreographers)? What evidence do you have to support your opinion?

3. Did the director's use of music and sound effects help or hinder the production?

4. Did the director cast the roles well?

5. What action in the performance do you believe was required by the script?

6. What action in the performance appears to have been invented by the director? Did that action help or hinder your enjoyment of the play?

7. What success (or failure) did the director have in structuring the dynamics of the performance?

8. Based on the reaction of the students in your group, do you think the director was a good stand-in for the audience during rehearsals?

9. Do you think the director was an interpretive or a creative artist?

The Designers' Vision

Designers create the visual and aural elements of a production that transport the audience to the world the playwright imagined and the director has interpreted. Designers turn the playwright's words into real sounds and sights that allow you to experience the play through all your five senses so you can suspend your disbelief. Aristotle may have believed that music and spectacle were the least important elements of theatre, but today we believe them to be vital to the theatrical experience.

Each production requires four major designs: scenery, costume, lighting, and sound. On Broadway and in most American professional theatre, it is standard practice for one specialist to do each of the four designs. In American college theatre, lighting and sound designs frequently are the responsibility of only one designer, and in amateur or community theatre, the director sometimes also designs the lighting and/or the sound. In European professional theatre, it is common for a **scenographer** to design scenery and costumes. There is no set number of designers, no "right" way for the designs to be created. The goal is to create the sights and sounds that increase your enjoyment of the production.

"Scenography" is a relatively new term that is best described by English designer Pamela Howard in her short and entertaining book What Is Scenography?

Remember that theatre is custom designed. Each production of *The Glass Menagerie* is unique, not only because the physical space of the theatres differs or because one production's budget is greater than another's, but also because a production's designers are unique creative artists who express their own vision.

HOW DO DESIGNERS COMMUNICATE?

Designers have to get their ideas out of their brain and into a tangible form the director and other designers can respond to. They turn the playwright's words into pictures and sounds, using verbal descriptions, two-dimensional drawings, three-dimensional models, samples of materials, and snatches of melody.

When the creative team is all meeting in one room, the immediacy of their communication speeds the process of achieving a production concept (Figure 9.1). Questions are answered. Wild ideas are thrown on the table and

Figure 9.1   Dutch director Neils Hamel is the center of attention, but TV monitors, scripts, and research materials fill the room for this production conference at the European Scenography Centre in London.

considered. Agreements are reached and old ideas tossed aside. A light bulb of inspiration shines on revelations and improvements. Each of the designers enthusiastically participates in the discussion. Continual exchanges, changes, and more changes are all part of this shared exuberance, leading the way to a unified concept that integrates each designer's vision with the director's interpretation of the playwright's creation. It is a very exciting process. The case study in Chapter 10 illustrates how it works.

ASIDE   Many funny theatrical disasters are the result of a failure to communicate. When he first described his production idea for Goldoni's eighteenth-century Italian comedy *The Servant of Two Masters*, the director was planning to do a traditional production so he requested historically accurate costumes. The costume shop had nearly finished building Linda's elaborate designs when she heard a rumor that the director had changed the production concept to a 1950s doo-wop musical! She looked in on a rehearsal and saw an actor wailing into a 1950s stand-up mike, with a backup group singing its heart out. The director had never communicated this radical change to Linda, and she wondered if the audience ever figured out what was going on (Color Plate 15).

In professional theatre today, designers regularly live far away from one another and work independently. Rarely are they all in one room, and they rely on technology to communicate. E-mail messages, along with scanned and digitally transmitted images, zip between computer screens. Technology speeds communication, but it also increases the likelihood of misunderstanding. Lighting designer Linda Essig tells the story of having designed the lights for a production based on the colors of the scene design that she had received over the Internet in a JPEG file. When she arrived at the theatre, the color of the set was different. Because the two designers' color monitors were calibrated differently, she had to redesign the lighting in a hurry. Miscommunication of images due to technology is as great a problem in today's theatre as miscommunication resulting from poorly written descriptions.

WHAT DO DESIGNERS DO?

All four designs require designers to do pretty much the same ten tasks, listed here.

● **FORESHADOWING**

Tom and Linda's Top Ten List of What Designers Do

1. Select a play to design
2. Read and analyze the script
3. Research the world of the play
4. Develop initial design ideas
5. Collaborate in developing the production concept
6. Prepare a first draft of the visual and aural designs
7. Solidify the production concept
8. Finalize the designs
9. Complete technical drawings, charts, and plots
10. Supervise the realization of the designs

Select a Play to Design

Designers are not at the top of the theatre's power pyramid and typically become involved in a production only after a play has been selected. Commercial producers, artistic directors of not-for-profit theatres, chairs of university theatre departments, and individual directors may be involved in the selection process. Designers rarely are. Designers "select" a play only by accepting or declining an offer that is tendered to them. Their decision can be influenced by the fee offered, the quality of the director and the other designers, the work schedule, and the budget available to them. Each design is a unique challenge and an opportunity for creative expression, so once they've embarked on a project, good designers quickly become excited about it.

ASIDE   Because he needs to make a living, a scene designer we know accepts every job that comes his way. "Only a crystal ball would stop me from accepting an offer," he says, "because if I could see the grief that was coming, I'd probably decline. Happily, I have 'Designer Amnesia'; it's like childbirth. You go through it, the results are sublime, and then you forget the pain and do it again."

Figure 9.2   Amanda adjusts the hem on Laura's "party dress" in excited anticipation of the Gentleman Caller's arrival.

Read and Analyze the Script

Designers read and analyze a script in two ways. They seek the same basic information about plot, character, genre, style, themes, and meaning that the director seeks, and they also analyze the script for information particular to their area of design. Scene designers, for example, note how many different locations are needed, any particular entrances that are required (a fire escape in *The Glass Menagerie*), and anything that is specified in the script by the playwright. What the audience sees and hears must match the playwright's words.

Costume designers study the script to learn where and when the play takes place—a palace in medieval England or an American tenement in the 1930s. They make a **character/scene plot** listing which characters appear in each scene, note when costume changes must happen (and how much time there is to make those changes), and write down all costume references in the script—for example, Laura's new party dress for her dinner with the Gentleman Caller in *The Glass Menagerie* (Figure 9.2).

Lighting designers study the script to learn where each scene takes place and what the season and time of day are so they can correctly identify the source of the lighting (the sun and moon for *Waiting for Godot;* the candles for *The Glass Menagerie,* as well as the street lights that shine through the window).

The sound designer reads the script to learn the specific sounds the playwright calls for (a ringing telephone) and to begin to imagine the ambient sounds that can be created to enrich the feeling of the action (the song on the record Laura plays on the Victrola in *The Glass Menagerie*).

Research the World of the Play

Designers do an extraordinary amount of research after they have read and analyzed a play and before they begin to envision their design. Each play

Figure 9.3   Americans recognize the Chrysler Building as part of the Manhattan skyline, but since the Hungarian audience this production of *The Glass Menagerie* was designed for might not recognize the St. Louis skyline, we're guessing the designer chose this backdrop, familiar from movies, to communicate the idea of "America."

introduces new challenges with respect to when and where the action is set and the production's theatrical style. A Surrealistic production of *Waiting for Godot* makes different demands on designers than a Realistic production of *The Glass Menagerie.* Plays set in unfamiliar historical eras or written about foreign cultures create fascinating challenges. When Hungarian scenographer Györghy Szegö designed *The Glass Menagerie,* he included a background that shows the skyline of New York City, not that of St. Louis. Perhaps he knew that his audience would recognize the Manhattan skyline from movies and that the skyline would represent America for them (Figure 9.3).

Designers must be very well educated in the history of art, architecture, interior decoration and furniture, clothing, theatrical costuming, and textiles; in the different illuminations created by oil, gas, candle, and electric lighting; and in the history of music. They must also be keen observers of the world we live in. Scene designer Joseph Varga spent a full day researching fire escapes for his design for *The Glass Menagerie* by taking photos as he strolled the streets and alleys of New Harmony, Indiana. He used details from several of those fire escapes in creating his design.

Designers are usually pack rats who collect objects over a lifetime that spark their imaginations and inspire their designs. Experienced designers acquire large libraries (Figure 9.4), which they use—along with university and public libraries and the Internet—to research information and illustrations they can share at meetings with the creative team. All these images help them develop their design.

Develop Initial Design Ideas

"My best work is my doodles on paper napkins in Italian restaurants," says a friend of ours. Designers absorb their analysis and research to stimulate their imagination so they can express their individual vision and share their early

Figure 9.4 The shelves of reference materials and the images pinned to the corkboard are only a portion of the research materials that Eric Sinkkonen uses when he imagines a design. His assistant, Mutsumi Takaki, is building a model under his close supervision.

A cardinal rule for designers: when flying to a production conference, never put your designs in checked baggage. We know two designers who lost their drawings and models and spent sleepless nights reproducing their work.

ideas with the creative team at the first major **production conference.** A scene designer might doodle a drawing of a set on a pizza-stained paper napkin, a costume designer might mark a dozen pictures from various books with Post-its, a lighting designer might take digital photos of the quality of light reflected on a river at dawn, and a sound designer might select samples of recorded music from a variety of sources. Whether these initial design ideas are visual or aural, they are the first small steps toward the designs that ultimately will be created. They are ideas that will stimulate the other designers and contribute to the collaborative process that the director will guide.

Collaborate in Developing the Production Concept

The first production conference is always exciting. Each member of the creative team arrives bursting with ideas and illustrations. Stacks of books, slide projectors, swatches of fabric, CD players, and stacks of drawings are scattered about a conference table, taped onto the walls, and popped out of backpacks. The director usually runs the meeting, presenting his or her ideas and then asking the designers to introduce theirs. Rather quickly, the formal or sequential order of presentations is abandoned. Everyone jumps in to offer helpful suggestions, raise questions, challenge ideas, and pose problems. The director facilitates this "Niagara Falls" of creativity while keeping the discussion focused on the interpretation, style, and genre of the production. The goal of this meeting is for everyone to leave with a shared sense of the production's basic interpretation, historical setting, theatrical style, and dramatic genre, those mutual understandings that will shape what the production will look and sound like and the emotional impact it will have on the audience. In theatre jargon, that's the **production concept.**

Prepare a First Draft of the Visual and Aural Designs

Now the designers start designing in earnest. They've assimilated the director's interpretation, integrated their analysis and research with those of their fellow designers, and, in the infectious enthusiasm of the creative collaboration, arrived at a production concept. They're ready to design the scenery, costumes, lighting, and sound.

Scene and costume designers sketch the scenery and costumes. Some do this manually, as you can see in Linda's drawing for *The Servant of Two Masters* in Figure 9.5. Costume designers draw each costume to be worn in the play and may select fabric swatches to attach to each drawing. Costume and scene designers sometimes render their designs on the computer and later build a **white model,** an unpainted, three-dimensional scale model of the set (Figure 9.6).

Lighting designers may **storyboard** the play. Using the scene designers' drawings, they make a drawing of each scene to illustrate where the light comes from and develop ideas for how the lights will help tell the story and shape the mood of each scene.

Sound designers select specific music and sound effects from existing sources or "build" on multiple tracks a particular effect, such as the human cries and metal clangings of a medieval battle.

During this period of their work, designers exchange suggestions with one another and confer regularly with the director.

EXPOSITION

The national union for designers is United Scenic Artists (USA). Like other unions, it establishes minimum fees for certain kinds of work, stipulates working conditions, and protects members against exploitation. Membership is available only to designers who pass a rigorous test or who can prove to a review board that they have a substantial body of professional achievements. They are then given a stamp that they place on all their designs to prove ownership (right). USA-829, a local branch of the International Alliance of Theatrical Stage Employees (IATSE, pronounced eye-AT-see), represents all stage employees, motion picture technicians, and workers in allied crafts, including props artisans and scene painters.

C.D. 693
COSTUME DESIGNER

SIGNATURE_____

The seal of United Scenic Artists. Each union member's stamp has a design category and an individual number.

Solidify the Production Concept

The second production conference is even more exciting than the first, because it is where the designers present their nearly finished designs for the

Figure 9.5 Linda's rough sketch of a costume for the title character Truffaldino, the wily scamp of a servant in Goldoni's eighteenth-century Italian comedy *The Servant of Two Masters.*

MULTI-PURPOSE KERCHIEF

JACKET & PANTS COVERED WITH PATCH POCKETS "CRUDELY" SEWN ON

C. D. - 693
COSTUME DESIGNER
SIGNATURE *L. Sarver*

TRUFFALDINO

first time. They see what their colleagues are planning and how their own work complements it. Once again, the director guides the meeting, and each designer's work is presented in turn—typically, scenery, costumes, lighting, and finally sound.

The scene designer describes the scenery, illustrating it with a **rendering** (a perspective drawing that gives the illusion of three-dimensional depth) and/or a white model of the set (Figure 9.7). The costume designer asks questions about the colors and textures of the set that will influence the costume design, the lighting designer discusses where lighting instruments can be

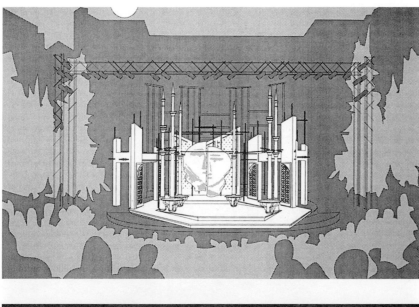

Figure 9.6   Eric Fielding rendered his set for *Othello* on the computer (top) and included a segment of the seating to illustrate what the set would look like on the stage from the audience's point of view. A small-scale, three-dimensional white model (bottom) helped the director envision the staging for the production.

hung, and the sound designer learns where speakers can be placed. Everyone raises both artistic and practical questions, and makes suggestions that might lead to adjustments in the scene design: how do the actors get up to that platform from offstage? can I hide a speaker inside the old Victrola? will the rough texture of the floor tear Laura's fragile silk dress?

Figure 9.7 Joseph Varga's perspective rendering for *The Glass Menagerie* at the Milwaukee Repertory Theatre shows how his design will look to the audience. The inclusion of characters in the drawing shows the size relationship between the scenery and the human figure. This scene depicts the Gentleman Caller dining with Jim and Amanda at the table while timid Laura sits closer to the audience.

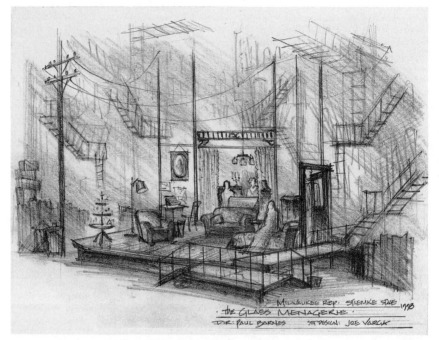

The costume designer shows renderings or **sketches,** drawings of each costume, as Linda did for the character Truffaldino in *The Servant of Two Masters* (Color Plate 16). Some sketches may be colorfully painted, while others may be line drawings with fabric swatches pinned to them. The director and the other designers ask questions and make suggestions that will help the costume designer finalize the designs in the weeks after the meeting: would a different color dress stand out better against the color of the wall? can the actor change costumes quickly enough? will the fabric absorb light or reflect it? where can the battery pack for the microphone be hidden in the costume without making an ugly bulge on the actor's body?

The lighting designer describes and demonstrates the colors and angles of the lighting design, sometimes clipping small lights onto the scene designer's model and sometimes making a computer presentation. Discussions about the practicality of the placement of lighting instruments, the emotional content of particular scenes, and the "look" of particular moments in the play are common.

The sound designer plays samples of the sound effects that have been "built" and the musical underscoring that has been designed to capture the mood of the production. Then the designer responds to questions and suggestions.

> **ASIDE**   You've probably heard the expression "He stole my thunder," meaning "I had that idea first." The phrase was first spoken in the eighteenth century by English playwright John Dennis, who used a very large metal mustard bowl to make the sound of thunder. His play was a flop, but when he attended another play a few months later, he heard the sound effect he had invented and exclaimed, "See how the rascals use me. They will not let my play run, but yet they steal my thunder!"

At the end of this second production conference, the entire creative team has a clear vision of what the production will be like. Each designer leaves knowing what to do next.

Finalize the Designs

The designers go "back to the drawing board" (back to their studios) and make the adjustments agreed to in the second production conference. The white model might be rebuilt and possibly painted. The costumes are redesigned as needed and the renderings fully painted. The lighting designer utilizes information about the colors and textures of the set and costumes to refine artistic and practical needs. The sound designer returns to the computer deck to alter the sound design (adding or deleting effects). All the designers remain in communication with one another, and all refinements, changes, and finalized designs are submitted to the director, who ensures that the designs achieve what the creative team has decided on.

Complete the Technical Drawings, Charts, and Plots

For the moment, the "creative" part of the designers' brains is put on hold. They shift gears, to prepare the technical drawings, charts, and plots that show how their designs will be realized. Some designers still do their drafting manually, but most use specialized computer software developed for architecture and adapted for use in the theatre. AutoCAD™ and Vector Works™ are the standards. Designers use this software to make the **technical drawings** that will convey their design ideas precisely and clearly to the artisans in the various workshops who will realize the designs. We think of designers as artists, but they must also be craftspersons with computer skills because they do a lot of detailed manual and computer-generated paperwork at this stage of the process.

The scene designer drafts a large number of technical drawings, including a scale line drawing of the **ground plan** that shows the scenery as it appears from above (Figure 9.8); a **front elevation,** or scale line drawing of a flattened two-dimensional front view of the scenery (Figure 9.9); a **cross section,** or scale line drawing of the scenery as seen from the side of the stage

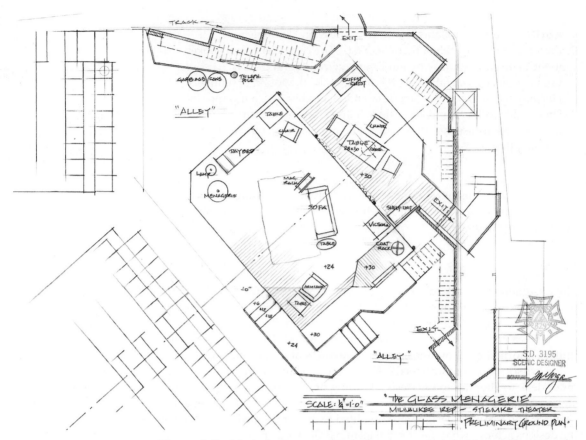

Figure 9.8 Many designers today draft on computers, but Joseph Varga's scale ground plan for *The Glass Menagerie* was drafted manually. Ground plans show the set from above, indicating how the stage is oriented toward the audience, where doors and stairways are located, and where furniture is placed. Whether drafted manually or printed out from a computer, ground plans are duplicated in blueprints that are used by the technicians who build the scenery and by the stage manager who tapes out the ground plan on the floor of the rehearsal room so the director and the actors can rehearse the blocking of the play.

showing where each piece of scenery will be installed in the theatre; and **working drawings** that show how each piece of scenery is to be constructed.

The costume designer makes line drawings showing the backs of costumes, trimming details, and the accessories that complete the design; a **costume list** itemizing what each actor will wear from the skin out; and a **costume plot** showing the order in which costumes are worn.

The lighting designer uses the scene designer's ground plan, front elevation, and cross section to draft—manually or on a computer—a **light plot**

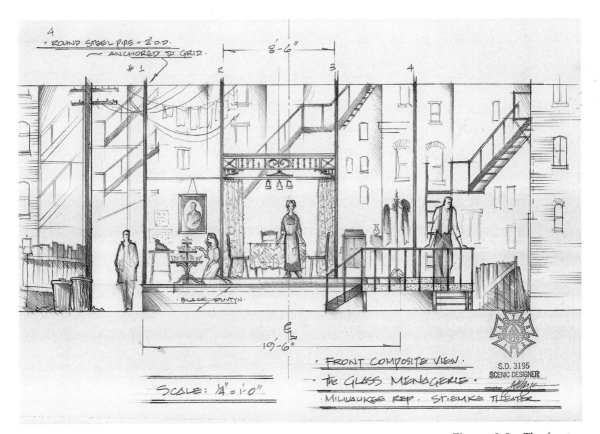

Figure 9.9 The front elevation for Joseph Varga's design for *The Glass Menagerie* shows a flattened two-dimensional view of the scenery. It is drawn to scale, with the human figure included to indicate the size relationship of the scenery and the actors.

showing where each instrument is hung (Figure 9.10); an **instrument schedule** listing each piece of equipment and the **color media** (or **gel**) that will be placed in front of it, along with how it will be connected to the computer light board; and a **cue sheet** listing what happens each time the lights change (and where in the script that happens).

> **ASIDE**   "Gel" is short for "gelatin," which is what color media was made from prior to the introduction of plastic. A trick used to be played on apprentice lighting technicians: they'd be handed a foot-square sheet of gel and told to "go wash this gel," and the entire crew would laugh as the horrified apprentice watched the gel dissolve in a bucket of water.

The sound designer uses a computer to make a **sound plot** showing where the speakers are placed and which channel each is connected to on the

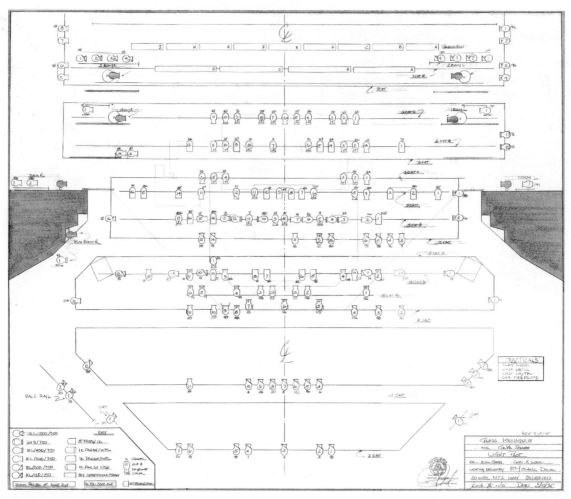

Figure 9.10 A light plot shows the various kinds of lighting instruments that will be used to create the design, where each instrument is hung, and where each is focused. This light plot for the GeVa Theatre's production of *The Glass Menagerie* is by F. Mitchell Dana.

computer sound board, and a cue sheet indicating what each cue is (a clock chimes ten and crickets chirp) and where in the script each sound effect occurs.

Supervise the Realization of the Designs

Now the designers' work is to make artistic decisions on the spot. From the time the designs go into the shops through their installation in the theatre and technical and dress rehearsals to opening night, each designer oversees the execution of his or her design to make sure that the vision is realized. Scene designers consult regularly with the **technical director** and **scene painter** about the construction and painting of the scenery. Costume design-

Figure 9.11   Do you recognize movie star Michael Douglas? He was only twenty-one when he played the title role in Pirandello's *Henry IV* at the University of California at Santa Barbara. Well, everyone starts somewhere. The lighting design sculpts Douglas and his fellow student in this production directed by Georgi Paro from the national theatre of (then) Yugoslavia.

ers meet daily with the costume shop staff about the construction of the costumes and also attend **fittings,** individual sessions when the actors try on their costumes. Lighting designers consult with the technical director and the **master electrician** about the hanging and cabling of the instruments and supervise the **focus session,** when all the lights are precisely aimed. Lighting is used to sculpt the figures on the stage, as shown in Figure 9.11, and to create a mood, as shown in Color Plate 8.

Actors rarely reveal their true measurements. Typically, men add 2 inches to their height and women take 10 pounds off their weight.

Sound designers supervise the **sound board operator,** who both assists in the installation of the sound equipment and operates the computer board during performances.

ASIDE   When the computerized sound board has an electric hiccup, it creates chaos on the stage. Wild jungle creatures are heard in the living room, or the TV news is broadcast "magically" across the endless prairie. Computers are a boon, but they can sometimes make a show a bust.

The final phase of the designers' work begins with the **load-in,** when the scenery is brought into the theatre and set up on the stage. Then the actors begin rehearsing on the set. The final rehearsals are run by the **stage manager,** who coordinates the work of everyone else and is in direct communication with the director. (You will learn more about this vitally important person in Chapter 14.)

During the final phase of rehearsals, scene designers supervise the decoration of the set and respond to notes about changes given by the director after each rehearsal. Lighting and sound designers enter their most intensive work period when rehearsals move into the theatre and onto the set. They design, set, and continually adjust each cue (in consultation with the director) through the sequence of technical rehearsals and previews to ensure that the visual and aural effects are correct, that the volume of sound is appropriate, and that the timing of the cues supports the emotion of each scene in the unfolding story. Costume designers attend all dress rehearsals, making any necessary adjustments.

The designers' creation is made real on opening night. The house lights dim, the curtain rises, and the audience thrills to the "magic of theatre" as the playwright's words are brought to life through the actors' performance, the director's interpretation, and the designers' vision.

EXERCISES

1. Create teams of four students each. Assign one student on each team the responsibilities of each of the four designers on a production: scene designer, costume designer, lighting designer, and sound designer. Have each member of the team make a comprehensive list of all the tasks carried out by that designer. The list should indicate the sequence in which the tasks are done during the preparation for a production and should include all the sketches, drawings, lists, plots, charts, renderings, and models that the designer is responsible for creating. Have the team members present their lists to the class, and encourage the other students to identify any items that have been duplicated or omitted. The goal of this exercise is to help students appreciate the quantity and sequence of the work that designers do.

2. After the class has attended a production, discuss the designs by exploring how each of the four designs did or did not support the production concept.

Putting It Together

In the previous four chapters you've read about the playwright's creation, the actors' craft, the director's interpretation, and the designers' vision. In this chapter we'll describe a "case study" of the creative process we followed when the Colorado Shakespeare Festival produced Shakespeare's *Troilus and Cressida.* The process should remind you of Stephen Sondheim's lyric "putting it together, bit by bit." It will help us if you know that the Festival was taking an enormous risk by selecting this title and that the stakes were dangerously high for the director and the designers as well.

THE CONTEXT

So many things can go wrong in creating a theatrical production that most productions fall short of success. They might fail financially, they might fail artistically, or they might fail totally. In Chapter 16, we describe theatre economics in detail, but for now just accept our word that the business of theatre is risky. We celebrate a baseball player who gets a hit three out of ten at bats, but we expect theatre artists to have a "hit" every time. Of course, they don't. In our own lifetime as theatregoers, we have seen very few "home runs," a great number of forgettably mediocre shows, and even a few legendary disasters.

> **ASIDE**   Are you familiar the teenage horror movie *Carrie?* Well, somebody had the not very bright idea of making it into a Broadway musical. The musical failed sensationally and closed after only one performance. Somebody lost $6 million that night!

The Festival took a big financial risk in choosing *Troilus and Cressida* because the play has earned a reputation for being a very difficult title to sell at the box office. Think about it. Which would you rather pay $38.50 to see: *Romeo and Juliet, Much Ado about Nothing, Two Gentlemen of Verona* or *Troilus and Cressida?* Yet each of the Festival's four productions had to earn the management's projected percentage of the season's total revenue, and *Troilus and Cressida* was projected to sell 60 percent of its tickets and earn $95,820. The Festival couldn't afford a financial failure. Pressure to succeed was built into the project from the beginning.

The career risk for us artists was equally great, because we were putting our reputations on the line by agreeing to do a play that has rarely succeeded. "You're only as good as your last show" is a theatrical truth, and we were gambling our reputations on our ability to create a production that would be good enough to bring in a hundred thousand dollars. If we failed artistically, then *Troilus and Cressida* would certainly fail financially, and we'd probably never be hired by the Festival again. Because word spreads fast in the theatre world, we'd probably have a tougher time getting hired elsewhere as well. Nobody could afford to be part of a **turkey** (theatre slang for a flop), yet nobody could predict how *Troilus and Cressida* would turn out. We all accepted the challenge. After all, that's what makes life in the theatre exciting!

For this "case study," we'll use the real artists' names. Here's a list to refer to as you read:

Playwright: William Shakespeare (and others, as you'll soon learn)
Director: Tom Markus
Scene designer: Joseph A. Varga
Costume designer: Linda Sarver
Lighting designer: Michael Wellborn
Sound designer: Kevin Dunayer
Leading actor: Richard Kinter (Pandarus)

SHAKESPEARE'S PLAY

You've never read *Troilus and Cressida?* You're not alone. After a lifetime in the theatre, Linda had never read it either. We've chosen it for our case study *because* it's unfamiliar. You're not likely to have preconceptions about what the play means or how it is traditionally produced, and that makes *Troilus and Cressida* a good play for us to use in describing a truly exciting and creative collaboration.

Shakespeare took his situation and characters from ancient Greek mythology. The story takes place during the Trojan War, in which a coalition of Greeks fought the army of Troy (on the western coast of modern Turkey). Another name for Troy is Ilium (ILL-ee-um), and Homer first told the story in a long poem called *The Iliad.* Many versions of the story have been written. It has been made into miniseries like *Helen of Troy* and epic movies like *Troy,* in which Brad Pitt stars as Achilles (a-KILL-eez). Each version tells a different part of the story, and each tells it a bit differently. Here's a short version that tells you everything you need to know to follow the plot of Shakespeare's play.

Helen, the beautiful young wife of an older Greek general, fell in love with the handsome young Trojan prince Paris (not to be confused with the

Helen was so beautiful that she has been described as having "the face that launched a thousand ships."

What idiot forgot to put the handle on the inside?!

Figure 10.1

city in France) and ran off with him. The Greek cities formed a coalition army and sailed their warriors to Troy to bring the unfaithful Helen back home.

The Greek army camped outside the strong walls of Troy. After ten long years of unsuccessful siege, the Greeks came up with a new plan. They built a large, hollow wooden horse and gave it to the Trojans as a gift. Greek soldiers hid inside it. After the Trojans moved the gift horse inside their city's walls, the Greek soldiers climbed out and opened the city gates to let in the rest of the Greek army (Figure 10.1). The Greeks rampaged through the city, slaughtering the Trojans. The Greeks won the Trojan War.

This is where we get the saying "beware of Greeks bearing gifts."

Shakespeare begins the plot of his play in the seventh year of the siege, with both sides exhausted from fighting and eager to end the war. The Greek generals, dissatisfied with the leadership of their general-in-chief Agamemnon (ag-a-MEM-non), are squabbling among themselves. Meanwhile, in the Trojan court, King Priam (PRY-um) listens to the advice of his eldest son, Hector, Troy's greatest warrior. Hector argues that Helen should be returned to the Greeks so that a quick peace can be reached, but Priam knows that Troy's honor is at stake and overrules Hector's plan. Elsewhere in Troy, Prince Troilus (TROY-lus), the younger brother of Hector and Paris, has fallen in love with Cressida (KRES-i-da), the beautiful and innocent niece of a corrupt Trojan nobleman named Pandarus (PAN-dar-us). Cressida resolutely resists surrendering her virginity to Troilus unless he marries her, but the wily Pandarus, who delights in bawdy songs and sexual escapades, succeeds in convincing Cressida to spend the night with her lover, Troilus, at her uncle's house.

Many schools, including the University of Southern California, have the Trojans as their mascot, the symbol of their honor.

We get our word "pander," a synonym for "pimp," from the name of this character from ancient Greek mythology.

Meanwhile, Hector challenges the greatest of the Greek warriors to one-on-one combat. It will be a contest to end the war. He expects his opponent to be Achilles, the mightiest Greek warrior, but Achilles is so angry at Agamemnon and so puffed up with his own importance that he has pledged never to fight again. As a scheme to shame Achilles and teach him humility, the Greeks' wisest general, Ulysses (you-LISS-eez), rigs a lottery to select the dumb brute Ajax to fight Hector.

The superhero Achilles could be wounded in only one place, and today we speak of our most vulnerable spot as our "Achilles heel."

Some time earlier, Cressida's father had fled the besieged city of Troy and defected to the Greeks. As his reward for changing sides, he asked two things of Agamemnon: to free some Trojan prisoners and to have his daughter brought

Ajax is now the brand name of a powerful household scouring powder.

to him in the Greek camp. Greek soldiers go to Troy under a flag of truce, and the handsome officer Diomedes (dye-OM-a-deez) finds Cressida with Troilus at Pandarus's house. The lovers swear undying faithfulness as Cressida is led tearfully away (but not before she reveals that she finds Diomedes attractive).

Cressida arrives at the Greek camp, where everyone is waiting for the fight between Hector and Ajax to begin. The generals take turns roughly kissing the aristocratic Cressida, treating her like a whore, but she is spirited and evades their advances with witty insults. As Diomedes leads her away from the generals, Cressida realizes that she will be safe only if she attaches herself to him.

Hector and Ajax have their big fight, but it ends in a draw. That night, the Trojans and Greeks celebrate the heroes' contest at an outdoor banquet where they drink rowdily in soldierly comradeship. While the others are carousing, Ulysses leads Troilus to Diomedes' tent, where the love-smitten young prince sees Cressida passionately kissing Diomedes. Agonizing over her faithlessness, Troilus returns to his city.

The next morning, the war resumes. Troilus fights like a madman, and Hector leads the Trojans toward what seems certain victory. Suddenly, from the Greek camp, Achilles unexpectedly reenters the battle. In a cowardly act of treachery, he stands back and watches while his private elite troops kill the unarmed and defenseless Hector. He ties Hector's corpse to his horse and drags the body around the walls of Troy, pretending he has killed the Trojan hero himself (Figure 10.2). Without Hector to lead them, the Trojans know

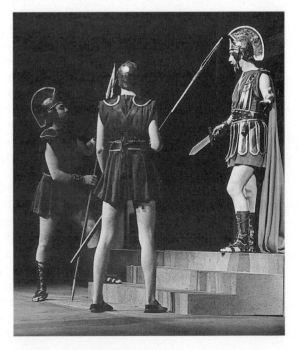

Figure 10.2   Shown here is Achilles, the mightiest Greek warrior, in a production of *Troilus and Cressida* that was set in the time of ancient Greece. He is wearing a historically accurate reproduction of Greek clothing. No, that's not Brad Pitt—it's Tom, many, many years ago.

COLOR PLATE 1 Georges Seurat's *A Sunday Afternoon on the Island of La Grande Jatte,* an example of pointillism, was the subject of Stephen Sondheim's Broadway musical *Sunday in the Park with George.* This painting must be viewed from a distance, because if you stand close to it you will see only dots of color and not the objects or shapes they create. Your eye "creates" the picture in the same way you "create" a theatre performance.

COLOR PLATE 2
Zoot Suit, by Luis Valdez, starred Edward James Olmos on Broadway. Marco Rodriguez (pictured here) played the lead role of Pachuco at the Goodman Theatre in Chicago. Olmos starred in the film version, which is available on DVD or video. *Zoot Suit* raises our consciousness about racial prejudice; it is based on a riot that broke out in Los Angeles in the early 1940s.

COLOR PLATE 3
Playwright Tony Kushner did not observe the three unities in *Angels in America*, and few modern playwrights do. Gerry Leahey's scene design for Florida State University's production was as visually spectacular as the design for the Broadway production.

COLOR PLATE 4 *Scapino!* is a fast-paced farce based on a seventeenth-century play by Molière. Count the doors and windows to discover how this set permits the characters to enter and exit quickly. Also count the violent actions that are about to happen.

COLOR PLATE 5 Jimmy Smits starred on Broadway in Cuban-American playwright Nilo Cruz's 2003 Pulitzer Prize–winning play, *Anna in the Tropics.*

COLOR PLATE 6 Othello loves his bride, Desdemona, yet he strangles her before the tragedy ends. Othello is a tragic hero who seems happy and successful at the beginning of the play but whose drive to maintain his honor eventually leads him to kill his wife and to commit suicide. (Colorado Shakespeare Festival)

COLOR PLATE 7   John Iacovelli's scene design for the Utah Shakespearean Festival's production of *Waiting for Godot* captures the ambivalent moods of this celebrated example of the dramatic genre of tragicomedy. It is also an example of the theatrical style of Realism.

COLOR PLATE 8   Laura talks with the Gentleman Caller in the Sacramento Theatre Company's production of *The Glass Menagerie,* directed by Tim Ocel and designed by Eric Sinkkonen. The cast is African American. The entrance from the fire escape stairs is down right, curtains can be drawn across the entry to the dining room up center, a curtained window is seen up left, a large portrait of the absent father hangs stage left, and the Victrola is down left. The lurid colored lighting appears to come from the neon signs of the dance hall down the alley and contributes to the mood of the play.

COLOR PLATE 9   Beate Czogalla's scene design for Georgia College & State University's production of *The Glass Menagerie* featured words and images projected onto the set. The legend "A Souvenir" refers to Laura's high school yearbook, and the projection of the "blue roses" refers to the nickname Jim (Andy Cisick) gave Laura (Mandy Butler) after she had fallen ill with pleurisy. See Figure 4.4 for more details about this scene design.

COLOR PLATE 10   Alaska's Perseverance Theatre's production of *The Glass Menagerie* illustrates the style of Postmodernism. It was directed by Peter DuBois, costumed by Katie Jensen, and lit by Vickki McGuire. The exciting scene design was by Robert Pyzocha. The entire interior of the theatre was painted so that the audience was surrounded by "wall paper" with a Southern Victorian pattern.

a. This picture shows the stage left area of the production. The dining room was down left, and the huge "cloud wall" was made of clear plastic stretched around a metal box. Inside the wall were fans that gently swirled smoke to suggest the dreamlike world of the play. Also inside the "cloud wall" was a very large photo of the absent father that could be seen when it was lighted and disappeared when it was not. The fire escape was on the upstage wall, just left of center, Tom spoke to the audience from there.

b. This picture shows the stage right area of the Perseverance Theatre's Production. A circle of Plexiglas on the floor was used to suggest the glass top of Laura's knickknack table (see Figure 4.21 for "How to Look at Modern Art"), and the glass animals were fixed to thin wires so they appeared to be floating in the air, as in a dream (or in Tom's memory). This picture shows the final moment of the play. Amanda (Anni Stokes) looks at the photo of her departed husband, while Tom (Jake Wald) asks Laura (Ekatrina Oleksa) to blow her candles out.

COLOR PLATE 11 These costumes and masks for the Classic Greek Theatre's production of *Oedipus the King* were inspired by ancient Greek sculpture. The proportions of the head to the body and the long, flowing drapery remind us of the Elgin marbles, the sculptures that originally were on the Parthenon in Athens and now are on display at the British Museum in London. The scenery in the background is geometric and symmetrical, in the style of Classicism.

COLOR PLATE 12 Giving a truthful performance requires an actor to convince the audience of the character's physical, vocal, and imaginative reality. Reviewer Jeff Baron wrote that actor Jack Axelrod had "the [vocal] ability to lengthen the word 'no' into five syllables. Axelrod superbly creates physical frailty: an almost imperceptible effort to catch his breath, a quick adjustment to keep his balance, a tired tilt of his head, a weakening in the knees. Whatever [emotional] substitutions, whatever techniques he uses, his portrayal is deep, true, and undeniably gorgeous." The actor is shown here playing Prelapsarianov, "the world's oldest living Bolshevik," in Tony Kushner's *Slavs!* at the Berkeley Repertory Theatre, directed by Tony Taccone.

COLOR PLATE 13 Patrick Stewart played the title role in an unusual production of *Othello* at The Shakespeare Theatre in Washington, D.C. Shakespeare wrote Othello as the only black-skinned character in the play, but an adventurous director reversed the races and cast African American actors in all the other roles instead. Stewart's Othello was the only white-skinned character.

COLOR PLATE 14 *Hairspray* is based on a cult movie. This picture illustrates the intricacy of the director's blocking (and the choreographer's dance).

COLOR PLATE 15   The doo-wop performance of Goldoni's eighteenth-century comedy *The Servant of Two Masters* illustrates what can happen when communication among the members of the creative team breaks down. The audience had a lot of fun but must have wondered about the disparity between the designs and the direction.

COLOR PLATE 16   The finished rendering of Linda's design for Truffaldino in *The Servant of Two Masters.* Compare this with the earlier drawing in Figure 9.5.

Troilus and Cressida

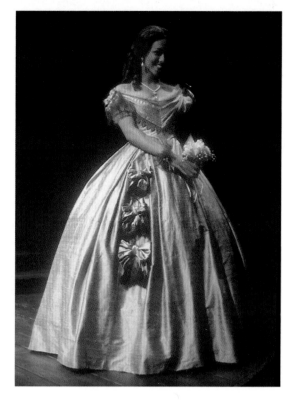

COLOR PLATE 17 This color rendering of Helen of Troy's ball gown has fabric samples of the dress material attached to it and is painted against a black-and-white collage of Civil War photographs similar to those used for the set. Compare this rendering to Figure 10.9 and to Color Plate 18, which shows the actual costume.

COLOR PLATE 18 In the gorgeous silk dress Linda designed for her, actress Noel True looked so beautiful as Helen that we all understood why Paris ran off with her and why the Greeks started a war to get her back.

COLOR PLATE 19 The glittering top hat, Stars and Bars vest, and comically bad wig brought visual delight to Pandarus's song-and-dance rendition of Andrew Marvell's lyric "Had we but world enough, and time / This coyness, lady, were no crime." This may be a long way from what Shakespeare imagined, but it was close to the audience's heart.

COLOR PLATE 20 The boxing match was one of the visual highlights of our production of *Troilus and Cressida*. This photo shows how the production concept was realized through the scenery, costume, and lighting designs. Agamemnon and Ulysses are in the foreground; Hector, wearing red long underwear, squares off against Ajax; a banjo player entertains the raucous crowd; and Achilles is on the right, wearing bright red trousers of a special unit of the Northern army called "Zouaves."

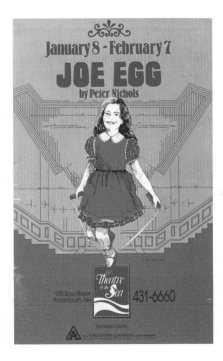

COLOR PLATE 21 This cheery and colorful cover of the program for *Joe Egg* at New Hampshire's Theatre by the Sea prepared the audience for a lighthearted evening so that they would enjoy the comedy in the early part of the play, before the mood turned somber.

COLOR PLATE 22 *TEXAS*, a historical drama with song and dance, is presented annually in this outdoor theatre that resembles an ancient Greek theatre. The natural setting and the circular acting space remain as vital today as they were 2,500 years ago.

COLOR PLATE 23
Shakespeare's Globe Theatre is a recently built open-air theatre in London located near the site of the original Globe Theatre where Shakespeare's plays were first produced. It is designed to look like an Elizabethan public theatre. Note the "groundlings" standing on three sides of the stage, the three galleries for seating, and the colorful decoration of the stage house. Performances in this theatre give audiences an exciting introduction to what theatre was like in Shakespeare's time.

COLOR PLATE 24 The Baroque court theatre in Cesky Krumlov, the Czech Republic, has an ornate proscenium arch, a beautifully painted ceiling, and a horseshoe-shaped balcony that provided excellent seating for the noble family that built the theatre. The backless benches on the main floor (the "stalls") provide a good view of the stage but are less comfortable. The five wings painted to suggest trees and the painted drop at the back of the stage are original eighteenth-century scenery.

COLOR PLATE 25 *The Producers* starred Nathan Lane and Matthew Broderick and was based on Mel Brooks's movie of the same title. Brooks wrote the music and lyrics and collaborated on the book. It is expected to be playing on Broadway for the next several years.

COLOR PLATE 26 *Seussical the Musical* is an example of a musical that failed commercially on Broadway but may yet return a profit for the producer and the investors from ticket sales for a touring production. Their hopes are based on the likelihood that people across America will buy tickets to see the Cat in the Hat and other beloved Dr. Seuss characters.

COLOR PLATE 27 *Rent* was produced Off Broadway in the late 1990s, but audience demand for tickets prompted the producers to move it to Broadway, where it has been a commercial, money-making hit for seven years. This picture shows the cast singing "La Vie Bohème," one of the musical's most rousing numbers. The touring production of *Rent* has entertained audiences in cities across America and has brought additional profits to the angels who invested in the show.

COLOR PLATE 28 *Urinetown* was a surprise hit that started Off Off Broadway and went on to win Tony Awards on Broadway and to tour most large American cities.

COLOR PLATE 29
Japanese director Shozo Sato directed *Macbeth* at Virginia Commonwealth University, and the designs and acting conventions were influenced by the traditional Japanese form of theatre called Kabuki. The fusion of Asian theatre practices and Western drama has become increasingly popular in recent years.

COLOR PLATE 30 *Show Boat* has been a hit each time it has been revived on the stage or in the movies, and the Broadway production in the 1990s proved that the 1927 musical by Jerome Kern and Oscar Hammerstein II remains great entertainment. *Show Boat*'s serious theme of interracial marriage is still pertinent today.

COLOR PLATE 31
The Lion King is based on the animated movie of the same title, and director and costume designer Julie Taymor found visually exciting ways to show both the live actors and the animal characters they play. Here, the dancing zebras demonstrate the power of spectacle in musical theatre.

COLOR PLATE 32   Andrew Lloyd Webber and Tim Rice's *Joseph and the Amazing Technicolor Dreamcoat* is based on a biblical story and is a precursor to the team's rock opera *Jesus Christ Superstar. Dreamcoat* was originally written to be performed by English schoolchildren. One of the most frequently produced rock musicals, it has been produced on Broadway twice, and a production starring Donny Osmond is available on video and DVD.

COLOR PLATE 33
Antonio Banderas starred in the Broadway revival of the musical *Nine.*

they are doomed. The Greeks are confident they will eventually win the war. Pandarus, suffering from venereal disease, ends the play by cursing love, sex, war, and heroes. He tells the audience that they are all pimps, just like him, and that he hopes they will get the same disease he is doomed to die from in another two months. The end.

Troilus and Cressida is an unfamiliar title and a very cynical play, so you can see why the Festival was taking a big financial risk when it chose to produce it. It is very difficult to make the play appealing to an audience, which is why we all were taking a big artistic risk as well. This is the play we were being paid to risk our reputations on. You can understand our reservations, but we're the kind of fools who rush in where wise men fear to tread, so we were very excited by the challenge.

GETTING STARTED

The Festival permitted Tom to choose his own scene and costume designers, and he was happy to have Joe Varga and Linda Sarver on the team. The Festival chose the lighting and sound designers. Tom had worked successfully with Michael Wellborn and Kevin Dunayer, so he welcomed them aboard.

We had been hired by early autumn for a production that would open the following July, so you might think we had plenty of time to do our work. But we all had other full-time jobs, and because we lived far from one another—in Wisconsin, New Jersey, Washington, and Utah—we would meet together only twice, in January and March. In between, we would have to communicate by phone, fax, e-mail, and FedEx.

Tom asked his collaborators to begin their own work immediately, well in advance of our January conference. Because this is a difficult and unfamiliar play, he suggested that everyone read it in the same way he had: begin by reading a brief synopsis of the plot of the entire play, next read a detailed synopsis of the first scene in Cliffs Notes, and then watch the video of the first scene in the BBC-TV production. Even though our production would differ significantly, watching the video version increased our understanding of the characters, the plot, and the tone of the play. Finally, each of us read the first scene in Shakespeare's play. We repeated the procedure of reading the synopsis of a scene, watching it on video, and reading Shakespeare's text until we had read the entire play carefully. Next Tom urged us to reread the play in one sitting. After that preparation, we felt ready to begin our individual research and analysis. Tom's direction in this first phase of our work was very helpful.

THE DIRECTOR'S RESEARCH AND ANALYSIS

About four years earlier, Tom had read a new translation of *The Iliad,* so that part of his research was already complete. Because he's been directing, acting, and teaching Shakespeare's plays for many years, he didn't need to research the playwright's life or read his other works. In the same way that each of you has a body of acquired knowledge and experience you can build on when you confront a new challenge, directors and designers have learned things during their careers that allow them to speed through some early phases of their work.

Tom read nine essays about *Troilus and Cressida* to learn how those critics and scholars analyzed its characters, themes, genre, style, structure, and meaning. They pointed out several intriguing themes Shakespeare explores: how time erodes our bodies and our spirits, how our romantic ideals and military code of honor are corrupted by our baser drives, how constancy is a delusion, how we destroy what we love with our cynicism, and how the world is a vile and scabrous place in which disappointment is the only certainty.

Tom was particularly intrigued with the reminder that the Greeks and Trojans were related. Some of them were cousins. The play is more about a family feud than about a war between foreign enemies. He had an intuition that this understanding might help him answer the question "How can we make an accessible and appealing production from such an unfamiliar and cynical script?"

Next, he researched previous productions, looking at photos, reading interviews of the actors and directors, and learning from the reviewers' evaluations. Happily, he had seen three productions of *Troilus and Cressida* in recent years and had acted the role of Achilles many years before. Once again, his accumulated experience sped his research.

He started to study the world of archaic Greece, but he quickly realized he wasn't ready to decide if that was when he wanted to set the production. He needed to learn more before making such an important decision. He began by analyzing the genre of the play. He learned that some scholars and theatre directors have interpreted *Troilus and Cressida* as a comedy, and it does have many funny scenes. Others label it a tragedy, because there are scenes of great sadness and it ends with the death of a noble hero. The sad and funny scenes are mixed together, and the audience doesn't always know if it should laugh or cry. Tom's analysis helped him understand the play as an early example of a genre that is common in modern times: tragicomedy (see Chapter 3).

Shakespeare's plays can be produced in many theatrical styles, from Realism to Postmodernism. *Troilus and Cressida* begins with a prologue that's spoken directly to the audience, and Tom felt those lines would work best if the production were done in the style of Theatricalism. He looked for additional ways to remind the audience that they were attending a play, not peeking through a keyhole at real events. He did *not* want them to suspend their disbelief (see Chapter 4).

His analysis of the play's dramatic structure showed Tom that the dramatic question is "Will Troilus and Cressida live happily ever after?" This question is posed at the inciting event when Cressida agrees to spend the night with Troilus. The turning point occurs when Cressida is taken away to the Greek camp by Diomedes. The resolution—where the dramatic question is answered with a resounding NO—comes when Troilus renounces Cressida after seeing her kiss Diomedes. Tom used the method described in Chapter 6 to distill the main plot to this single sentence: "This is the story of Troilus and Cressida, who fall in love, are separated by the cynical and corrupt forces of the militaristic society in which they live, and who discover they must betray each other just in order to stay alive." The meaning of the play, as he interpreted it, was stated this way: "War corrupts our values and destroys our happiness." He felt that this statement is very relevant in today's world, and he was encouraged that he had found a way to make this play speak to our audience.

He sent his analysis of the play's genre, style, themes, structure, and meaning to the four designers and included a list of his sensory responses to the play. This marked his effort to direct the production at an early stage of its development by guiding his colleagues to the same emotional responses to the play that he had experienced.

SIGHT: Beautifully dressed women cheering a parade of flags that are torn to shreds and held up by rusted swords that are dripping with blood.

SOUND: Stirring martial music drowning out the distant shriek of a child being tortured.

SMELL: Heavy, sweet perfume masking the stink of decaying corpses.

TASTE: The sweet-sour acid when my dinner comes back up.

TOUCH: The smooth forearm of a young man where a jagged bone has ripped through the skin.

THE DESIGNERS' RESEARCH AND ANALYSIS

While Tom was being analytical (and disgusting), we designers were doing a very different kind of research and analysis. Ours was much more practical. Each of us read the play to gather the information we needed to create our individual designs.

Joe figured out where every scene takes place. On Shakespeare's stage, the scenery didn't change for every new location (see Figure 15.11), and changes were signified by what the actors said or by a symbolic piece of furniture. There are fifteen different locations in *Troilus and Cressida*. Joe made a chart showing which scenes take place in King Priam's court, which in Achilles' tent, which in Pandarus's house, and so on. His chart showed the flow from one location to the next, and for each scene he made a list of the props indicated in the script—a letter, a sword, a lantern. Figure 10.3 shows Joe's quick pencil sketch of a possible design idea.

As costume designer, Linda needed to know a lot about the characters so she could imagine what they would wear. She made descriptive lists of the traits of each character based on what is said in the script and on her understanding of the characters' social and economic status, their profession, their individual psychology, and their relationships to other characters. She made a chart showing where each scene takes place and what's happening at that point in the story. She made a character/scene plot showing which characters appear in each scene to help her track each character's costumes through the

Figure 10.3 Joe Varga's initial design idea shows a set made of rough stone with gigantic ruined columns and broken steps. His quick pencil sketch conveys visually how seven years of warfare have battered and eroded the once majestic city of Troy.

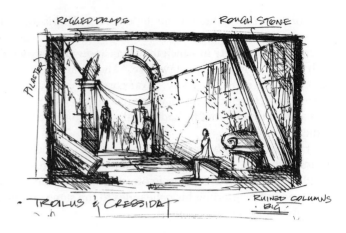

play so she would know when they changed clothes (and how fast they had to change). It also showed her which characters might be "doubled," that is, which two roles could be played by one actor. She also made a list of all the references to costumes in the dialogue so she knew what Shakespeare wanted the actors to wear. Figure 10.4 shows the rough sketch of a design idea that Linda drew to get a feel for the historical period.

Lighting designer Michael Wellborn made a chart showing the location, the time of day, the mood, and the light source for each scene: is it inside a tent at night and lit by a torch or outside at twilight and lit by the setting sun? Later, he would use this chart to plan his lighting design.

Sound designer Kevin Dunayer made a list of every sound mentioned in the script—each fanfare, the musical accompaniment for each song, the off-stage clanging of swords—as well as a list of every place he felt musical underscoring would enhance the mood of a scene. Kevin also located a rare CD titled *Music of Ancient Greece,* a music historian's reconstruction of ancient Greek music played on authentic instruments. He planned to play it for us at our first conference.

We were all gearing up for our first meeting in Colorado, when Tom shocked us with his brainstorm.

SOMETIMES A GREAT NOTION

Tom had had a flash of inspiration, the kind of creative thinking that sometimes makes a director seem brilliant and other times makes him a fool. He'd heard himself humming the folk song "Two Brothers," and instantly he knew how to do *Troilus and Cressida*.

Two brothers on their way,
One wore blue and one wore grey,
As they marched along their way,
All on a beautiful morning.

"TROILUS and CRESSIDA"
HELEN III·1
WITH PARIS
ROUGH SKETCH

Figure 10.4   Here is Linda's first impression of what Helen of Troy should look like. Helen is dressed in ancient Greek clothing for a passionate love scene with Paris.

Blue and gray—the American Civil War. In spite of his initial excitement, Tom analyzed his brainstorm carefully and objectively. The Civil War was a conflict within the American family, not with a foreign enemy (he remembered that the Greeks and Trojans were closely related). It was a war in which the soldiers' bodies and the nation's spirit were worn down by *time* (he remembered that time is one of the main themes in Shakespeare's play). It was a bloody war in which the South held to the outmoded value of "honor" (like the Trojans) while the North's cynical militarism ground out a cruel victory (Grant's brutal war of attrition was similar to the Greeks' siege of Troy). It was a war that corrupted America's values, a war in which our innocence died, a war in which the only certainty was despair. It was the Trojan War writ anew with American blood. It was the world of *Troilus and Cressida.*

Here was a way to make this cynical play accessible and exciting for our audience. Tom sent his idea to his designers. Initially, we were cautious. We knew that a lot was at stake, and we didn't want to make a distastrous mistake. After some reflection, we all embraced his idea and accepted his direction. Our excitement about the production increased tremendously.

> **ASIDE**   Linda designed *Romeo and Juliet* some years ago and, for no sensible reason she could understand, the director set it in the world of *Star Wars,* with Juliet looking like Princess Leia and Friar Lawrence dressed as Obe Wan Kanobe. That kind of production makes designers say, "I sure hope the director knows what he's doing."

BACK TO THE DRAWING BOARD OF RESEARCH

We still had enough time, so we set aside our research about ancient Greece, put our drawings in a file for use in some future play, shelved that intriguing CD of ancient music, and began to research the Civil War era. Ken Burns's brilliant television documentary was our starting place, and it remained a major source of inspiration for the next several months.

Tom prepared a script. The Festival feared that the play's difficult language would be hard for the audience to understand, so Tom edited Shakespeare's text, shortening it and eliminating some of the confusing subplots. He simplified the language, substituting familiar words for those that were arcane, though he never broke the meter, forced an image, or wrenched the syntax of Shakespeare's language. He wrote new lines to clarify the story and strengthen characters. When he had finished, we all could understand the text and we were confident the audience would know what was going on as well. We hoped Shakespeare's ghost would accept Tom as coauthor and that we could avoid the kind of failure an edited script frequently had brought down on more talented heads than ours.

Tom substituted songs from the Civil War era for the bawdy Elizabethan songs sung by Pandarus, and he inserted a song composed by playwright Robert Potter—an up-tempo musical setting for Andrew Marvell's poem *To His Coy Mistress.* Marvell was a contemporary of Shakespeare, so his language seemed to belong in the play. Also, his poem deals with time and unrequited love—two major themes in the play. The list of coauthors grew longer.

In preparing the script, Tom borrowed the use of spoken quotations and projected scene titles from Ken Burns's television documentary. These additions confirmed Tom's decision that our *Troilus and Cressida* should be done in the style of Theatricalism.

The designers researched the visual world of the Civil War (particularly the photography of Mathew Brady), the civilian dress of the 1860s and the military uniforms worn by both armies, and the music of mid-nineteenth-century America in preparation for exploring Tom's bold idea in greater depth.

CONCEPTUALIZING THE PRODUCTION

The January production conference brought us together for the first time. Tom's job as director was to organize how we presented our individual research and analysis and to ensure that before we left town we would have a shared interpretation and a clear vision of our production concept. We designers taped maps of famous battles and photos of life on Southern plantations to the walls of the meeting room as we listened to *Songs of the Civil War* played by The 97th Regimental String Band. Their instrumentation, the familiar melodies, and the vitality of the music expressed the spirit of our concept in a way no words or pictures ever could. Joe laid out books of Mathew Brady's photography and taped on the wall some pencil sketches he had done. Linda shared photographs of elegant high-society dresses. Michael described the kind of illumination provided by lanterns and candles. Kevin played snatches of battle sounds—horses neighing, rifles firing, and the distant trumpets of a cavalry charge.

As the meeting progressed, ideas tumbled freely out of each of us. Nobody was territorial. We shared a common quest. Joe explained to Michael how the light from a lantern could project the silhouette of Cressida kissing Diomedes through the canvas of his tent, and Kevin introduced the fact that baseball games were played between Southern and Northern teams in the no-man's land between the picket lines. Tom pointed out photographs of soldiers playing chess. Michael puzzled over some lines in the script that he thought Tom needed to clarify, and Linda (smiling like the Cheshire Cat for having found The 97th Regimental String Band) shared copies of the original published uniform regulations for both the Confederate and Union armies. Tom, who had been waiting for the proper moment, passed around photos he had taken at a Civil War reenactment he had attended a few weeks before (Figure 10.5). Before we knew it, we were caught up in the swirl of new ideas, surprising inspirations, bold suggestions, bad ideas, heated discussions, and laughing agreements. Through them all emerged three truths: (1) the Civil War was the first war to be photographed, and photography must play an important part in the design of the production; (2) music was a vital grounding for the emotional world of the production, and we wanted live musicians on the stage; (3) the play should be as energized and virile as possible, no matter how sad or bleak the story.

We reached important decisions over the next two days. We agreed on the location, season, hour of day, and mood for each scene, including a chandelier-lit ballroom for a big dance scene Tom wanted to stage in King Priam's court. Joe's set would be on one level, without a balcony, and would provide many entrances and exits. The floor would be painted to suggest a chess board and would include a painted emblem of crossed Union and Confederate flags based on the logo for the Civil War reenactment Tom had attended—and printed on the T-shirt he wore to the meeting (Figure 10.6). Joe would incorporate photography in the scene design, and a large LED sign would hang overhead on which we could flash the titles of the scenes or

Figure 10.5 Many people make a serious hobby of re-enacting Civil War battles, and they take on the role of historical persons. This reenactor wears the historically accurate wool uniform, socks, and shoes of a Confederate soldier and has groomed his facial hair in the correct style for the 1860s.

Figure 10.6 The T-shirt sold at the Civil War reenactment displays the Stars and Stripes of the United States flag crossed with the Stars and Bars of the flag of the Confederacy. This emblem became a dominant logo for our production.

Grant's portrait is on the fifty-dollar bill.

appropriately ironic comments, like General William Tecumseh Sherman's famous "War is all hell!" The LED sign fitted the style of Theatricalism that we all embraced (Figure 10.7). Tom agreed to stage the action so that actors entered through the auditorium from time to time, and he planned for many speeches to be delivered directly to the audience, solidifying the style. Linda would design selected characters to look like the Civil War icons that we recognize: King Priam would resemble Confederate President Jefferson Davis, Ulysses would look like General Ulysses S. Grant, and Pandarus would wear the white linen suit of a Southern plantation owner. The character of Thersites (thur-SITE-eez), who speaks the prologue and has the most cynical lines in the script, would not be a professional clown (as Shakespeare wrote him) but instead would be a photo-journalist covering the war and would look like Mathew Brady (Figure 10.8). Michael would light each scene to make the time and place specific, and he and Kevin would devise special effects for the sounds of the explosion of guns and cannons during the battle scenes.

We'd been in Colorado for three days, we'd conceptualized the production, and as theatre artists we'd had a "Rocky Mountain high." We returned home to our other jobs, but we continued our individual work on *Troilus and Cressida.*

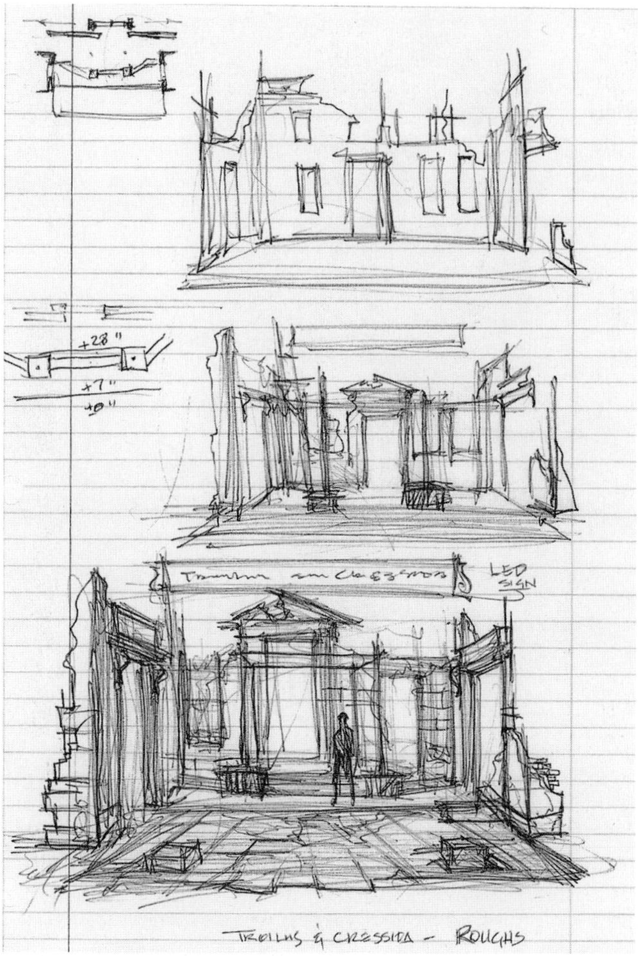

Figure 10.7 Joe doodled during the production conference. You can see here how his design idea developed through three stages from drawing to drawing. His final design was based on these rough drawings.

BETWEEN CONFERENCES

For the next two months, we refined our concept by sending pictures and written comments back and forth. Joe sent Tom a drawing of a chandelier, Tom e-mailed Joe his responses, and then Joe revised his drawing. Joe came up with the exciting idea of making a collage of photographs of the campgrounds and battle sites and then "mapping" those black-and-white images onto the walls of the set. We all knew this idea was a "keeper" as soon as we heard it. Linda showed Tom pencil drawings of the costumes, and he offered suggestions. Figure 10.9 shows her revised line drawing for Helen of Troy. Her research uncovered the surprising information that two regiments of Union Sharpshooters wore dark green uniforms. Everyone associates the color green with jealousy, so we chose the Sharpshooter uniform for the character

Sharpshooters used the finest rifles of the day, manufactured by a company named Sharps. We still call marksmen "sharpshooters."

Figure 10.8 Linda made a collage of images of the famous Civil War photojournalist Mathew Brady to show what the character of Thersites would look like.

of Diomedes because that helps the audience see him through Troilus's jealous eyes when the handsome Greek officer leads Cressida away—and later leads her astray. Michael researched various kinds of pyrotechnic devices that could be put in hidden pockets in the stage floor and would explode with bursts of light and smoke during the battle scenes. Kevin created sound effects to accompany those bursts, Joe found places in his set to put the electric triggering devices, and Tom planned his staging to ensure that the explosions would be fired when no actor was standing near them.

THE SECOND CONFERENCE

When we reconvened in Colorado in March, we felt in our bones that Tom's Civil War idea made perfect sense. Now we were eager to see and hear each other's ideas. Joe presented a three-dimensional white model (Figure 10.10) as well as a rendering of the set (Figure 10.11). Linda passed around her color rendering for each character (Color Plate 17) with fabric samples attached so

Figure 10.9 Linda's design for Helen of Troy's ball gown sparked a lively debate. Historically accurate skirts were very large, but Tom argued for skirts that would take up less space on stage. This drawing shows how they compromised on a mid-size skirt.

Figure 10.10 At the second production conference, Joe and Tom used the white model of the set to discuss Tom's imagined blocking of the actors.

we could understand how the costumes would move. Tom provided a list describing the props he imagined using in each scene—including letters, rifles, a picnic basket, a chess set, a megaphone, a baseball glove, and a big tripod camera for Thersites that would flash when a picture was taken. Michael gave a resoundingly explosive demonstration of the available pyros (it had to be done outside with a fire marshal supervising the demo). He talked through

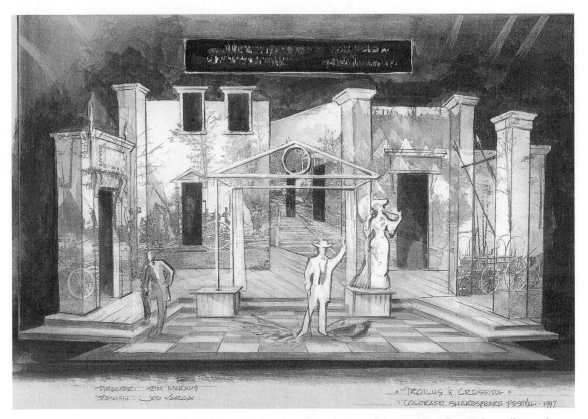

Figure 10.11   Joe's painted rendering of the scenery shows the collage of photographs he selected to be "mapped" on the walls of the set. The size and placement of the LED sign are shown at the top of the rendering. The pavilion in the center of the stage is a minimalist version of the architectural style known as Classic Revival, which used ancient Greek design motifs; buildings in this style were popular in the 1860s. Notice how Joe has incorporated the crossed-flags logo from the Civil War reenactment into his design.

the play scene by scene with Joe, Linda, and Tom to ensure that the colors and angles of his lighting design were compatible with the overall design concept and would complement the scenery and costumes, as well as the mood of the blocking Tom was developing. Kevin played more specific samples of battle sounds, and he and Tom confirmed where the cues would be placed in the script. Tom provided written directions for the choreographer, who would stage a formal dance, and for the fight director, who would arrange all the fights—including the boxing match between Hector and Ajax that was one of the highlights of the production. At the end of the two-day conference, our concept was fully refined. We were ready to move forward, more convinced than ever that our production concept would please the audience.

FINAL PREPARATIONS

Each of us worked individually during the next two months. Tom developed his staging ideas in preparation for working with the actors in rehearsals and checked regularly with the others to ensure that everything was progressing on schedule and as planned. Joe drafted the technical drawings—the ground plan, elevation, cross section, and **painter's elevations** (Figures 10.12a–d).

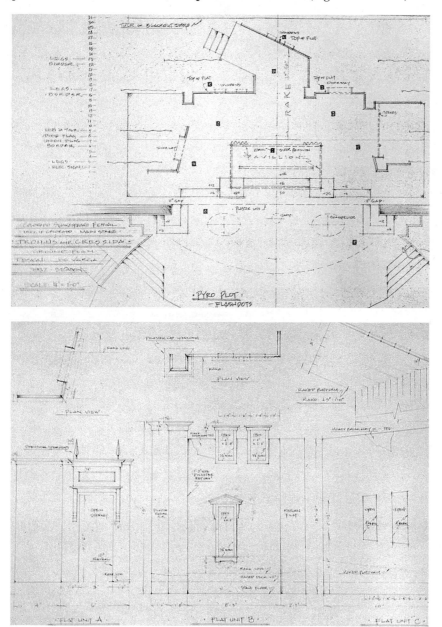

Figure 10.12a This ground plan for *Troilus and Cressida* shows the set from a bird's-eye view. You can see the position of the LED sign, the location of the pavilion that will be elevated on a 12-inch-high platform with one step on either side, and the placement of the pyrotechnic explosives.

Figure 10.12b This technical drawing is an elevation that shows the various walls in a flattened two-dimensional front view. The written notes give the technicians important information that will guide them in building the set.

Figure 10.12c This technical drawing is a cross section that shows the placement of the scenery in the theatre. You can see that there's not enough space to lower and raise a large chandelier between the pipes with scenery and drapes hanging from them.

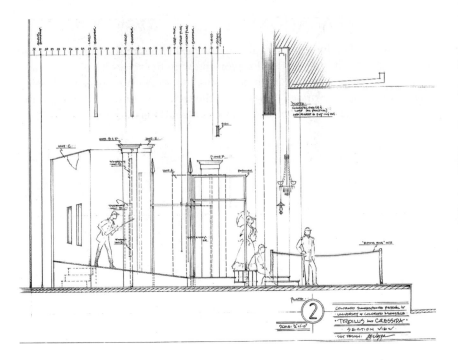

Figure 10.12d Painter's elevations are small-scale paintings that the designer provides to guide the scene painter. They are usually very colorful, but the walls of Joe's set called only for the mapping of the black-and-white photo-collage. The scene painter projected Joe's elevation on the blank walls to paint the images.

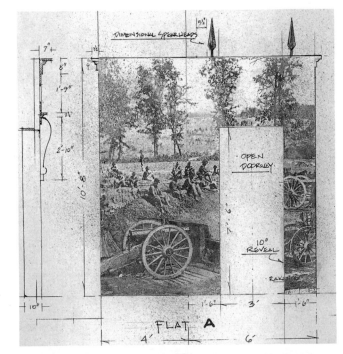

Cue #	Speaker	Description	Source	Level	Notes	Pg #

(Colorado Shakespeare Festival 1997 — Sound Score & Cue Sheet)

Colorado Shakespeare Festival 1997
Sound Score & Cue Sheet

Production: *Troilus & Cressida*
Director: Tom Markus
Sound Designer: Kevin Dunayer

Cue #	Speaker	Description	Source	Level	Notes	Pg #
10	All	Pre-show	B	-3.5	at 1/2 hour pre	
A/F	All	Out Q 10	B		at 5 min pre	
C/A		Corp Announce	A	-4.0		
11	All	Slow Music	B	-3.5	Auto Follow pre	
20	1-4/7	Lincoln 1	A	-3.5		1
		Slow Mus. Out	B			
30	5 & 6	Battle #1	C	-5.0		1
40	All	Explosion #1	B	-3		2
		Battle Out	C			
50	1-4/7	Whitman 1	A	-3.5		2
70	6	Bonnie Blue	B	-25		4
90	6	Artillery 1	B	-10		4
100	6	Artillery 1.5	B	-10		4
120	1-4/7	Sherman 1	A	-5.0		5
130	6	Retreat	B	-15		9
140	L-5 & 6	Dixie	A	-25	slow fade up	9
145		Pan L to Center	A			10
147		Pan to Left	A			11
148		Out Q	A			11
170	2	Hail to Chief	A	-15		12
180	1-4	Male #1	B	-15		12
200	2	Dist. Trumpet	A	-15		14

Figure 10.13 The first page of sound designer Kevin Dunayer's cue sheets for *Troilus and Cressida*.

Linda purchased fabric for the costumes that would be built, as well as the necessary trimmings and accessories. She arranged for the costumes that would be rented or borrowed from other theatres, pulled some costumes from the Festival's storage, and ordered custom-built military uniforms from a company that supplies historically accurate uniforms for Civil War reenactors.

Michael drafted his light plot showing where each instrument would be hung and focused and made a first draft of a cue sheet. Kevin worked in his sound studio in New Jersey to create more of his complex and multilayered sound effect cues and also made a first draft of his cue sheet (Figure 10.13).

REALIZING THE PRODUCTION

The best-conceived productions can crash and burn on the road to opening night, so we all gave our entire energy to realizing the production, starting on the day in mid-May when the entire company moved into our temporary

"Build period" is theatre jargon for the time between the day the shops start working and the first technical or dress rehearsal.

apartments in Boulder, Colorado, and began our work in earnest. The rehearsal and build period of a production never fails to reaffirm Murphy's Law: "Everything that can go wrong will go wrong." We were experienced enough to know that, despite our smooth sailing thus far, we edged closer to disaster with each passing day.

In the first two days, the acting company auditioned and Tom cast the roles. In a fully professional theatre, casting is done weeks in advance. The Colorado Shakespeare Festival's actors, however, are recruited from professional training programs and graduate schools across the country, and they audition after they arrive. The four directors meet to cast the season's four plays, often compromising their own productions for the benefit of the Festival. Tom was uneasy about several of the actors who would be playing major roles in our production. He grew more concerned when he learned that his plans to include a banjo player in the production were threatened. The prominent bluegrass musician and recording artist Pete Wernick had agreed to do the show, but now we discovered he had scheduled concerts that conflicted with some performances. Tom auditioned several substitutes, and we realized that three different musicians would be performing at one or another performance during the season. That meant allocating precious rehearsal time to accommodate the three banjo players. It also meant designing and building additional costumes. And that meant a strain on the budget.

ASIDE   Pete Wernick is known as "Dr. Banjo." Check out his Web site, www.drbanjo.com, to learn about his CDs, videos, banjo camps, T-shirts, and concert schedule.

The designers met with the crews in their respective departments to explain the needs of their designs and to answer the artisans' questions about exactly how the designers wanted things to look.

Rehearsals began with a presentation to the acting company. Tom talked about the production concept and explained how the script had been revised, Joe displayed the rendering and model for the set, Linda showed her costume renderings, Michael described how his lighting design would contribute to the mood, and Kevin played samples of the music. We listened quietly while the actors read through the play, breathing first life into our new version of the script. Then each of us went off to supervise the work in our own area.

Actors contributed their creativity throughout the six weeks of rehearsal. Early on, we determined that the Trojans would speak with a soft Southern accent and that the Greeks would have a variety of regional accents (Figure 10.14). Thersites (carrying his camera and looking like Mathew Brady) would have a strong New York accent; when he spoke the prologue, the audience would be jarred out of their expectations of "Shakespeare" and invited into the more familiar world of our play (Figure 10.15). The decision to use

Figure 10.14   In the Trojan palace, Hector wears his Confederate uniform as he seeks his father's blessing before going into battle. The Trojans spoke with a soft Southern accent. At the left of this photo, you can see how King Priam was made up to look like Confederate president Jefferson Davis. He wore a dressing robe for this predawn scene.

regional accents meant that additional precious rehearsal time had to be given to the voice and dialect coach.

Richard Kinter, the professional guest actor playing the flamboyant Pandarus, is an accomplished musical theatre performer. He suggested that his Act One finale be a song-and-dance number in the tradition of nineteenth-century vaudeville. He asked for a backup group with banjo, guitar, spoons, and washboard, and he asked Linda to design a showman's glitter-covered top hat and a breakaway vest that would reveal the red, white, and blue of the Confederate Stars and Bars. It was wonderful, but it meant that five more costumes had to be created. The budget was being stretched tighter and the labor force pushed harder.

While Tom rehearsed the actors, we designers made artistic decisions on a daily basis, supervising the painters, technicians, prop crew, electricians, and costume shop staff. Linda oversaw the construction and alteration of the costumes and supervised the fittings every time the actors tried on their costumes. She discovered that the military uniform that had been rented for one of the important officers—the only uniform of the correct rank—was several sizes too big for the actor. Because the costume couldn't be changed—and the actor couldn't gain 40 pounds in four weeks—she solved the crisis by designing a "fat suit" for him to wear, a fitted, polyester-batting, pillowlike undergarment that padded the actor to fit the oversize costume. The actor's vanity was bruised, but the character looked great!

Joe discovered that the chandelier he had designed was too big and wouldn't fit on the stage. What would happen to Tom's gala ball scene in Priam's palace? In a flurry of the kind of creativity-on-demand that long ago earned him the affectionate nickname "Design-o-matic," Joe designed and substituted the handsome battery-powered sconces seen in Figure 10.16.

Figure 10.15   Thersites, costumed and made up to look like Civil War photojournalist Mathew Brady, spoke the prologue directly to the audience in his native "Noo Yawk" accent.

Figure 10.16   This sketch and photograph show the wall sconces for the ballroom in King Priam's palace, which had red-white-and-blue bunting draped through the crossed torches. These were Joe's quick-fix solution to the problem of the too big chandelier. The actor wearing the "fat suit" is on the right side of the photo.

Lighting designers call their pencil sketches "storyboards," borrowing the term from the movies.

Michael watched rehearsals to learn where the actors would play each scene and sometimes sketched a scene's staging so he could refine his lighting design.

Kevin asked members of the acting company to record the various narrated speeches that introduced the scenes. He also worked with his crew to place the microphones and speakers for the production.

Written reports of changes, developments, and problems were distributed daily to keep everyone current. Weekly meetings ensured that everyone was communicating, that problems were being anticipated and solved, and that everything was on budget and on schedule. Whenever Murphy's Law popped up, everyone contributed ideas until a solution was found.

TECHNICAL AND DRESS REHEARSALS

All of our work came together in the final week of rehearsal. Under Tom's supervision, we were "putting it together, bit by bit" in our effort to "make a piece of art." The actors moved out of the rehearsal room and onto the stage for the technical rehearsals, in which the lighting and sound cues were rehearsed and refined. The LED sign exploded in a storm of sparks. It was Friday night, and the sign couldn't be repaired until after the first preview. With the ironic supertitles missing, many of the production's transitions would seem awkward. Our ability to judge the audience's reaction on Monday would be impaired, and we'd have less time to make adjustments between

Figure 10.17   The title *Troilus and Cressida* suggests a love story like that of Romeo and Juliet. Here, the title is displayed ironically on the LED sign above actor Richard Kinter as he speaks the diseased and dying Pandarus's final curse at the audience.

the final preview and opening night. Figure 10.17 shows the relationship of actor Richard Kinter and the working LED sign as Pandarus delivered his final speech on opening night.

Costumes were added for the dress rehearsals. Color Plate 18 shows the beautiful silk dress worn by Helen. At the first dress rehearsal, however, the actress's silk skirt caught on the rough edges of the set. Sandpaper solved that crisis. Then we realized that we were still using the modern baseball glove we'd been using in rehearsals. Hastily, the prop department tried to research what an 1860s baseball glove looked like, but they found nothing. The prop crew made their best guess and designed and built a glove, and we hoped it would look believable to the audience. (A year later, while watching Ken Burns's television documentary about baseball, we were delighted to discover that they had guessed correctly.)

The fire marshal wouldn't let us use the flash powder in Thersites' tripod camera. We substituted a hidden battery-powered strobe light and a rubber bulb that the actor could squeeze to emit a puff of talcum powder. Necessity is the mother of theatrical invention!

Throughout these final rehearsals, the creative and interpretive artists exchanged ideas continually, and lightning-fast decisions required compromises that we all knew benefited the production. Finally, we watched two preview performances during which we all took notes about the audience's reactions so we could make final adjustments prior to opening night.

ANOTHER OPENING, ANOTHER SHOW

The collaborative process suggested in Chapters 6 through 9 and described in this chapter was completed on opening night. It was time to share our creation with the Festival's audience (Figure 10.18). Even though we all had a lot of experience behind us, each opening night breeds a terror in the director and designers that is just like the actors' stage fright. Suddenly, we were afraid that every decision we had made was WRONG!

Our terror level rose enormously just hours before opening night. Actor Richard Kinter came to Tom's apartment in the early afternoon, looking ashen. He said, "I'm afraid I have a hernia." Without him, the show could not open. We were in a panic! Richard was rushed to the emergency room, diagnosed with a hernia, given a prosthesis to wear, told it would be safe for him to go on that night, and sent back to the theatre. He remained terrified. Moving very cautiously, he put on his makeup and got ready for his first entrance.

Kinter played his first scene very, very, cautiously, but as the show went on he gained confidence, and by midway in the first act he was giving a terrific performance. Color Plate 19 shows his Act One finale, the song-and-dance number that was a show-stopper. We all sighed with relief.

To our delight, the audience greeted our production with laughter, attentive silences, and enthusiastic applause for the entrance of the swirling ballroom dancers and the boxing match between Ajax and Hector (Color Plate 20). If the reviewers' responses are any measure of achievement, we had

Figure 10.18 This joyous love scene from early in the play shows how the audience saw Troilus and Cressida (Hayden Adams and Cheyenne Casebier) on opening night.

an artistic success. One reviewer wrote that the production was "thoughtful, innovative, and effective," and another described it as achieving "a vitality and sense of creativity that make this play the sleeper hit of CSF's 40th season." At the end of the season, we were delighted to learn that our production of this extremely risky play had attracted a fraction over its projected attendance and had, thankfully, sold enough tickets to bring in a hundred thousand dollars.

We didn't kid ourselves that we had hit a home run with *Troilus and Cressida,* but we were really happy we hadn't struck out. In the final analysis, we think it's fair to say we had a modest "hit."

EXERCISES

1. After your class has seen a production of a play by any classic playwright that has been interpreted and conceptualized in an unexpected manner, discuss what you did and did not like about the concept. Offer reasons for your opinions, stating specific examples whenever possible. The purpose of this exercise is to develop your analytic skills as well as your understanding of the creative process.

2. After the class has read a play by Shakespeare, select a team of five students. One student takes the function of director, and the others become the scene designer, costume designer, lighting designer, and sound designer. Spend a class session conceptualizing a production of the play while your fellow students listen. Before the next class, have each member of the creative team do individual research and analysis to develop the concept, while the other students reflect on the strengths and weaknesses of the concept as it was developed in the previous class meeting. In the next class meeting, each member of the creative team should make a presentation to the class describing how his or her research supported the interpretation and concept previously developed. Then have the creative team answer questions from the class about their research and the production concept. The point of this exercise is to explore the creative process. You are unlikely to develop a concept that all students like or agree with.

The Audience Joins In

If you attended the theatre early in the term, you may have been assigned to read Chapters 11 and 12, as we suggested in the Overture. The chapters in Act 3 describe how *you* join in the process of creating theatre. You are the audience, and the audience enters into the creative process when the curtain rises.

Act 1 addresses how to understand and evaluate theatre, and Act 2 describes how the playwright, actors, director, and designers collaborate to prepare a production. Keep in mind what we wrote in the Overture—theatre doesn't happen without an audience. Now it's your turn. Creating the theatrical experience is about to become *your* responsibility.

In Act 3 we'll help you learn how to locate the performances that the creative and interpretive theatre artists have worked long and hard to prepare, and we'll guide you to getting tickets and making yourself comfortable in the auditorium. Then we'll explore with you the kinds of stages you're most likely to discover when the curtain rises. Finally, we'll describe the surprising variety of people and jobs that make up the "backstage" world.

It's time to imagine going to the theatre. You're the audience. Join in.

CHAPTER 11

Finding Theatre and Getting Tickets

You know where and when the football team plays because you've seen notices in the paper. You also know how to find out what's at the movies and what rock groups are playing at the local night spots. How do you go about finding theatre?

No matter where you live, you will find eager and informed theatregoers. You might not think, for example, that Salt Lake City is a particularly vibrant theatre town. Yet at 3:00 A.M. on a recent February morning when **tickets** were to go on sale for the national tour of the musical *Les Miserables*, 125 people were already in line at the box office. When the box office opened at 7:00 A.M., hundreds more who had been sitting in their parked cars joined the rush. In a matter of a few days, all 32,000 tickets for the engagement were sold. Why? Because these people wanted to go to the theatre and knew how to find it.

FINDING OUT WHAT'S PLAYING

Theatre is a business, and like a rock concert or a football game, it wants to sell tickets. Because theatre is a small business with little money to spend, it places its advertisements strategically, aiming them at the portion of the public that is interested in theatre, and also relies heavily on free public announcements. For a show that is in hot demand, such as *The Phantom of the Opera*, tickets are snapped up. More commonly, theatres make an effort to inform buyers of where they are, what they are offering, and how tickets can be bought. We'll explore how and where theatres place ads and announcements informing you how to find theatre where you live.

FORESHADOWING

The Five Ways Theatres Inform Audiences

1. Direct mail
2. Print ads and announcements
3. Radio and television ads and announcements
4. Telemarketing
5. The Internet

Direct Mail

Direct mail is theatre's most efficient and cost-effective way of advertising. Theatres develop lists of persons who are likely to be interested in theatre, and they mail attractive brochures directly to those people's homes. Where does a theatre get its lists? It starts with the name and address of everyone who purchases a ticket to that theatre. Now you know why you're asked for yours when you buy a ticket. Next, it secures the mailing lists of other arts organizations. The theatre swaps its list with the ballet, which swaps its list with the opera, which swaps its list with the symphony, and so on. The relatively small cost of preparing and mailing a brochure generates the largest proportion of a theatre's ticket sales, making this mode of advertising the centerpiece in a theatre's marketing strategy.

Print Ads and Announcements

Print ads are comparatively inexpensive, and theatres place print ads in many places. Marquees are the most obvious form of print advertising (Figure 11.1),

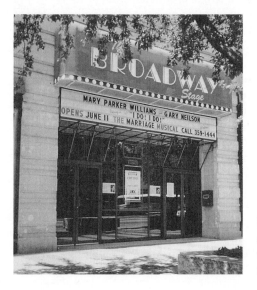

Figure 11.1 This marquee is an obvious form of print advertising for the opening of the musical *"I Do! I Do!"*

Figure 11.2   A large form of print advertising, this enormous banner was hung on the wall of the Pioneer Theatre Company's stage house to advertise its 2003–2004 season. It was seen by hundreds of commuters daily.

but there are others. Newspapers carry display ads for season tickets just after the Labor Day holiday, when people are setting their schedules following summer vacation; newspaper ads for single productions can be found at any time of year. These ads commonly are located near the ads for other forms of entertainment, such as movies. Print ads also appear in magazines that appeal to upper-middle-income families and in glossy monthlies such as *San Diego Magazine* and *Virginia Today.* Because people who go to one kind of arts performance are likely to enjoy another, theatres commonly place print ads in programs for the ballet or the opera. Billboards and signs on public transportation are yet another place you'll see print ads. Commercial theatres in New York and elsewhere place ads on buses, in subway stations, and on huge billboards visible to commuters (Figure 11.2). You are likely to have seen a poster, or "window board," yet another form of print ad that theatres use. Posters are aimed at pedestrian traffic and are placed in windows that large numbers of people pass by. You may also have seen table tents and handbills. The former are found on tables at restaurants and motels; the latter are handed to you as you walk down the street.

Print ads are an inexpensive way to attract the impulse buyer. As a public service, most newspapers also print a column—commonly titled "Calen-

Figure 11.3 The hit musical *Pippin,* starring Ben Vereen, opened in 1972 and was the first Broadway show to advertise with television commercials.

dar"—that lists events you can attend. Printed announcements of this kind usually give the name and address of the theatre, the phone number to call for tickets, and the names of the plays being presented.

Radio and Television Ads and Announcements

Radio stations sell ads by time. A thirty-second spot costs less than a sixty-second spot, and an ad broadcast during the evening news costs more than one that airs at 4:47 A.M. Because radio advertising is more expensive than print advertising, many small theatres can't afford to advertise by radio. In contrast, commercial theatre productions like *The Phantom of the Opera* buy a lot of air time. If you haven't heard radio ads for theatre, maybe you don't listen to stations that play classical music or golden oldies. Theatres have to be selective about where they spend their advertising money, and they rarely place ads on radio stations that play rock, rap, country, or New Age music. While theatres would like to advertise regularly on radio, they can't afford to very often.

What is true for radio is even truer for television. If you have seen TV ads for theatre, they were probably for the big commercial productions playing on Broadway or on tour. TV advertising, a relatively new mode of advertising, began with the Broadway musical *Pippin* in 1972 (Figure 11.3), and television ads are now commonplace in New York, particularly for large musicals that hope to sell $800,000 worth of tickets each week.

EXPOSITION

In 1972, Stephen Schwartz's soft-rock musical *Pippin* was not selling many tickets during preview performances, and audiences were walking out at intermission. The gossip in the theatre community was that the show had "flop" written all over it. Facing the possibility of closing the show and losing all their money when the negative reviews came out, the producers had two brainstorms. First, they omitted the intermission so people didn't have a polite time to leave. Second, they launched a major ad campaign on television. They made an energetic and colorful TV commercial that showed their star, Ben Vereen, singing and dancing. The strategy worked. The show was a box office hit despite its generally unfavorable critical response.

Some theatres provide information through announcements that they don't have to pay for. All radio and television stations are licensed by the Federal Communications Commission (FCC), an agency of the U.S. government. One of the FCC's regulations is that the airwaves belong to the people and that in order for a station to secure a license to use the public airwaves—that is, to broadcast—the station must put a certain portion of its total air time in the service of the public. The announcements it makes are called public service announcements (PSAs), and various stations broadcast different kinds of PSAs: a lost and found for pets, a listing of school closings, a calendar of arts events. What's true for radio is also true for television, but PSAs aren't broadcast as frequently on television as they are on radio. Although PSAs may help the theatre get the word out in a general way, they aren't much help to you if you want to learn the specifics about what's playing.

Telemarketing

You're probably as hopeful as Tom and I are that the recently passed federal and state laws making telephone solicitation illegal will be enforced. Then maybe dinner hour and Saturday morning sleep-in won't be interrupted by people trying to sell us auto glass. The phone calls won't stop entirely, of course. Not-for-profit businesses are exempt from the new regulations, so we will still get calls asking us to vote for a candidate, give to a charity, or buy tickets to the symphony. These calls are made by telemarketers, and theatres are among the many businesses that have learned that **telemarketing** is an inexpensive and highly efficient way to reach their buyers. A theatre builds a list of prospects and engages a group of telephoners who make an appealing sales pitch.

ASIDE If you have a pleasing telephone voice and a charming yet aggressive personality, you can make money by working for your local theatre company. The hours are convenient (usually from 4:00 in the afternoon until about 8:00 in the evening), and if you are good at it you can make a handsome commission on top of your hourly wage. But before you embark on this job, be certain that you can take rejection—you'll get a lot of it. Some people will hang up on you, others will be rude, and more than a few will insult the product you are trying to sell them. "I subscribed last year, and I *hated* the shows" is something you'll hear often.

Here's an experience Tom had when he tried to help out with a subscription drive:

—Hello?

—Hello. I'm calling from TheatreVirginia, and I hope this is a convenient time to chat with you. Do you have a free moment?

—Yes, I suppose so . . .

—Wonderful. Well, we're looking through our files, and we see that you haven't renewed for next season. We know you won't want to miss out on the seven terrific shows we'll be doing, so we wanted to call and remind you that you could renew now and keep the good seats you had this past year.

—Oh dear, I don't know . . .

—Have you been out of town? I notice you didn't return your renewal form when we sent your brochure in the mail last month.

—No, you see . . .

(About here I realized that her voice was very frail and that she was probably quite elderly and perhaps in poor health.)

. . . you see my husband passed away just before Christmas and I don't have any way to get out of the house at night and I can't see to drive very well, and so I don't think I can come to the theatre anymore.

Several hours later, after I'd made the umpteenth call like that, I grew very depressed. So many older folks in failing health, with no family or friends, and here I was trying to sell them theatre tickets! I told my managing director that the experience was too depressing and that I was sorry but I just couldn't continue. He laughed heartily. "That's because you're not a real salesman," he teased. "If you were, you'd say something uplifting like 'Gee, I'm sorry to hear that you lost your husband, but you know if you'd subscribe to our next season you could meet lots of new folks at the theatre and maybe find yourself a new husband.'" We both laughed, I told him he was a heartless swine, and I admitted I wasn't a "real salesman." I went back to directing plays and let him get on with the business he did so very well—the business of selling subscriptions.

The Internet

The Internet has quickly become an important marketing tool for theatres across America, and you can get information from their Web site and buy tickets on-line. The Internet is used to augment direct mail, print ads, radio and television spots, and telemarketing and is the newest of the five ways theatre uses paid advertising and announcements to tell you where you can find a performance. Because the Internet continues to expand rapidly, some of the information we provide here may change by the time you read it, but you surfers know that a vast ocean of information is waiting for you. Dive in!

Try both "theatre" and "theater"; that small spelling difference will result in two completely different sets of hits.

The standard route is through your preferred search engine, and we've become addicted to Google. You'll speed your search if you name a specific play or theatre (for example, New Stage) and find its home page. Most Web sites will tell you what the play is about, give a synopsis of the plot, tell you who the leading actors are, and show some photos of the production. Some will play songs from the production or show clips of the action. If you enter only the word "theatre," you will receive more hits than you may want to sift through. While you'll stumble onto some interesting and unexpected information this way, some tips can help you find theatre.

EXPOSITION   *Theatre Web Site Addresses*

Theatre Direct International: broadway.com
American Theater Web: americantheaterweb.com
Theatre Central: playbill.com
Theatremania: theatremania.com

Large cities, New York and London, for example, have specialized sites for cyber-minded theatre lovers who want to stay up-to-date on their favorite plays and players. The home page for Theatre Direct International (TDI) offers you the hottest stage news involving Broadway and Off Broadway productions, as well as productions in London. TDI raises the curtain on a virtual playbill of information, including show openings and schedules, cast lists, ticket availability, and even a bit of theatre gossip. Check out this site even if you're not going to the theatre. It's amazing to see the number and variety of theatrical offerings in places where theatrical tourism is a large part of the local economy.

ASIDE   Would you like to know what the critics said about a play before you buy a ticket? Just type in the name of the play and add the word "review." You'll get lots of unrelated hits—including reviews of the show's CD—but you'll find the critics' reviews among them.

Maybe you're not headed for New York or London but want to find out what's happening in your hometown or during your visit with friends on the Mississippi Gulf Coast. The sites that we've suggested list theatre events in nearly every city across the country. These sites invite you to select the name of a city to learn what plays are available there. The American Theater Web site, for example, provides links to not-for-profit theatre companies all over the country. Each entry includes a summary of the theatre company's work and productions along with a link to the theatre's own Web site for more detailed information. The range is impressive—you can locate information on everything from small community theatres in Texas to the Arena Stage in Washington. Although the big commercial houses of Broadway are not on the site, it offers links to several dozen not-for-profit companies in New York City.

The third Web site, Theatre Central, is the hub of theatre on the Internet. It gives information about both international theatre and American theatre and may even list the plays in your hometown. The site lists Broadway, regional theatre, national tours, and summer stock. It has fascinating stories, permits you to buy tickets on-line, and offers numerous links.

The fourth Web site is Theatremania. Here you can find information about every play on Broadway, Off Broadway, Off Off Broadway, on tour, and at regional theatres. The site provides reviews and salient information about each production and also has a link to ticketmaster.com in case you want to purchase tickets through that firm. (Ticketmaster is described in more detail below.)

More theatres each day are setting up their own Web sites. You'll need a little time and some trial-and-error searching to find them, because their address is often a condensation of the name of the theatre company. When you hit on one, you'll find e-mail and snail-mail addresses, phone and fax numbers, season schedules, performance dates, titles of current productions, ticket prices, and names of the directors, actors, and designers. Some sites even list audition dates in case you're an actor looking for a job. A theatre's Web site may include graphics of its productions, background information about its plays, director's notes, reviews of its productions, or links to related sites.

Some particularly successful commercial productions maintain official Web sites for fans of that show, giving background information about the play. Search by entering the name of the play. For example, entering *Phantom of the Opera* will link you to a site that offers the dates a touring production will be in your city, photos of the cast, a video, music, history, reviews, the story of the play—everything you could want, including a gift shop, an e-mail club, and a 24/7 chat room. Hop on the Internet and find out if the national tour of your favorite musical is headed your way.

TICKET TIPS

Theatres sell tickets in two basic forms: **single tickets** and **season tickets.** It's the same practice used by sports teams and symphony orchestras. You can buy one or more tickets for a particular performance, or you can buy one or more tickets to each production in the series a theatre company presents in a season. In the commercial theatre, on Broadway, and in many large cities, theatres produce one show at a time so only single tickets are available. A season ticket admits you to the same seat for each production of the theatrical season, and typically you select the week of the run and the performance of the week you wish to attend—for example, the second Tuesday night of the four-week run of each production. At the time of purchase, you receive your ticket for each production and know that you will always have the same seat and will always go on the same day of the week. People who attend the theatre with friends and make a social or business occasion of their theatregoing prefer this way of buying tickets. Most theatres do three things to make season tickets attractive: they offer you the opportunity to purchase your tickets before single tickets go on sale so that you have an excellent chance of getting good seats, they offer the tickets at a discounted rate, and they offer you the right to exchange your ticket for any other performance of a production. They can't guarantee you a comparably good seat in exchange, of course, but you are able to reschedule at your convenience.

Some variants on these two forms of tickets might be of interest to you. You can purchase **group tickets** (typically, twenty or more) for a particular performance at a discounted rate. If you belong to a sorority, a club, or a professional organization that would enjoy seeing a play, you can purchase group tickets at a reduced price. Alternatively, some theatres sell a **pass** as well as a season ticket. A pass is good for a specified number of admissions, say five. By presenting your pass at the box office, you can get five seats to one performance, one seat to any five performances, or any combination of five seats. You can get tickets only on a space-available basis, so you can't be certain where you'll be sitting. Some people prefer the pass to the season ticket because they can take friends or business associates to selected performances and can avoid productions they think they may not like. Flexibility is important for people who have strong feelings about what they don't want to encounter in the theatre.

How do you actually go about buying your ticket? The surest way is to go to the theatre's box office. Box offices usually are open a full working day six days a week, but some are not, so phone before you go. The box office clerks are more than happy to accept your cash or major credit card, and some local theatres will accept a personal check. The box office usually displays a sign describing the different prices for seats in various parts of the theatre. The front rows cost more than the back of the balcony, and a seat in the center costs more than one on the side. If you are a student or a senior citizen and can produce appropriate identification, reduced price tickets may be available to you. Theatres rarely announce these discounts, so you have to inquire about them.

Theatre ticket prices are tied to the general economy and can go up and down like the price of gasoline. The first Broadway show to charge $100 for the best seat on a Saturday night was *Miss Saigon,* but that price is now the standard for musicals like *Hairspray* and for "hot ticket" dramas like the re-

Most theatres have special policies. Some don't admit children under age five, some require a ticket for children even if they sit on an adult's lap, and most will permit you to reserve a space for a person in a wheelchair.

vival of Eugene O'Neill's great American drama *Long Day's Journey Into Night* that starred Brian Dennehy, Vanessa Redgrave, Phillip Seymour Hoffman, and Robert Sean Leonard. Back balcony seats sometimes cost only $25.00 mid-week. As a rule, musicals cost more than plays, and ticket prices for dramas and comedies range from $100.00 down to $35.00.

As you travel about the country, you will find that there are no fixed prices for theatre tickets. Some patterns can be observed, however. Ticket prices in the city we live in are a fair guide to those in other cities. For a tour of a major commercial production like *The Full Monty,* ticket prices range from $80.00 down to $30.00. For the resident professional theatre company, prices range from $42.50 down to $20.00. For local amateur theatre companies, prices range from $30.00 down to $12.00. For plays presented at a university, prices range from $10.00 down to $6.00.

You can see the advantage of buying a season ticket to a theatre that charges $42.50 a seat. Instead of paying $297.50 for a seven-play season, you might pay only $250.00. If you're buying four seats together, you would save $165.00. Season tickets—whether for the theatre season or the football season—are as wise a choice for those who attend regularly as newspaper subscriptions are for those who read the paper daily.

Sometimes going to a theatre's box office is inconvenient. Many people buy their tickets on-line, but you can also purchase tickets by telephone if you are willing to pay a service charge and you have a major credit card. Theatres will mail the tickets to you or hold them at the box office, where you can pick them up just before the performance. In many large cities you can purchase tickets from agencies that are conveniently located in hotel lobbies and department stores. Other ticket agencies can be found by looking under "Tickets" in the phone book. Companies such as Telecharge and Ticketmaster sell you tickets with an added commission; they will mail the tickets to you or have them held at the box office.

For the bargain-minded theatregoer, discounted tickets for same-day performances are available in large cities such as New York, London, and Paris at special box offices in central locations. In New York, the TKTS booth is located in the heart of the Broadway theatre district (Figure 11.4). Using cash or traveler's checks, you can buy tickets there at half or three-quarters the face value of the ticket (plus a $3.00 service charge); tickets are available to most Broadway shows if you are willing to stand in a short line and are flexible about what you want to see. In addition, most resident professional theatres outside New York offer **student rush tickets** at a greatly reduced price. These tickets usually are available only thirty minutes before curtain time. Student rush seats are often the same price as a movie ticket—between $6.00 and $8.00—and you might get excellent seats!

You can buy theatre tickets over the Internet for theatres that have a Web site. If you have a credit card, you can choose the performance you want to see and view the available seats on a seating chart (the same way you choose a seat on an airplane). Then you select the seats you want and buy your tickets with a click. Your tickets will be mailed to you or held for you at the box office.

Figure 11.4   The TKTS booth in midtown Manhattan sells discounted tickets for that day's performances of Broadway and Off Broadway shows.

Commercial productions, particularly Broadway shows and national tours, sell tickets through Internet companies that either add a service charge or (sometimes) offer a discount. Here are some we recommend:

anytimetickets.com	Provides hard-to-get tickets to shows on Broadway and in Las Vegas for people who are willing to pay a $50 service fee
ticketmaster.com	Charges a service fee of less than $10 for Broadway and Off Broadway shows, for tours, and for theatres in big cities; can link to Ticketmaster from the informational Web site theatremania.com
telecharge.com	Sells tickets to many shows that its competitor Ticketmaster does not and charges a comparable service fee
BroadwayBox.com	Offers discounted tickets for Broadway shows

We want to let you know about one final way to buy tickets. Sometimes tickets for a popular show that is sold out can be purchased from people who have extras. However, be wary of scalpers who offer tickets at incredibly inflated prices. Their tickets sometimes are phony and won't be accepted by the theatre, and their transactions are illegal in most states. If you are eager to see a popular show, you might take a chance on encountering someone standing in front of the theatre trying to sell tickets bought for friends whose car broke down.

A ticket is a legally binding contract with the management of the theatre. In consideration of the money you paid (and the price is printed on the ticket), you are guaranteed a particular seat for a particular performance of a particular play. No one else may occupy your seat. What happens if the management doesn't deliver what the ticket guarantees you? You might get your money back. Each theatre has its own procedures and policies.

When you've found a play you want to see and have bought your tickets, you're ready to join the theatre artists who have completed their work and are waiting for you to join them in creating a theatrical experience.

EXERCISE

Divide the class into four groups, and let each group select a leader who will distribute the work within the group. After each group spends a week researching one of the following forms of theatre advertising, the leader of each group should make a report to the class on the quantity, quality, and location of the group's particular area of research.

1. Research print ads, naming the newspapers, magazines, posters, or marquees and describing the size, color, and "sales point" of each ad. If possible, illustrate the report with examples.

2. Research radio ads, giving the station, the time of day, the length, and a description of each ad.

3. Research television ads, giving the station, the time of day, the length, and a description of each ad.

4. Describe how the group used the Internet to learn about theatre performances in your city during this past week and report on the results of the search.

12 CHAPTER ● ● ● ● ● ● ● ● ● ●

Take Your Seats, Please

Once you have purchased your ticket, you're ready to experience theatre, ready to appreciate the results of the collaboration of the playwright, actors, director, and designers. In this chapter, we offer you a number of things to consider—both before and during the **performance**—that will increase your enjoyment when you attend the theatre.

WHEN TO ARRIVE

Broadway performances usually begin at 8:00 P.M. for an evening show and 2:00 P.M. for a matinee, but some Broadway shows begin at 7:00 P.M. Many performances outside New York start at 7:00 P.M. on Sunday and at 7:30 P.M. on weeknights. Still other theatres offer shows at 5:00 P.M. or 9:00 P.M. Double-check the curtain time printed on the theatre ticket. If your ticket is being held at the box office, phone the theatre or check the ad.

Allow yourself ample time to get to the theatre. Give yourself some leeway if you're traveling by public transportation or if you suspect it will take you a while to park. Some theatres post directions on their Internet Web site. Unlike the movies, theatre doesn't show fifteen minutes of coming attractions before the performance begins, nor does it offer a "next show" that allows you to see the part you missed if you arrive late.

When is "late"? Performances usually begin some two to five minutes after the announced curtain time, so don't be surprised if your watch reads 8:04 and the house lights haven't yet dimmed. Managements start slightly late on purpose to ensure that the audience is seated before the performance begins. You are late if you arrive after the performance has begun, and ushers are instructed to keep you in the lobby until some suitable point in the play when your entrance will least disturb those who arrived on time. Some theatres have a video monitor in the lobby so you can watch what you are missing, but more often you will just twiddle your thumbs until you are admitted—possibly as much as thirty minutes into the action. To enjoy the show fully, plan to be prompt.

You will increase your enjoyment if you arrive twenty minutes or so before curtain time. Not only will you have a chance to visit the rest room (thereby avoiding the hordes during the fifteen-minute intermission), but you will also have time to read the program.

> **ASIDE**   The bus was caught in traffic, so we arrived after the curtain had gone up on the Broadway musical *Ragtime*. The usher admitted us only after the opening musical number (we missed the spectacular start to the show), and as we made our way down the aisle a woman hissed, "you should be ashamed of yourselves." We were very embarrassed and plan never to be late again.

DECIDING WHAT TO WEAR

You want to dress appropriately—not too fancy, not too casual. If you're not certain what to wear, be comforted. Most theatregoers have faced the same dilemma.

Fashions and customs change from country to country, from decade to decade, and from theatre to theatre. Not long ago, people wore tuxedos and formal dresses to the Broadway theatre, every lobby had a cloakroom at which gentlemen checked their opera cloaks (not coats, mind you), and every seat had a wire gizmo under it to hold the gentleman's top hat. (You'll still find these gizmos under the seats in some older theatres.) American culture today is increasingly informal, and we tolerate a wide range of dress. Theatregoers are not expected to show up in tuxedos, but even the most tolerant among us are more than a little taken aback when we see something distasteful—like the woman we saw recently at a Broadway show with her hair put up in big pink sponge curlers.

As a rule of thumb, you should dress for the theatre as you would dress to eat at a restaurant, and you should let the price of the theatre ticket and the theatre's location serve as a guide for how to dress. If you are going to an expensive restaurant or if you paid $80.00 for a theatre ticket to a commercial touring production at a downtown theatre, you should expect most of the audience to be dressed nicely in business suits and party dresses. If you are going to a neighborhood restaurant or if you paid $30.00 for your theatre ticket to a summer theatre festival, you should expect the audience to be more casually dressed in open-collar shirts and slacks and in blouses and skirts. If you are heading for the local pizza parlor or if you paid $8.00 for your ticket to a college production, jeans and sneakers are the dress of the day. Because we live in a permissive culture, no one will say anything if you show up at a college play in a nice suit or at your city's professional theatre company wearing jeans. If your goal is to blend in with the rest of the audience so that you feel comfortable, then common sense, our guidelines, and consultation with friends who are regular theatregoers should help you choose which hangers to take out of your closet.

BEFORE THE PLAY BEGINS

At the theatre, you can see the flow of people moving inside. A window at the box office has a sign reading "Reservations" or "Will Call" where you can pick up your tickets if they are being held; you might need to show your credit card and a photo ID. As you join the crowd heading toward the auditorium, you might be able to check your coat so that you don't have to sit on it or wad it up under your seat. You also may be able to rent a hearing device if someone in your party has a hearing loss. Signs might be posted advising if there are loud noises in the production, such as simulated gun shots (which can be painful for people who wear hearing aids), if a flashing strobe light is used (which can be dangerous for people with pacemakers), if characters smoke on stage (though cigarettes are usually herbal), and if the play contains "adult" themes or language that might be inappropriate for children.

As you move through the lobby, someone will take your ticket, tear it in half, give you back the ticket stub with your aisle, row, and seat number printed on it, and point you toward the correct aisle. Finally, an usher will hand you a **playbill** and show you to your seat.

EXPOSITION
· · · · · · · · · · · ·

Did you ever wonder why your ticket is torn? Theatre's a money-making business, and careful accounting is important. Directors of Broadway plays earn 1.5 percent of the weekly gross, so they want a precise accounting of what that gross is. Your ticket stub is a part of the accounting process that determines what the director is due. For a hit Broadway musical, the director's 1.5 percent can exceed $10,000 a week.

· ·

The playbill contains three kinds of information: what you ought to read before the play begins, what you might enjoy reading afterward, and advertisements. Playbills come in various sizes and shapes, from the one-page photocopied cast list you might get at your nephew's school play to the oversize, glossy souvenir program you might buy at a summer Shakespeare festival. But all provide you with some essential information. The most common form is a five-by-eight-inch booklet.

Toward the middle of the playbill you will find the title page, like the one shown in Figure 12.1 from Peter Nichols's comedy *Joe Egg*. The title page tells you the name of the play, the author, and the key artists who created the performance—the director, the designers, and other specialists, including the casting director, dramaturg, and stage manager.

Figure 12.1 This title page from the playbill for *Joe Egg* at New Hampshire's Theatre by the Sea gives the name of the theatre company, the title of the play, and the names of the playwright, director, designers, and other key artistic collaborators.

presents

JOE EGG
by **Peter Nichols**

Directed by
Tom Markus

Set Design by
Ray Recht

Costume Design by
Lisa C. Micheels

Lighting Design by
Jon Terry

Production Stage Manager
Dori Eskenazi

Stage Manager
Harriet L. Sheets

SPONSORED IN PART BY
The Kingston-Warren Corporation.

*"JOE EGG is presented by special arrangement with Samuel French, Inc."

Theatre by the Sea is a professional company operating on a League of Resident Theatres (LORT) agreement with Actors Equity Association, and is a constituent member of Theatre Communications Group, Inc. and the American Art Alliance.

ASIDE   *A Day in the Death of Joe Egg*, by English playwright Peter Nichols, was a box office hit in 1967 in London and New York, and in 1971 was made into a film starring Alan Bates and Janet Suzman; it is available on video. *Joe Egg* is frequently produced in America's regional theatres, and the playbill illustrations in this chapter are from one of those productions. *Joe Egg* has had two important Broadway revivals. Jim Dale and Stockard Channing starred in the play in the 1980s, and the 2002 London revival starring popular comedian Eddie Izzard and British star Victoria Hamilton transferred to Broadway, where both actors were nominated for Tony awards. *Joe Egg* is a very funny and deeply moving modern play that you will want to see when it's performed where you live.

A little farther into the playbill is the cast page, which lists the cast of characters and the actors who play them. Here you can read the characters' names, their jobs, their relationships, and other information about them that will help you understand what unfolds on the stage. You can peruse the cast list for the names of actors you have seen before. Many programs have a separate performance page telling where the action is set, when it takes place, and whether there will be any intermissions. If the number of actors in a play is small, the cast page and performance page are sometimes combined, as in Figure 12.2.

If you take time to read the title page, the performance page, and the cast page, you will be marginally prepared to enjoy the show. But the playbill includes much more information that you might enjoy reading before the performance begins. Most programs contain bios that briefly describe the previous accomplishments of the artists who created the performance. You might learn that the leading role will be played by an actor you've seen in the movies, that the director's career has taken her to Broadway, or that the costume designer has won an Emmy. Bios are published to give you some background on the artists, and many theatregoers enjoy reading them. Figure 12.3 shows some bios for *Joe Egg*. In reading them you will learn that two of the actors appeared recently on Broadway and another was in the movie *Terms of Endearment*.

Toward the back of a playbill you will usually find the staff page, which lists the people who work at the theatre and helped create this particular production (Figure 12.4). You may not have any keen interest in learning the name of the assistant house manager or the master electrician, but you will be impressed by the number of people it took to create the performance you're about to enjoy. This completes the first kind of information—what you ought to read before the play begins.

EXPOSITION

Theatre is what economists call a labor-intensive industry, which means it takes a lot of people to create a performance. Automation hasn't changed how theatre has been done for thousands of years. An actor is still needed to play

Figure 12.2 The cast page gives the names of the characters and the actors. Characters are listed on the left, actors on the right. If the cast is small, the information usually found on the performance page—where and when the action is set and whether there are any intermissions—is frequently placed on the cast page.

♪ THE CAST

JOE EGG

(in order of appearance)

Bri . . . . Ian Stuart
Sheila . . . . Johanna Morrison
Joe . . . . Briana Campbell
Pam . . . . Alexandra O'Karma
Freddie . . . . David Pursley
Grace . . . . Virginia Downing

★ ★ ★ ★ ★

PLACE:
Brian and Sheila's living-room

ACT I
An evening in winter

There will be one intermission

ACT II
Later the same night

★ ★ ★ ★ ★

a role, a dresser is needed to help with quick costume changes, a carpenter is needed to build the set, and an usher is needed to show you to your seat. Theatre is like the proverbial iceberg—80 percent is unseen. Although you may remember the actors when you leave the theatre, you will rarely think about the fight choreographer or the props-running crew. Without them, however, the show couldn't go on.

Figure 12.3   Actors' bios in the playbill give information about their professional careers.

♪ WHO'S WHO

ALEXANDRA O'KARMA (Pam) has appeared in numerous productions in New York City, including *THE HOMECOMING* at the Jewish Repertory Theatre, *KNITTERS IN THE SUN* at the Lucille Lortel (for which she garnered the Villager Award for Distinguished Performance), *I AM A CAMERA* at the American Jewish Theatre, and *A MONTH IN THE COUNTRY, WARBECK, CINEMA SOLDIER* and *A FLEA IN HER EAR* at the Colonnades Theatre Lab. Last spring she created the role of Liz in the world premiere of *FUGUE* at The Long Wharf. Other regional credits include Lady Macbeth at the Tennessee Repertory Theatre, *TO KILL A MOCKINGBIRD* at Indiana Rep , *THE CHALK GARDEN* at the American Shaw Festival, *MAN AND SUPERMAN* at the George Street Playhouse, Terence Feely's *THE TEAM* at the Hartman Theatre, for which she created the role of Selina Proby, and multiple summer stock productions with Michigan's Cherry County Playhouse and Ohio's Kenley Players. Ms. O'Karma appeared on HBO television this past fall as Anna Daley, opposite Tommy Lee Jones, in the BBC production of *YURI NOSENKO, KGB*, and on PBS' American Playhouse series, starring in *REFUGE*.She can also be seen in *TERMS OF ENDEARMENT*, playing a nasty New Yorker named Jane.

DAVID PURSLEY (Freddie) is a veteran of numerous regional theatres including the Virginia Museum Theatre, the Old Globe of San Diego, Seattle Repertory Theatre, Stage West of Springfield, Massachusetts, the Dallas Theater Center, the Arizona Theatre Company, the Barter Theatre, and Nassau Repertory Theatre. His roles have ranged from Horace Giddens in *THE LITTLE FOXES* and Teddy Roosevelt in *TINTYPES*, to Malvolio in *TWELFTH NIGHT* and the bogus aunt in *CHARLEY'S AUNT*. Recently he played the title role in *TARTUFFE* for the North Carolina Shakespeare Festival, and directed their production of *LOVE'S LABOUR'S LOST*. He made his Broadway debut in the Tony-nominated Brecht-Weill musical *HAPPY END*, which starred Meryl Streep and Christopher Lloyd, and he has been in numerous Off-Broadway productions including *PEACE, WINGS*, and *THE THREE MUSKETEERS*. For two seasons he was the Artistic Director of the Cortland New York Repertory Theatre, and has appeared at Radio City Music Hall and at the White House. A graduate of Harvard, he also holds a Master's Degree from Baylor University/Dallas Theater Center.

IAN STUART (Bri) recently spent fourteen months in the comedy hit *THE FOREIGNER* at New York City's Astor Place Theatre, where he gave over 440 performances as "Froggy." Other New York credits include Broadway's *CAESAR & CLEOPATRA*, with Rex Harrison and Elizabeth Ashley; *THE ACCRINGTON PALS* at The Hudson Guild; *MISALLIANCE* at The Roundabout; *COUNT DRACULA* at Equity Library Theatre; *THE JACK THE RIPPER REVIEW* at Manhattan Punch Line. He has extensive regional theatre credits playing leading roles for Hartford Stage Company, Repertory of St. Louis, Pennsylvania Stage Company, Virginia Museum, Delaware Theatre Company, Nassau Repertory, The Barter. He has also played King Arthur in *CAMELOT* and Captain Von Trapp in *THE SOUND OF MUSIC*. Television credits include numerous soaps, most recently "Payson" in *ONE LIFE TO LIVE* and "Dr. Sossaman" in *ALL MY CHILDREN*. Also a director, with more than 30 productions to his credit, he recently staged an acclaimed revival of Pinter's *BETRAYAL* for Connecticut's Boston Post Road Stage Company in Fairfield.

The second kind of information you will find in a playbill is information you might enjoy reading either before the performance (if you arrive early at the theatre) or after the performance to enrich your appreciation of what you've seen. It is background information written by a theatre's **dramaturg,** a literary consultant whose other work includes translating plays, doing research for directors and actors, and reading new plays that are being considered for production.

The third kind of information you'll find in the playbill is advertisements. The ads can give you a sense of who will be sitting next to you. If a resident

Figure 12.4 This staff page from the *Joe Egg* playbill lists the names of all the personnel who worked for Theatre by the Sea. This page contains many more names than the cast page does. As you can see, theatre is a labor-intensive business.

$ THEATRE STAFF

Artistic Director   TOM MARKUS

ADMINISTRATION

Management Advisor	IRA SCHLOSSER
Administrative Assistant to the Directors	VICTORIA KASABIAN
Development Director	TOM BIRMINGHAM
Administrative Assistant	GAIL McDOWELL
Marketing/PR Coordinator	MICHAEL REZNICEK
Marketing Associate	KAREN A. HEENAN
Marketing Volunteer	PHYLLIS GIGLIO
Business Manager	MONIQUE DI BEASE
Box Office Manager	DRIKA OVERTON
Box Office Assistant	MICHAEL J. TOBIN
Box Office Assistant	CAROL ST. CLAIR
Box Office Assistant	JO ELLEN SCULLY
Box Office Assistant	DOUGLAS D. WERTS
House Manager	JAMIE REYNOLDS
Concessions Manager	SHARLENE HAMMOND
Bartender	MARC CONNORS
Custodian	GARY REYNOLDS

ARTISTIC/PRODUCTION

Production/Facilities Manager	JOHN LAWRENCE BECKER
Production Stage Manager	DORI ESKENAZI
Stage Manager	HARRIET L. SHEETS
Assistants to the Stage Managers	BARBARA ROLLINS
	MELISSA WENDER
Lighting Designer/Master Electrician	JON TERRY
Electrics Intern	MERRITT CROSBY
Properties Director	JOEL PORTER
Properties Intern	MARYANN GORMAN
Costume Shop Foreman/Designer	LISA C. MICHEELS
First Hand	JOY MISSAGGIA
Wardrobe Coordinator	JANE M. CARVILLE
Graphic Design	DIANE DRAPER
Set Construction	BOB SCENIC

professional theatre company's playbill contains ads for cars and jewelry, then your fellow audience members probably will be middle-aged and affluent. If the ads are for bookstores and coffeehouses, expect a younger, university audience. If the ads are for fast-food restaurants and toy stores, you'll probably see a lot of children in the audience.

The playbill is your ticket to what the business world calls "added value." If you read the dramaturg's information after you have gone home, you'll get even more value for the dollars you spent on the ticket. If you look through the ads, you might find a restaurant you'd like to eat at after the performance. Even if you look at nothing more than the cover of the playbill, you will form a fundamental image that will help you prepare to enjoy the play. The graphic image on the cover of the *Joe Egg* playbill shows the title character as she is seen in her one happy moment in the play (Color Plate 21).

From the graphic image on its cover and the written information in its pages to the types of advertisements it carries, the playbill is a valuable tool that will assist you in appreciating the experience you are about to have.

About three minutes before the performance begins, the theatre gives a signal. In some theatres, the lights in the lobby dim two or three times. In other theatres, a bell or buzzer sounds. Some theatres play a recorded voice asking you to "take your seats, please." If you are in the rest room, visiting in the lobby, or checking your coat, now is the time to move promptly to your seat.

In the final moments before the houselights dim, stop to consider what you are hearing and seeing. Many theatres prepare you for the performance by playing music that has been carefully chosen to put you in an appropriate mood. If you notice the music, ask yourself what mood it creates and how it prepares you for the performance to come. At the same time, note what you see. If the stage has a curtain, it will be attractively lighted—though it won't give you any particular information. If there isn't a curtain, you'll be offered a first view of the stage set, usually attractively lit to express the mood of the play. It can be fun to study the set and guess at the kinds of characters and actions that will enliven it.

Announcements will be broadcast informing you if any roles will be performed by understudies and reminding you to turn off all cell phones and pagers, that the taking of photos is prohibited, and that no smoking is allowed in the auditorium. The final words you'll usually hear before the performance begins are "Enjoy the show."

DURING THE PERFORMANCE

Our mention of promptness raises the subject of theatre etiquette. There are no absolute laws about how to behave at the theatre, but there are some established practices. Common sense should keep you from doing anything that will disturb the audience around you or the actors on the stage. In recent years, columns on the subject of audience etiquette have appeared in the theatre sections of newspapers from New York to Seattle addressing the concern that a culture weaned on television is in danger of losing its sense of public courtesy. One article described a man who talked back to the characters in a play, and another described a woman who brought her pet chimpanzee to the theatre. The people sitting around her complained because the woman talked throughout the performance, loudly repeating the dialogue to the chimp. The usher asked the woman to leave, but he later admitted he thought it a shame because the chimp had behaved well. The columnist urged theatregoers to treat both actors and audience as they themselves wished to be treated, and she provided a list of rules for good audience behavior. Another journalist adopted Old Testament diction and provided a list of ten commandments for theatregoers. Linda and I offer our good-humored variation on their lists here.

The first recorded instance of an audience "hissing" a play was Bernard de Fontenelle's Aspar. *The Paris audience disliked it in 1680, and it turns out they were right—the play has long since been forgotten.*

Ten Commandments of Theatre Etiquette

1. THOU SHALT ARRIVE PROMPTLY. Get to your seat before the performance begins. You don't want to be disturbed by a late arriver, so don't disturb others.

2. THOU SHALT NOT SPEAK DURING THE PERFORMANCE. Laughing at jokes and applauding the actors is encouraged, but don't repeat the dialogue or explain the plot to your companion. You're not at home watching TV. You paid to listen to the actors, not your neighbors, so don't make them listen to you.

3. THOU SHALT LEAVE THY CHILDREN AT HOME. It's unfair to your children to bring them to a show that bores them or has language that disturbs them, and their fidgeting intrudes on those who paid to enjoy the play. Many theatres will not admit children under age five. Save your children's theatregoing for a performance intended for children.

4. THOU SHALT LEAVE THY RECORDING DEVICES AT HOME. Copyright laws prohibit recording a performance, so using your still or video camera is illegal as well as bothersome to those around you. The clicking sound is irritating to your neighbors, and the flash is dangerous for the actors.

A new law in New York City fines people $50 if their cell phone rings in a theatre.

5. THOU SHALT TURN OFF ALL ELECTRONIC DEVICES. Beepers, pagers, alarm watches, cell phones, CD and DVD players, portable radios, and other noisy electronic gizmos have no place in the theatre. If you are a doctor on call, leave your name and seat number with the house manager.

A scientific study proved that the sound you make unwrapping a cough drop is equally loud whether you do it fast or slowly. And if you do it slowly, the crackling sound disturbs the audience for a longer duration.

6. THOU SHALT NOT EAT OR DRINK IN THE THEATRE. Unlike movie actors, whose recorded performance keeps going no matter what noise you make, actors on stage are distracted by what they hear in the auditorium. No outside food or drink is allowed, and you will contribute to an enjoyable experience if you refrain from rattling wrappers.

7. THOU SHALT NOT PUT THINGS ON THE STAGE. The stage is not a resting spot for your handbag or your playbill or your feet. These items are ugly for the audience to look at and dangerous for the actors.

8. THOU SHALT NOT RIFFLE THY PLAYBILL. Do not smack your playbill nervously against your leg, roll and unroll it, or scrape your teeth with it. Open it in advance to the performance page so you can check for important information (if you can read in the dark), or put it under your seat or in your bag.

9. THOU SHALT KEEP THY FEET OFF THE SEATS. Don't drape your legs over the seat in front of you, and don't walk on someone else's seat to get in or out of yours.

10. THOU SHALT REMAIN IN THY SEAT UNTIL THE END. The end means the end of the curtain call. If you are ill or bored and must

leave before the play is over, leave as quietly as you can and during
an interval if at all possible. It is extremely discourteous to the actors to
head for the door before the performance has entirely ended.

After that formidable list of *don'ts,* here's an important *do:* do laugh, cry,
gasp, and applaud! Participate in the event and contribute to the experience.
What you do during the performance affects the people around you as well
as the actors, and it contributes to your own enjoyment. Remember that the
actors can hear you laugh, see you cry, feel your silence. Theatre is a live
event, and an unresponsive audience can kill it. Keep in mind that theatre is a
collaborative medium in which the playwright's intent, the director's conception, the actors' interpretation, and the designers' vision blend with the
audience's perception to yield a new and unique experience at each performance. Do your part to make your performance a success.

EVERYBODY HAS A FIRST TIME

There's a first time for everything, including going to the theatre. Can you recall the first time you went to a play? Who took you? What did you see? Did
you enjoy it? Tom's first experience was in Chicago, at the Goodman Theatre.
Linda describes her first experience this way: I was five years old when I attended a stage version of *The Wizard of Oz,* and it scared the wits out of me. I
remember clearly that I sat about four rows back on the left side of the balcony. I was intensely caught up in Dorothy's adventures. I laughed at her an-
tics and clenched my fists when she was in danger, but when the flying
monkeys swooped across the stage, I panicked and ran shrieking out of the
theatre. Happily, I had an adult there with me, or I might be running still. On
that Saturday afternoon, someone taught me how to dress, what to take with
me, how to behave, and what would happen when we got to the theatre. That
matinee performance set in motion a lifelong habit, and now, as an adult, I go
to the theatre about thirty times each year.

Years later, Tom and I took my brother and his wife to see *The King and I.*
My brother is a very successful electrician, but the day of the performance he
was quite anxious about what he should wear. He asked if his wife should
buy a fancy new dress. I said they looked fine and paid little attention to his
nervousness. When we entered the theatre, our two pairs of seats were in different locations, so I handed my brother his tickets and said "See you at intermission." Tom and I zipped off to our aisle seats. A moment later I was
astonished to find my brother crouching in the aisle beside me. He whispered,
"How do we find our seats?" A thunderbolt struck me—my fifty-three-year
old brother had never been to the theatre! Theatre is my job and my passion,
and I had long ago forgotten that first-timers don't know how to dress or
what to do. I pointed him toward a helpful usher who showed them to their
seats. They loved the experience so much that he is now a regular season
ticket subscriber to the theatre in his hometown. He buys ten subscriptions so

he can take his family and friends. He considers theatre an essential part of his life, and he loves sharing this cultural enrichment and great entertainment with his grandchildren. That's the powerful effect theatre can have on a person who has learned "how to go to the theatre."

Well, you've taken your seat and the curtain is going up. Now it's your turn to contribute to the creation of the theatrical experience. You're as ready as you can be to join the laughter and applause. We hope you enjoy the experience as much as my brother does, because, as the lyric we quoted in the Overture reminds us, the performance is "a chance for stage folks to say 'hello.'"

EXERCISES

If your instructor has assigned the entire class to see a play, afterward you can do these exercises.

1. Describe the audience at the performance you attended. What was their general age? How did they dress? How did they behave during the performance?

2. How many people were listed on the staff page of the playbill? If the page provided a breakdown between the two groups, how many people were on the theatre's permanent staff and how many were connected with this particular production?

3. What did you learn from the bios in the playbill that was of particular interest to you?

4. If there was a director's note or a dramaturgical essay in the playbill, give a synopsis of it and explain how it enriched your appreciation of the play.

5. Compare your experience the very first time you went to the theatre to your experience the first time you attended a play for this course.

The Curtain Rises

A theatre building is like an iceberg that's 80 percent underwater—there's a lot the public never sees. You'll want to begin by familiarizing yourself with the **front of house,** the theatrical term for everything on the audience's side of the curtain. After you've learned about the **public spaces** (those areas "above the water line"), we'll describe the five most common theatres and explain how each shape of theatre influences your experience. At the end of the chapter, we'll describe the scenery you'll see when the curtain rises. Then you'll be ready to learn about the **support spaces** (those areas "below the water line"), so in Chapter 14 we'll take you on a **backstage** tour.

PUBLIC SPACES

We call "public" all those spaces that accommodate the audience. Let's start with the box office where you buy your ticket. It's a secured room where a lot of money changes hands, and you can approach it either from the street or from the lobby. When you enter the theatre, you're in the lobby, a waiting space out of the sun or rain where you can sit to read your program or visit with your friends. Theatres decorate and arrange their lobbies to make you comfortable and to put you in a good mood. Lobbies vary greatly depending on the theatre's size, when it was built, and whether the building was originally designed as a theatre. You might find a place to check your coat or a concession booth selling beverages or souvenirs, and there are always rest rooms for your convenience. Some theatres have parking facilities, elevators, and restaurants. A few newer theatres have special patron lounges for donors who have given money to the theatre.

Beyond these public spaces is the **auditorium.** An auditorium literally is a "place for hearing." The word has the same Latin stem as the word "audit." When you say "I will audit that class," you mean that you will hear what the professor has to say. When you take your seat in the hearing place, you are an auditor. You are also a spectator who has come to *see* the play (the same stem as the word "spectacle"). Curiously, the ancient Greeks called the "seeing place" where they sat to watch a performance a **theatron** (THEE-a-tron). Because we use the word "theatre" to describe the whole building, we have

Theatre slang also refers to the auditorium as the "house," and you may hear an usher ask the supervisor (or house manager) "How full is the house tonight?" The term "house" is short for "playhouse," and actors will describe an unruly audience as a "tough house."

come to accept the word "auditorium" to describe the portion of the theatre where we sit to experience a play.

A lot of words are used to describe different portions of the auditorium, and these words may be useful to you when you are buying tickets. In America we call the main floor the **orchestra;** in England it's called the **stalls.** Most of us use the word "orchestra" to describe a large group of musicians who play classical music, but "orchestra" was the name in the ancient Greek theatre for the large circle where the chorus performed, the "dancing place."

The orchestra can have rows of seats that reach from one side of the auditorium to the other without interruption or rows of seats that are divided by aisles into sections (typically, two aisles create a center section and two side sections). The arrangement with uninterrupted rows of seats is called **continental seating,** presumably because it first became popular on the European continent. The arrangement with aisles is called **American seating.** To ensure that audiences can leave a theatre quickly in the case of fire or other emergency, federal regulations require that theatres with continental seating have a space of three feet between rows so that you can easily pass in front of a seated person. Theatres with American seating can have the rows closer together, but no one can be seated more than seven seats from an aisle.

In recent years—and in response to federal legislation—theatres have created places where persons in wheelchairs may be seated. These seats commonly are located at the back or side of the orchestra. If you or your companion uses a wheelchair, specify that at the time you purchase your tickets.

Above the main floor you may encounter the **box seats, mezzanine, loge, dress circle,** or **balcony.** In order to choose (or find) your seats, you need to know the differences among them. A box seat is in a special area partitioned off from the general seating. While a box seat may be more expensive than a seat in the orchestra, it might not give you a better view of the stage. Traditionally, a box seat is a better seat from which to be seen, which is why in bygone times people were content to pay more for such seats. In the eighteenth and nineteenth centuries, theatregoing was a major social event, and the rich and famous, wearing their most fashionable new outfits, went to the theatre to be seen. The theatres they went to had boxes just under the level of the balcony and placed all around the sides of the auditorium. The boxes closest to the stage were considered the most desirable, even though they provided a limited view of the stage. Abraham Lincoln was seated in a box (Figure 13.1) when he was assassinated by actor John Wilkes Booth. There are still boxes in older theatres in New York and London. Before you buy tickets for box seats, inquire whether they have an "obstructed view," which means they are behind a column or afford only a partial view of the stage.

All seating on floors higher than the orchestra used to be called the balcony—first balcony, second balcony, and, in some theatres, a third balcony or **gallery.** Slang terms for the gallery include the "nosebleed section," "paradise," or "the Gods" (because the seats are so high up that they seem near to heaven). Each balcony was entered from a separate lobby, and the highest balcony was entered from a separate exterior door that led to an entirely sep-

Figure 13.1 The Presidential Box of Ford's Theatre in Washington, D.C., provides a limited view of the stage but lets the audience see the people seated in it. In 1865, Abraham Lincoln was assassinated while seated here, and the assassin leaped from the box down onto the stage.

arate stairwell. These separate entrances can still be seen in many older European theatres. The gallery seats originally were intended to accommodate the serving classes, because the snobby upper classes didn't want to mingle with their social inferiors even while entering a theatre.

Today, the desire to inflate the price of balcony seats has led producers to inflate the words they use to describe various seating areas. The word "mezzanine" used to mean a small balcony halfway up, just under the first balcony—not quite as good a seat as on the main floor, but better than one in the balcony. Now the word is used sometimes to describe the first balcony and sometimes to refer to the back rows of the orchestra. The word "balcony" is reserved in many theatres today to describe only the very back rows of the upper seating. When you are considering balcony seats, *caveat emptor* ("buyer beware"). You can be sure to get the seats you want if you can look at a seating chart when you buy them, either at the theatre's box office or on its Web site.

The word "loge" comes from an old French word for a booth of seats in the opera house, but it is used today to describe theatre seats that are located at the very front of the first balcony. There's no widely accepted use of the word "loge," however, and you'll encounter it only occasionally. To avoid confusion, inquire at the box office about where loge seats in that particular theatre are actually located.

Another term used to describe the front seats of the first balcony is "dress circle." It is still used in England and in some American opera houses. You can infer that this term refers to the seats where, in earlier and more elegant times, people "dressed" for the theatre. The elegant women who sat in the dress circle wore floor-length evening gowns, and the gentlemen wore white tie and tails. In the English theatres of the nineteenth century, the dress circle provided the best view of the stage as well as the best view into the royal box. The seats in the stalls on the main floor were looked down on, both literally and socially; they were entered from a lobby that was below street level, because the entire theatre building was built down into the ground. The entrance to the dress circle was from the street-level lobby, allowing the wealthy patrons of the "carriage trade" to get out of their horse-drawn carriages and into the theatre with the greatest of ease while their coachmen went around to the side entrance to climb the stairs to "paradise."

KINDS OF THEATRES

Each of the five kinds of theatres you're about to encounter has its descriptive name, each is best suited to a certain kind of performance, and each provides you with a particular kind of experience. Some types may be familiar to you, while others may be unlike anything you've ever seen.

FORESHADOWING

The Five Kinds of Theatres

1. Proscenium arch theatre
2. Arena theatre
3. Thrust theatre
4. Black box theatre
5. Found space theatre

Proscenium Arch Theatre

The most common form of theatre architecture in our time is the **proscenium arch theatre.** It's a theatre with all the seats facing in the same direction—like those in a movie theatre—and with an ornate frame around a stage that is temporarily hidden from your view, usually by a beautiful curtain. Almost every Broadway theatre, most theatres on college campuses, and most

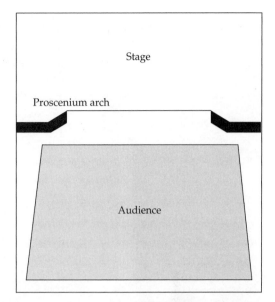

Figure 13.2   A proscenium arch theatre (left) has a frame around the top and the two sides of the stage through which the audience watches the actors on the stage. The schematic drawing above (right) is called a "ground plan." This ground plan for a proscenium arch theatre shows how the proscenium arch separates the stage from the audience.

large theatres in cities across America are proscenium arch theatres. The word "proscenium" (pro-SEEN-ee-um) needs explanation. "Pro" comes from the ancient Greek word meaning "in front." We say we are making "progress" when we are in front of where we were a few moments ago. **Skene** (SKAY-nay) is the name the ancient Greeks had for the freestanding building in which the actors changed costumes or waited to make their entrances. The place in front of the skene, where the actors performed, was called the "proskene" by the ancient Romans, and a division was made between the proskene and the auditorium where the audience sat. In the seventeenth century, the two became separated by an archway. The audience watched the play through the kind of picture-frame arch shown in Figure 13.2, which we call the "proscenium arch."

When you take your seat, you recognize that you're in one large space that is divided into two parts: one part for the spectators and one part for the performers. The audience all faces one direction, as in a classroom. A proscenium arch theatre might be large enough to seat 3,000 or so small that it seats fewer than 100—size is not a defining factor. The stage is usually raised up a few feet off the ground and is separated from the audience by the arch that spans the stage. This arch creates a sort of three-sided picture frame around the stage and hides the backstage area from the audience's view. The audience watches the performance through a frame. A proscenium arch theatre is sometimes called a "keyhole stage," to suggest the notion that the audience is peeking through a keyhole into a world that otherwise would be unseen. Many proscenium arches reflect the style of the seventeenth century and are decorated with ornately sculptured plaster painted to look like a gold picture frame (Figure 13.3).

Figure 13.3 This beautiful proscenium arch theatre has an ornately decorated three-sided picture frame that separates the stage from the auditorium. You can also see the orchestra pit in front of the stage, the box seats on the side wall, and the mezzanine seats in front of and slightly lower than the curved balcony.

Proscenium arch theatres are best suited to **representational performances,** the type of performance in which the audience understands the "convention of the fourth wall"—do you remember that from Chapter 1?—the situation in which both the actors and the audience pretend the room represented on the stage has a fourth wall that has been removed so the audience can observe the action. In a representational performance, the actors "represent" believable characters who live in their own world, and the actors do not acknowledge the existence or presence of the audience. Most plays written in the last hundred years call for representational performances, which is why proscenium arch theatres are the most common type.

Representational performances in a proscenium arch theatre allow you to identify with the characters and to be completely involved in the action. You forget yourself for a while. Your experience can best be explained by the phrase "the willing suspension of disbelief," explained in Chapter 1. It is easiest to pretend that the drama is really happening when we are peeping into the world of the characters, and the frame around the stage—the proscenium arch—helps us to do that.

Have you ever been to a theatre that is very much like a proscenium arch theatre but doesn't have an arch—a theatre with no frame around the stage? This variation of the proscenium arch theatre is called an **end stage theatre**

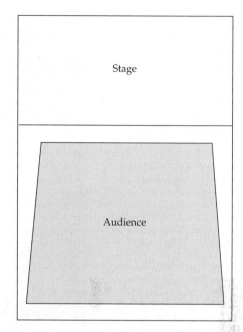

Figure 13.4 An end stage theatre (left) does not have a proscenium arch separating the audience from the stage. The ground plan of an end stage theatre (right) shows the stage at one end of the space and the audience facing it at the other end, with no architectural separation.

because the stage is at one end of the space, with all the seats facing it (Figure 13.4). End stages usually are built in spaces not originally intended as theatres. Virtually all the characteristics of a proscenium arch theatre are found in an end stage theatre, although usually there is very little offstage space. End stage theatres also lend themselves to representational performances and to the willing suspension of disbelief (Figure 13.5).

Stage Directions   When you read a play or hear actors talk, you'll encounter the terms "upstage," "downstage," "right," "left," and "center." Those of us who work in the theatre imagine the stage as being divided into six areas (Figure 13.6). Actors and director can communicate directions quickly—and playwrights can indicate where they imagine a scene taking place—by using the terms that describe these six areas. The areas are frequently referred to by letters, for example, UC (up center) and DR (down right). The terms "upstage" and "downstage" came into use centuries ago when plays were performed outdoors or in halls that weren't built to be theatres and had flat floors. Spectators couldn't easily see over the person in front of them, so the actors shrewdly built their stages on a **rake**—that is, the stage floor was built on an incline and slanted toward the audience. It was easier to see actors standing farthest from the front of the stage because they were higher off the ground (upstage). We all know that actors want to be seen and heard, so you would be correct in supposing they all want to play their important scenes DC (downstage center).

To "upstage" an actor is to stand farther from the audience (behind the actor) and do something inappropriate that draws the audience's attention. Actors hate being upstaged!

Figure 13.5 The scenery reaches to the side walls and ceiling of this end stage theatre. Note that the offstage space is a hallway beyond the doors to the room and that there's no room above the stage for scenery in this theatre without a proscenium arch.

Figure 13.6 The nine areas of the stage in a proscenium arch or end stage theatre.

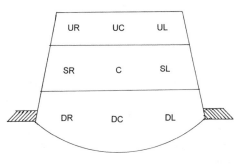

The directions "left" and "right" are always given from the point of view of an actor facing the audience on the stage of a proscenium arch or end stage theatre. When an actor stands close to the audience and on your left side, she is standing DR. The terminology and directions may seem confusing at first, but we who work in the theatre are used to the terms and never give them a second thought. You say "cross right" and I do, even though I move to *your* left.

Arena Theatre

When you first enter the Alley Theatre in Houston, Texas, you see that the stage is in the center and the seating is all around it. No proscenium arch separates the audience from the actors, and you can look across the stage to see

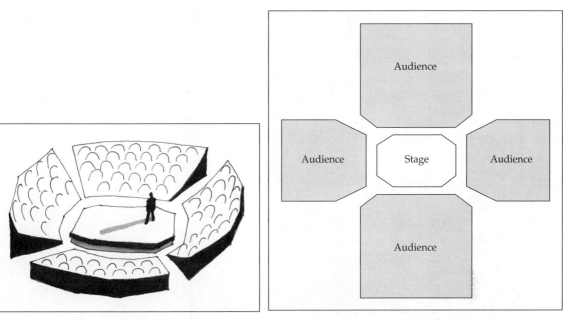

Figure 13.7 An arena theatre (left) has seating all around the stage, and the actors enter through the same aisles the audience uses. As this ground plan (right) shows, the whole audience at an arena theatre sits close to the stage.

the people seated on the other side, as shown in Figure 13.7. The **arena theatre** is aptly named: it's the architectural descendant of the ancient Roman arenas where the audience sat on a comfortable ring of seats while gladiators fought to the death on the earthen circle before them.

The arena, a popular form of theatre today, is a development of the twentieth century. For three hundred years, the proscenium arch theatre was the only kind of theatre people in Western civilization knew about. Around the turn of the twentieth century, many theatre artists began to experiment with the impact theatre might have if different spaces were used. From these experiments came the arena theatre, also known as "theatre-in-the-round," which became popular in the mid-twentieth century.

Arena theatres can be square, like the renowned Arena Stage in Washington, D.C., or round or even oblong, like the Penthouse Theatre in Seattle. They can seat hundreds, like the Alley Theatre in Houston (Figure 13.8), or fewer than ninety, like the arena theatres on many university campuses. Whatever their configuration or size, arena theatres have three traits in common: intimacy, a proper **aesthetic distance,** and minimal use of scenery.

Intimacy Intimacy is the most evident trait of an arena theatre. Because audiences are seated on all sides of the stage and because the actors must be heard by patrons they do not always face, these theatres-in-the-round are usually quite small. No seat is very far from the stage. The proximity of the actors to the audience encourages a subtlety in the actors' work that leads the audience to laugh at comic lines or funny expressions. Comedies are especially successful when acted in arena theatres.

Figure 13.8 The Alley Theatre in Houston arranges its 296 seats on the four sides of the stage.

Proper Aesthetic Distance   The phrase "proper aesthetic distance" describes the condition under which the audience is close enough to the stage to be emotionally involved and yet far enough away to remain physically apart. A demonstration of our natural desire for a proper aesthetic distance is the way we relate to someone telling a story. As we listen to a storyteller—and this is as true of children in a kindergarten class as of adults listening to a tour guide—we keep a small distance between ourselves and the storyteller. If the storyteller walks away, we move closer. If the storyteller moves toward us, we retreat. There's a distance at which we feel comfortable, a distance that seems natural. As an audience in the theatre, we want to be physically and emotionally far enough away from the stage to retain our awareness that we are watching a play, and at the same time we want to be physically and emotionally close enough to share the characters' emotional lives. When that happens, we are at the proper aesthetic distance to enjoy the performance. If we are too close, we see the actor's sweat through the character's makeup and lose our ability to believe. If we are so far away that we can't see or hear, we lose our proper involvement. The balance is a delicate one, and for us to enjoy theatre most completely we need the proper aesthetic distance. The fixed seats in most theatres prevent us from adjusting our distance from the stage, but arena theatres provide the desired aesthetic distance more often than proscenium arch theatres.

EXPOSITION

The first time you go to an arena theatre, you might find yourself more interested in the audience than in what happens on the stage. You will appreciate the action on the stage more completely after you have seen enough arena theatre productions to ignore the distractions. You will become adept at disregarding everything in your line of sight that interferes with your concentration on the play, and you will become skilled at imagining a fourth wall through which you peep at the action on the stage. Only when you are able to suspend your disbelief sufficiently to experience a representational performance fully will you find the intimacy of the arena theatre to be a fair exchange for the illusion that is more successfully created in a proscenium arch theatre.

Minimal Use of Scenery   The stage of an arena theatre has very little scenery. The audience sees only a suggestion of the play's fictional location from the treatment of the floor, the selection of furniture, and the fragments of hanging scenery that suggest the physical environment. It is almost impossible to create an illusion of a real place when the audience sees that the room has no walls or doors. As a result, the kind of performance that is best suited for this shared space, where audience and actors have no arch separating them, is **presentational performance.** As opposed to representational performance, presentational performance is a performance in which the actors openly acknowledge the existence of the audience and "present" the play to them. Actors speak directly to the audience and sometimes wink when delivering punch lines to jokes, and they sing directly to them in musicals. There is no convention of the fourth wall in a presentational performance, and the audience does not willingly suspend its disbelief. Quite the contrary—the audience understands that it is participating in a theatrical performance, not peeping into another world.

ASIDE   Presentational performance is more common in live theatre than in television or movies. One wonderful exception is the film made from the eighteenth-century comic novel *Tom Jones* and starring Albert Finney. If you want to have a good time, rent it from your local video shop. You will find that the characters sometimes look directly into the lens and speak directly to you or wink at you. They break through the convention of the fourth wall that you are accustomed to in movies and offer a film example of presentational performance.

Figure 13.9   The areas of an arena stage are sometimes referred to by comparison to the hours on a clock.

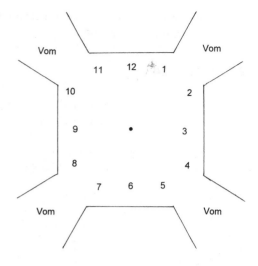

Paradoxically, representational performances are often successful in arena theatres. Why do you suppose that's so? What is there about theatre that permits audiences to believe in a fiction when there is very little visual support for the illusion? The answer must be that we have learned the conventions of representational performance so well from our years of seeing plays in proscenium arch theatres and on movie and television screens that we are able to imagine a fictional world even when we see little evidence of one. We can see that the room has no walls and can see the audience across from us, yet we can believe in the illusion. We share the characters' joys and agonies, but we are never tempted to leap onto the stage and enter their world.

Stage Directions   Because the audience surrounds them, actors face in all directions at some moment during a performance in an arena theatre. As you can imagine, the stage directions used for proscenium arch theatres don't work. They are replaced with directions related to the furniture or to the entrances ("stand near the table" or "cross to the doorway"). Stage areas are described as the hours on a clock face (Figure 13.9), with a particular spot chosen as "12," and directors ask actors to "cross to seven o'clock, a couple of steps in from the edge of the stage."

Thrust Theatre

Let's visit the Guthrie Theatre in Minneapolis, the most celebrated **thrust theatre** in America (Figure 13.10). When you first walk into the auditorium of the Guthrie Theatre, you can see why it's called a "thrust theatre." The audience sits on three sides, and the stage thrusts itself into the space where in a proscenium arch theatre there would be seats. In the thrust theatre, as in the arena theatre, actors and audience share a single space. No arch separates them, and there's not much opportunity for using scenery to represent the

Figure 13.10 The thrust stage creates a close relationship between the actors and all 1,441 patrons of the Guthrie Theatre in Minneapolis. The audience sits on three sides of the stage, and no one is more than 55 feet from the stage.

play's virtual place. Instead, the back wall of the stage suggests where the action of the play is taking place. Actors enter and exit through the doors in the back wall and also through the aisles, which pierce the banks of seats in much the same way the aisles in a football stadium pierce the rows of seats in the grandstands (Figure 13.11). The movement of the characters through the audience's part of the theatre increases the sense that audience and actors are part of the same world.

EXPOSITION

Aisles in thrust theatres are called "vomitoria," from the Latin word "vomitus," from which we also get our word "vomit." In this case it describes the way the actors exit, or are "disgorged" from, the theatre. You'll hear theatre people refer to a vomitorium by the shortened name "vom." You might hear a director tell an actor to "exit through the vom."

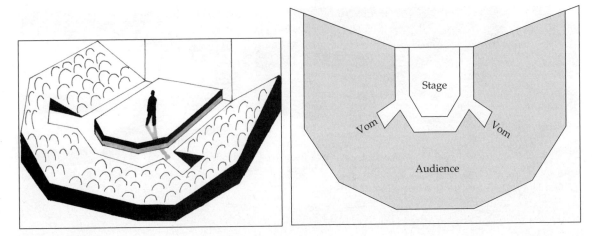

Figure 13.11 A thrust theatre (left) has a stage that "thrusts" into the area where seats would be in a proscenium arch theatre. The audience sits on three sides of the stage. This ground plan of a thrust theatre (right) shows the vomitoria that go under the audience's seats. Actors can enter and exit through these "voms."

The plays best suited to a thrust theatre are those classics written before the proscenium arch theatre was introduced—before the concept of theatrical illusion became dominant and representational theatre became the norm. The great classics by Shakespeare and Molière and the ancient Greeks have a scale of grandeur that calls for the presentational style and can best be achieved in the spacious reaches of a thrust theatre. These plays invite you to help in their creation when the characters speak directly to you. The opening speech of Shakespeare's *Henry V*, given by a character named Chorus, captures the excitement of presentational theatre on a thrust stage. Chorus tells the audience to pretend when they hear someone talk about horses that they can actually hear hoofbeats. He goes on to say that it's the audience's job to imagine how the king is dressed, what the different locations look like, and how much time passes between the scenes. Quite simply, Chorus asks the audience to use its imagination in creating the performance it will experience, just as *The Glass Menagerie*'s narrator, Tom, urges his audience to imagine the world in which his story takes place.

When you're in the audience of a thrust theatre, you'll experience the same kind of intimacy you experience in an arena theatre. However, the audience in a thrust theatre is not divided into small clusters as it is in an arena theatre. Instead it has the same sense an audience in a proscenium arch theatre has—a sense of being one solid, unified mass. The stage thrusts forward into the audience, and the play seems urgent and immediate.

Black Box Theatre

In the last few decades, **black box theatres** have been built on most university campuses and also as part of the large complex operated in London by the Royal National Theatre. When you first walk into a black box theatre, that's all it is—a large, empty box of a room with its floor, walls, and ceiling painted black. It's well furnished with lighting and sound equipment but has no fixed arrangement of audience seats or the actors' stage. It's just an empty space until someone decides how to arrange the stage and the seating for a particular production.

Black box theatres became popular in the 1960s when theatre artists experimented with the very nature of theatre. Productions in arena and thrust theatres had proved that the relationship between the performer and the actor could be manipulated with fascinating results, and some artists carried the experiments to extremes. *The Empty Space,* a hugely influential book by English director Peter Brook, describes the value of a neutral space in which the theatrical experience can be studied.

In order to conduct experiments, theatre artists need a neutral space that can be modified to meet the needs of any type of performance. This neutral space, much like a scientist's laboratory, is a functional space in which all sorts of theatre can be created. A black box theatre is usually quite small, rarely holding more than two hundred people, and it can be easily altered to have end stage seating for one performance, three-sided thrust seating for another, and full arena seating for yet another. In more experimental productions, audiences and actors can be placed high up on platforms near the ceiling or down low in pits below the level of the permanent stage floor.

All sorts of plays are well suited to black box theatres. Performance is limited only by the artists' imaginations. Your experience as a member of the audience will be an exciting one because you will be very close to the action and may well encounter an experimental production that stretches your experience of what theatre can be.

A particularly exciting kind of theatrical experiment conducted in a black box theatre is **environmental theatre** (Figure 13.12). It was defined by scholar and director Richard Schechner (SHEK-ner) through a sequence of productions he directed in New York in the 1960s and 1970s and in an essay he wrote titled "Six Axioms of Environmental Theatre." Two traits of environmental theatre are that multiple actions happen simultaneously and that the performers' and the audience's spaces are continually readjusted, with no portion of the black box theatre reserved exclusively for spectators or performers. The entire theatrical space is used by both, as illustrated in the photo of Schechner's production of *Commune* (Figure 13.13). The actors might perform a scene in the representational manner one minute and switch to the presentational manner the next, not only speaking directly to the audience but even telling people to move from the platform they're sitting on so the actors can play their next scene there. Environmental theatre violates the traditional distinctions between auditorium and stage. The flow of the players' action causes the flow of the audience, which could happen only in a black box theatre that has been imaginatively arranged with platforms of various shapes and levels that permit the actors and audience to continually alter their relationship.

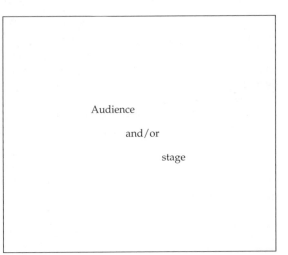

Figure 13.12   A black box theatre can be arranged many ways. This drawing for an environmental theatre production (left) illustrates the variety of levels and platforms used by both the audience and the actors. This ground plan for a black box theatre (right) shows that there is no fixed location for the audience or the stage. It is an empty room that can be arranged in many ways.

Figure 13.13   Richard Schechner's environmental theatre production of *Commune* was staged in a black box theatre in New York City named the Performing Garage. It got this unusual name because it had previously been a garage for cars. The audience moved about on platforms, ramps, and ladders, and the actors moved among them, sharing the same space. The interaction of actors and audience purposely removed any sense of aesthetic distance and created a sense of a shared experience. As you look at this photo you may not be certain who's an actor. During the performance, audience members were frequently surprised when the person who had been standing next them suddenly spoke and became a part of the performance.

ASIDE   *Dionysus in 69* is the most notorious example of environmental theatre, and celebrated film director Brian De Palma's video
of Richard Schechner's stage production is an exciting introduction
to this kind of theatrical experiment. The video can be ordered on the
Internet through www.amazon.fr or www.fnac.com.

Many of Schechner's productions benefited from the work of Latino designer Jerry Rojo, who also oversaw the creation of the Möbius Theatre at the
University of Connecticut (Figure 13.14). The Möbius Theatre was named
after August Möbius, the eighteenth-century German scientist who gave us
the Möbius strip, an ideal image for an impermanent and continually changing space.

Figure 13.14   The Möbius Theatre at the University of Connecticut is a black
box theatre in which an arrangement of platforms and stairs has been installed.
These spaces permit several actions to happen simultaneously, and the places in
which the actors perform and the audience sits can be continually readjusted
during a performance.

ASIDE   You can make a Möbius strip. Tear a 1-inch strip from the long side of a piece of paper so that you have a 1×11-inch piece. Hold the two ends together to make a circle, and then flip one end over so there's a twist in the paper when you rejoin the two ends. Stick the two ends together with some tape. Now put your finger anywhere on the paper and move it around the circle, tracing your path. You'll discover that there is only "one side" to a Möbius strip. This strip, a subject of significant study in mathematics, is a useful image for a theatre space in which there is a continual flow of audience and performers from one place to another. The Möbius Theatre was well named.

As you might expect, most environmental theatre performances have scripts that are created specially for the productions. Should you ever find yourself attending an environmental theatre production, you will witness a unique and very unusual theatrical experiment.

A fine example of environmental theatre was *Orlando Furioso,* an Italian production that toured to New York. It dramatized a famous narrative poem titled *Orlando Furioso,* which means "Orlando gone berserk." The poem is an adventure story that is the Italian equivalent of Homer's *Odyssey.* The production took place under a huge inflated tent, the kind set up temporarily in city parks to cover tennis courts and held up by air blown into its plastic walls. It looked like a huge modernistic igloo. Nearly a thousand people were admitted, and inside were three permanent, freestanding stages: one long rectangular one at each end and a small square one in the very center that looked like a boxing ring. All three stages were some 5 feet off the ground so the audience could see what was happening on them as they walked around the huge enclosure. The story of *Orlando Furioso* follows the hero as he lives through a sequence of wild adventures involving dragons, evil kings, and virtuous maidens. Parts of the play happened on all three stages simultaneously, and the audience walked toward whichever one interested them. From time to time, one or more additional stages were rolled into the common space. These square stages were mounted on wheels, and stagehands screamed "*Attenzione!*" as they slammed into the crowd (that's Italian for "Watch out!"). Everyone moved out of the way as fast as they could, and the relationship of audience to performers to performing space was continually changing. It was a colorful, raucous, and exciting event. It was environmental theatre, and it could only have been produced in the neutral space of a black box theatre— or, in this case, a white dome theatre.

Found Space Theatre

Theatre can be performed anywhere. Audiences could take a seat in the food court of a neighborhood mall, lounge on the lawn of a college campus, or make themselves comfortable inside someone's home. Although performances traditionally are given in one of the four kinds of theatres we've already discussed, some performances take place in what is called a **found space theatre.** As the name indicates, theatre can be performed in a space that was not intended for use as a theatre—a parking lot, a railroad station, a shopping mall. Why would someone do theatre in a found space? For one of two reasons: to take the performance to the audience instead of the audience to the performance, or to find a rare location that is organic to the performance.

Instead of hoping that an audience will buy tickets to an established theatre, some artists take their performances to the audience. We've seen a puppet version of the opera *La Traviata* performed on a subway car in Paris, a mime performance at a cable car stop in San Francisco, and a historical pageant celebrating the fifteenth-century Christian defeat of the Moors on a pedestrian mall in Barcelona. Following their performances, the actors passed the hat for contributions, and the delighted crowds gave generously. Not all performances in found spaces are light entertainment, however. Many American theatre artists who take their performances to public places are political activists who believe that short, provocative plays are an effective way of engaging people in political debate. These artists hope to change public opinion and influence the policies and practices of society. This kind of theatre was common in the 1960s and 1970s, when **guerilla theatre** was performed on college campuses, in shopping malls, and in the lobbies of state legislative buildings. Guerilla theatre protested loudly against America's military involvement in Vietnam and the treatment of Mexican American laborers in California. Many people believe that these so-called **agitprop** plays contributed to a reversal of American policy in Southeast Asia and to the fair treatment of workers in the agricultural fields of California. Politically oriented plays like those written by Luis Valdez for El Teatro Campesino are not very common today, but you may still come across them from time to time.

The second kind of found space theatre is created by artists who believe that conventional theatres do not provide the ideal setting for their plays. One New York group was En Garde Arts, a site-specific company that performed in the ponds and on the bridges in Central Park. This group also turned the scaffolding on the outside of a Victorian nursing home into a jungle gym and its courtyard into a circus ring. En Garde's producer, Anne Hamberger, explained, "I believe in going to where people live rather than waiting for them to come to us."

Found space theatre is not just an urban phenomenon. Community Performance Inc. creates celebratory events with the participation of the citizens of rural communities and has installed stages inside existing buildings such as the Yoder Dairy Barn in the Mennonite community of Warwick, Pennsylvania (Figure 13.15). We've never seen a production by Community Performance Inc. or En Garde Arts, but we have seen a passion play about the life of Christ performed in Spanish on the steps of a cathedral in Spain (Figure 13.16). The close relationship between the audience lining the sides of the steps and the actions taking place on the "stage" in the center made for a very moving experience.

Figure 13.15 The Yoder Dairy Barn (top) in Warwick, Pennsylvania, was the site for a Community Performance Inc. production titled *The Warwick Mennonite Centennial Oral History and Folk Opera.* Using the interior of the Yoder Dairy Barn as a found space, designer Joe Varga created a dynamic setting (bottom) of platforms and ladders for the performers and seating levels for the audience. Note the theatrical lighting instruments hung from the rafters and the actor seated high above the main stage, between the windows.

Found spaces are best for plays that are short and easily understood and that don't depend on complicated scenery or technology. Your experience at this kind of performance can vary widely. Sometimes you will be delighted by the entertainment, and other times you will be challenged by the political content. In either instance, you'll realize how little is needed for the creation of the theatrical experience. Today we depend on the sophisticated technology used in proscenium arch, arena, thrust, and black box theatres, but thousands of years ago, when the first actors gathered their tribe together near the campfire to tell their stories, they used a found space.

Figure 13.16   The steps leading up to a Spanish cathedral provided the found space for this performance of *The Way of the Cross,* a religious passion play. In this scene, Jesus is driven toward Mount Calvary by a Roman soldier who is wearing a highly theatrical costume. The audience of nearly a thousand stood and sat along the sides of the stairway to experience the performance.

SETTING THE STAGE

Thus far we've been describing the architecture of five kinds of theatres and the spatial relationship between the audience and the stage in each. But you don't usually see a theatre naked. The stage is usually dressed up with some kind of scenery. Like the different kinds of theatres, different kinds of scenery can influence your experience of the performance.

Many plays take place in one location and have a single set. Whether the action takes place outdoors under a tree (*Waiting for Godot*) or indoors in an apartment (*The Glass Menagerie*), the scenery doesn't change throughout the play. Other plays take place in a variety of locations. For those plays, either the scenery must change several times during the performance or the set must be a neutral structure that permits the audience to imagine all the different locations in the action. Theatre has five standard kinds of scenery, and any kind of scenery could be installed in any kind of theatre. Because you're probably most familiar with proscenium arch theatres, we'll ask you to imagine that you are seated in the center of the orchestra, looking at the stage.

The Five Kinds of Scenery

● FORESHADOWING

The Five Kinds of Scenery

1. Box set
2. Realistic exterior
3. Two-dimensional painted set
4. Unit Set
5. Projections

Figure 13.17 This box set is for Neil Simon's comedy *The Prisoner of Second Avenue.* The action takes place in an apartment in New York City. The side walls are angled slightly so that the audience in the side seats can see the full stage.

Box Set If you think of a dollhouse, you'll know immediately what a **box set** looks like: a room with a wall missing. The box set has a ceiling, three walls, and a floor. Many modern plays, particularly those that take place in a living room or kitchen, use box sets. When you see a box set, you can expect a representational performance that strives to convince you that you are seeing a "slice of life," because you're being asked to pretend that you're looking into a real room. In some cases, a set won't have a ceiling or the precise right angles you'd find in a real room, but it's still considered a box set even when the walls are free-standing and slanted so that the audience seated at the sides of the auditorium can see the whole stage, as in Figure 13.17.

ASIDE   You may have heard the term "drawing room comedy." A drawing room is an earlier name for the room we call a parlor or living room today. It's short for "withdrawing" and refers to the room a family withdraws to for privacy, as opposed to the room in which the family receives guests. If you visit older homes in the South or East, you may find a sliding double door between two parts of the living room; the part farthest from the front door is the drawing room. The action of a drawing room comedy is set in a family's private room, hence the name. A drawing room comedy is almost always performed in a box set.

Realistic Exterior   The action of some plays takes place outdoors. When performed representationally, those plays require scenery that imitates locations like the side of a mountain or the countryside next to a lonely road. The box set is used to create an illusion of an interior, and **realistic exterior scenery** is built to create an illusion of nature. The scenery is made from wood, muslin, Styrofoam, or some other material shaped and painted to create a three-dimensional illusion that will help the audience suspend its disbelief.

Two-Dimensional Painted Set   Many productions use scenery that is painted to create a decorative background instead of scenery that is built to create a three-dimensional illusion of reality. **Two-dimensional painted scenery** is painted on surfaces fixed to a frame. Each unit is called a **flat.** Flats placed on the side of the stage parallel with the proscenium arch are called **wings.** Although the wings do not make a solid wall, they are spaced so the audience can't see offstage. Actors enter through the gaps between the wings, because there is no pretense that the set is a real place. Hanging at the back of the stage is a large painted cloth called a **drop.** Two-dimensional scenery, frequently called **wing and drop scenery,** is illustrated in Figure 13.18. The wings and drop might be painted to indicate an exterior (a tree by a road where Didi and Gogo wait) or an interior (the parlor of the Wingfield's apartment). When you see a two-dimensional painted set, you can expect a presentational performance that never asks you to suspend your disbelief. Today, two-dimensional scenery is used for ballets, musicals, and plays written in earlier centuries when two-dimensional scenery was in fashion.

Unit Set   A **unit set** is a permanent structure that remains in place throughout a performance and does not represent a recognizable place. An architectural arrangement of levels and platforms, it provides an audience with a way to imagine whatever location the play requires, as you can see in the design shown in Figure 13.19. When the dialogue says that the action takes place in the king's throne room, the actors kneel before a throne on one side of the unit set, and the audience imagines the throne room. When the action moves to a hill overlooking a battlefield, the actors place some banners on a platform

Figure 13.18 This cutaway drawing shows how two-dimensional wing and drop scenery is arranged on a stage.

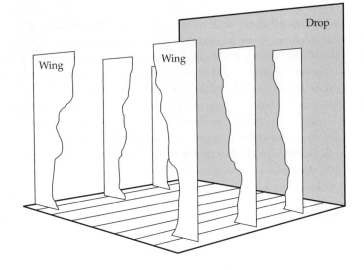

Figure 13.19 Designer Eric Fielding created this unit set for a play about Galileo. It permitted actors to stand on the small platforms at the sides of the stage, but most of the action took place on the large disk in the center. The small, interior disk could be lowered to make one solid floor, or it could be tilted to create a dynamic acting space, as in this photo.

Figure 13.20   Projected scenery can be seen on the rough hanging wooden panels. "Late Morning, Three Days Later" tells the time of this scene, and photos from the Civil War suggest the location of the scene. The play, *Mother Courage,* has many scenes, and the use of projected scenery allowed swift location changes.

on the other side of the unit set, and the audience imagines the hill. When you see a unit set, you can expect a performance that is presentational one moment and representational the next. Unit sets are most commonly used for episodic plays such as those by Shakespeare.

Projections   Modern technology has increased the kinds of scenery you can see at a performance. Today you might see images projected onto the front of flat scenery or projected through translucent screens from behind. **Projections** can create the illusion of a real place or the unrealistic suggestion of an imaginary place. While some projections are commonplace, others are experimental. When you see a set that uses projections, you might be in for an unusual performance. Figure 13.20 shows how actual photographs from the Civil War era projected alongside words announcing the title or time of the scene combined with realistic props like a wagon to create the style of Theatricalism for a production of Bertolt Brecht's antiwar play *Mother Courage.*

How Scenery Moves

There are very few directions scenery can move. It can move horizontally, off-stage. It can move vertically, out of the audience's sight above the proscenium arch or down through a trapdoor to a room beneath the stage. It can move in a circle, spinning around on a big turntable. Modern theatre uses one or more of these methods to change the scenery from what you see one moment to what you see the next.

Four Ways Scenery Moves

1. Wagons
2. Flies and elevators
3. Slip stage
4. Revolving stage

Wagons   Scenery can be built on **wagons** that roll off the stage. Although an entire box set could be put on a wagon, more frequently a wagon carries only a portion of a set. The horizontal movement of scenery is not very fast. While wagons are the preferred way of moving heavy scenery, they are usually used for moving scenery during an intermission.

Flies and Elevators   Scenery can be set on **elevators** that lower beneath the stage, or it can be rigged to fly upward into the empty space above the proscenium arch, called the **"flies."** The drop at the back of a wing and drop set commonly is flown out to reveal another drop behind it that is painted to indicate the location of the next scene. This vertical movement can happen at the same time that an entire set of six wings slides offstage, revealing another set of wings in place behind them. The new wings augment the scene painted on the new drop. In this way, a new location is revealed in a matter of seconds.

Slip Stage   The floor can be built with a **slip stage** in it, a portion that can slide offstage. Furniture (or actors) can be standing on the slip stage when it moves, and a new location and scene can be created by this movement.

Revolving Stage   A large turntable or **revolving stage** can be placed in the center of the stage, with new scenery coming into view as the old scenery disappears (Figure 13.21).

Hybrid Scenery and Technological Innovations

If someone can imagine it and a theatre can afford it, it can be done. You will see productions that put a box set on a turntable and surround it with wing and drop scenery. You will see a unit set built on elevators that raise and lower the platforms as the action unfolds. You will see wing and drop scenery with projections that change the imaginary location without the wings ever moving. Popular musicals like *Les Miserables* and *The Phantom of the Opera* thrill

Figure 13.21 When the audience first looked at the stage, they believed that the action of the play would take place outside a realistic house (top). This is English scenographer Pamela Howard's design for Tennessee Williams's *The Rose Tattoo.* Imagine the audience's surprise when the platform the house was built on began to turn like a giant lazy Susan, changing the scenic setting from the exterior to the interior of the house (bottom).

audiences with elaborate and innovative set designs that are a combination of every imaginable kind of scenery. The way this **hybrid scenery** moves brings gasps and applause.

Robert Edmond Jones was one of the first great American scene designers. His book *The Dramatic Imagination* remains an inspiration today. Decades ago, Jones foresaw that the tools with which we create theatre would always be evolving, and he wisely wrote that a theatre designer's job is to express the timeless themes of the playwright by using the newest and best tools available.

In the past twenty years, advances in technology have expanded the impact of spectacle on our theatrical experience. Disneyland's *Haunted Mansion* uses holograms to create its theatrical illusions. Broadway's *The Lion King* projects both prerecorded computer graphics and real-time video onto actors' costumes. Some of the most exciting recent innovations have been created by Cirque du Soleil (SERK due so-LAY; the name means "circus of the sun"). This astonishingly imaginative team of theatre artists creates entertainments you might have read about, seen on television, or thrilled to in person in Las Vegas. Using computerized controls, their production of *O* at the Bellagio casino in Las Vegas floods a huge stage with water deep enough for divers to plunge into and within seconds raises a floor through the water that dancers can use to perform ballet. Simultaneously, singers rigged on wires fly upward out of the audience's sight as real-time videos of their flight are projected onto huge screens. One of Cirque du Soleil's most recent entertainments, *A New Day,* features pop singer Celine Dion and uses the kind of abstract images in its visual design that first were introduced to theatre by the Surrealists, later became familiar in Postmodern theatre, and now are seen daily by viewers of MTV-style music videos.

None of us can imagine where the technological revolution will lead or how theatrical performance will develop in the future, but dedicated experimenters are exploring the boundaries of what live theatre can achieve. Among them is the Institute for the Exploration of Virtual Realities (i.e.VR) in the Department of Theatre at the University of Kansas. In 1995, i.e.VR presented the first of many exciting productions—Elmer Rice's *The Adding Machine,* a play written in 1923 and originally conceived in the style of Expressionism (see Figure 4.27).

ASIDE Like many university-based science labs, i.e.VR breaks new ground daily. Its goal is to explore how virtual reality and related technologies can be applied to theatre production and performance. You can learn more about their exciting work at these Web sites:

www.ku.edu/~mreaney/machine/
www.ku.edu/~ievr/

i.e.VR's production of *The Adding Machine* unfolded in technologically produced three-dimensional environments, and the audience confronted live actors alongside computer-generated characters. The paths taken within these virtual worlds were not prerecorded but rather were improvised by the backstage technicians. The virtual worlds themselves were created through a combination of real-time computer graphics and theatre-quality projection equipment. The audience wore polarized glasses that facilitated the illusion of virtual locations and of special effects that had never before been experienced in live theatre.

The Adding Machine focuses on the character of Mr. Zero as he tries to find happiness in a dehumanized society. Playwright Rice predicted that technology would turn us into machines, but i.e.VR's use of computers as an artistic medium rather than as a dehumanizing force supported and illuminated Mr. Zero's story. A celebrated illustration of how technology served the meaning of the play was the production's second scene, in which Mr. Zero is fired from his job as an accountant by the character known only as the Boss. The live actor playing Mr. Zero was onstage interacting with the virtual character of the Boss, while the actor playing the Boss performed offstage in front of a video camera. The innovative technology made it possible for the Boss to

Figure 13.22   An experimental production of Elmer Rice's Expressionistic play *The Adding Machine* was directed by Ronald A. Willis at the University of Kansas. The designer/technician who used the technology of virtual reality was Mark Reaney. The audience wore polarized glasses and could see the projection of an offstage actor at the same time that it saw the physical reality of an actor onstage (top). The virtual reality technology permitted the audience to see the Boss through Mr. Zero's eyes, one of the major traits of the style of Expressionism. As Zero became more and more frightened of being fired from his job, the Boss grew larger and larger (bottom).

grow larger as Mr. Zero perceived him growing into a greater and greater threat, and the scene ended with Mr. Zero seeming to dwindle into a "zero" of insignificance as the Boss's laughing face grew to fill the stage space (Figure 13.22).

We hope you're asking yourself what Aristotle would have thought of i.e.VR's production of *The Adding Machine*. As you learned in Chapter 2, Aristotle classified spectacle as the sixth and least important of the elements of theatre. While it seems clear that technology can greatly enhance the element of spectacle, Linda and I think it has value *only when it used in the service of the playwright's creation.* New technology tempts theatre artists to experiment. Though they certainly don't have to use the newest technology in order to create compelling theatre, their experiments sometimes create exciting breakthroughs. In our experience, however, technology is too often used to distract audiences from the play, to provide visual stimulation primarily as a means of disguising a banal drama that will not have a lasting impact on how we understand our world or how we live our lives—and that, we old-fashioned folks believe, is what theatre should aspire to. It is what theatre does best.

EXERCISE

Divide the class into six groups and have each group select a leader. Each group will research one of these kinds of theatre space: proscenium arch theatre, end stage theatre, arena theatre, thrust theatre, black box theatre, and found space theatre. The group leader will determine whether Internet research or an on-site visit with a camera will best accomplish the goal of preparing written descriptions and visual images to illustrate a report to the class that describes the size, appearance, and location of the nearest example of the group's assigned kind of theatre space.

Backstage Revealed

By now you must be curious about what goes on in the 80 percent of the theatre "below the water line" of the iceberg. Come "backstage" with us, and we'll show you where we do most of our work and introduce you to the people we work with.

WHAT'S IT LOOK LIKE?

There are two ways to get backstage: through the **pass door** and though the **stage door.** The pass door is inside the theatre and leads backstage from the public spaces. The stage door is the outside door the actors use when they arrive at the theatre. In 1930s movies, "stage-door Johnnies" collect beautiful chorus girls at the stage door; today it is where fans wait to get autographs after a performance. Either door will lead you into the **stage house,** the name for the entire structure that includes the stage and the offstage areas you can't see from the auditorium.

Many theatres, including the Royal National Theatre in London and the Oregon Shakespearean Festival, sell tickets to backstage tours to satisfy the curiosity of the general public.

EXPOSITION
• • • • • • • • • • •

Many backstage terms have a nautical origin because they were introduced by the sailors hired by theatres to work backstage in the eighteenth century. The stage floor is called the **deck,** and the **crew** has to **swab** it before each performance. The ropes that control the scenery are called the **rigging,** and they are run through **pulleys** and connected to a **winch** that's **anchored** to the deck.

• •

The first thing most people want to do when they visit backstage is walk out onto the stage and stare into the auditorium—they want to feel what it's like to be an actor. The experience can be intimidating as you look at a thousand empty seats and imagine them filled with paying customers who will make you feel embarrassed if you make a mistake. Would you want to face all those faces eight times a week? It takes courage to be an actor.

If you look to either side of the stage, you'll see the **wings,** the parts of the stage the audience can't see. Much of the scenery that is not on stage is

Figure 14.1 Scenery is attached to a batten by lines. Cables attached to the top of the batten run up to pulleys that are fixed to the grid and then run across to a pulley at the side of the stage house and down to an arbor (a sort of cage) in which the counter-balancing stage weights are placed. A rope attached to the bottom of the arbor runs down to a pulley anchored below the deck and then back up over a pulley at the grid and down to the top of the arbor. A stage-hand can pull that rope to make the counter-balanced scenery move up or down. A lock near the stage floor allows the rope to be secured so the scenery won't slip up or down.

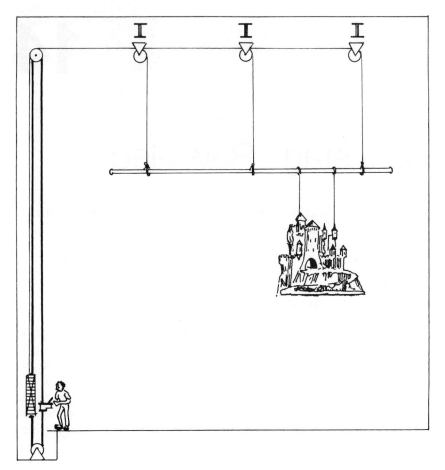

stored here. You'll also see **prop tables** and **changing booths** for quick costume changes. Actors make their entrances from the wings, so called because these areas are at the sides of the stage in the same way a bird's wings are at its side. Scenery can also be raised up through the stage floor through trapdoors, or "traps," from an empty **trap room** beneath the stage. Overhead, hidden from the audience by the top of the proscenium arch, is a space called the **fly loft,** or "flies," that houses drops, drapes, lighting instruments, and scenery waiting to be lowered into the audience's view.

The basic principle of how scenery is raised and lowered is diagrammed in Figure 14.1. Lines are tied from a piece of scenery to a **batten,** a long metal pipe that stretches the width of the stage parallel to the front of the stage. Long cables are tied to the top of the batten, and sent up over pulleys attached to the **grid** (a network of steel beams high above the stage floor), across the grid to another pulley at the side of the stage house, and down to an **arbor,** where a crew member attaches it to a metal weight equal to the weight of the scenery. By balancing the weight of the scenery and the weight of these metal **stageweights,** scenery can be flown out of sight of the audience—when the batten and scenery

Figure 14.2   A dressing room is equipped with mirrors, bright lights, and shelves for hats and wigs. It is where the actors put on their makeup and change into their costumes.

are down on the stage floor, the counterweight is up in the air; when the scenery is up in the air, the counterweight is down on the stage floor. This balancing act, gives the whole system its name: **counterweight system.**

ASIDE   A small church we know performs a passion play in a theatre each Easter telling the story of Jesus. The same actor plays the role of Jesus year after year, and underneath his costume he wears the kind of flying harness that actors use for the role of Peter Pan. At the show's joyous ending, Jesus blesses the crowd and ascends gracefully into heaven—in reality, into the fly loft out of the audience's sight. One year he couldn't perform, and an understudy played the role of Jesus. The play went smoothly until near the end. Nobody had stopped to think about the counterweight system. The new Jesus was a skinny little guy who weighed a lot less than the regular Jesus. When the counterweight system was released, Jesus shot up out of sight like a bullet. The audience heard a loud crash and a cry of "Oh, *#!#@!" and watched as one sandal came floating down from the grid.

In addition to the stage, wings, and flies, "backstage" includes **dressing rooms** (Figure 14.2) where the actors change clothes and put on their makeup as well as the **green room,** the room where the actors relax when they're not onstage.

ASIDE   Theatre historians don't agree on where the name "green room" came from. One widely held belief is that the waiting room in

(continued)

London's Drury Lane Theatre was painted green in the seventeenth century and that actors carried that descriptive name for the waiting room with them when they traveled to other theatres.

The **crossover** is the route actors use to get from one side of the stage to the other without being seen by the audience. Usually it's a space behind the scenery, on the deck, or in a hallway at the very back of the stage house. In some older or makeshift theatres, actors have to go outside the building to cross to the other side of the stage.

ASIDE   Early in Linda's career as a costume designer, she worked at a theatre that didn't have a crossover. To get to the other side of the stage, actors had to exit the theatre by the front door and go around the block to enter through the back door. Next to the back door was a pool hall, a regular neighborhood hangout for workingmen. The highlight of their evening was to watch Romeo, wearing tights, race past the pool hall windows for his next entrance. His appearance always brought whistles and catcalls.

WHO'S BACKSTAGE?

How would you go about getting a new lamp for your home? You'd probably go to the store, buy a lamp you liked, take it home, screw in a bulb, plug it in, and turn it on. How many people does it take to turn on your light bulb? One—you. Now imagine that you're watching the technical rehearsal for a production of *The Glass Menagerie.* Imagine a group of people on the stage, in deep discussion about a table lamp.

The **property master** has brought three lamps on stage. One was bought new, one was built by the **prop crew** according to the property master's design, and an old one was brought up from the theatre's storage room. The director and the scene designer choose the lamp they feel is most appropriate in terms of design and most practical in terms of how it will be used in the production. The scene designer likes the fabric on the lamp shade, but it has a small torn spot. A member of the **wardrobe crew** promptly pulls out a needle and thread and fixes the problem. The prop crew adds the lamp to its checklist to ensure that it will be on the set at each performance and placed properly so the actors know where the switch is. A **carpenter** cuts a small slot in the baseboard of the scenery wall to accommodate an electrical cord, and an **electrician** wires the lamp to an offstage outlet. A member of the prop crew provides a new bulb. An electrician climbs a ladder to hang a stage lighting instrument that will be focused on the area of the stage around the lamp to augment its illumination. The master electrician plugs both the new stage lighting instrument and the lamp's offstage plug into **circuits** that are controlled by the **computer dimmerboard.** The lighting designer selects the color to be used, supervises the focusing of the new stage lighting instrument, and sets the level of illumination for both sources of light in each scene. The stage manager writes the cues for when the lamp will be turned on or off into the **promptbook,** and the **computer dimmerboard operator** enters these cues into the cue sheets. The director shows each actor how to pantomime turning the switch so the audience will believe their character is turning the light on or off, when in fact the stage manager will give the cue to the computer dimmerboard operator who will push the button that actually turns the lamp and the lighting instrument on or off.

How many theatre people does it take to turn on a light bulb? Twelve—the director, scene designer, property master, prop crew member, electrician, stage carpenter, lighting designer, master electrician, computer dimmerboard operator, wardrobe crew member, stage manager, and actor. We hope this good-humored illustration of who's backstage and the departments they work in has given you a heightened appreciation for the labor-intensive and collaborative nature of theatre.

⬤ **FORESHADOWING**

The Production Manager and the Backstage Areas

1. Production manager
2. Scenery
3. Properties
4. Costumes
5. Lighting
6. Sound
7. Stage management

Production Manager

The **production manager** is the link between the artistic and managing directors and the heads of the six production departments. The production manager is a middle-management supervisor responsible for scheduling, budgeting, and communications between the department heads, a vitally important person who ensures that the artistic quality and logistical requirements of the production are achieved.

Scenery

The technical director (usually called the "TD") is the head of the scene shop, and oversees the construction, painting, and installation of all the scenery. The TD coordinates the scene shop's work with the production manager and interprets the technical drawings provided by the scene designer (described in Chapter 9) to make sure the carpenters understand exactly how the scenery

Figure 14.3 A scene shop is equipped with tools for carpentry and welding and for working with plastics.

is to be built. The TD orders materials and supplies, assigns work, fixes schedules, and monitors progress. The **scene shop manager** (sometimes the same person as the TD) supervises the work of the carpenters (sometimes called "technicians") on a daily basis. Depending on the number of workers in the scene shop, the technicians may have special expertise in welding, hydraulics, or working with plastics.

The scene shop, the largest backstage space in a producing theatre, is a tall open room with sufficient space to build large units of scenery. As Figure 14.3 shows, the scene shop is filled with heavy equipment, including hydraulic scaffolds, saws, drills, and welding tools. When technicians work with metals or plastics, they wear protective masks and work in a specially designed area, because these toxic materials require special ventilation.

The TD also supervises the **charge artist,** the head of the crew of scene painters. This crew paints everything from the decorative flowers on a lamp shade to large canvas **backdrops** fastened to a **paint frame,** a vertical wooden frame that is attached to a pulley system so the scene painters can paint a backdrop by raising or lowering it.

Properties

Because the prop crew uses many of the same tools as the scene shop, the **prop shop** is usually adjacent to the scene shop. The prop shop builds, buys, and maintains all the items used in the play, from furniture to firearms to food

Figure 14.4   Val Kilmer holds the realistic skull that the Colorado Shakespeare Festival's property shop crafted for *Hamlet,* in which he played the title role.

Figure 14.5   A costume shop is equipped with cutting tables, dress forms, and a variety of sewing machines. Costumes for each play are made or custom-fitted to each actor by the costume shop staff.

(Figure 14.4). The property master heads the prop crew and makes artistic decisions in coordination with the scene designer and also makes budgetary decisions in coordination with the production manager.

Costumes

Figure 14.5 shows a typical **costume shop,** equipped with **dress forms** on which costumes are shaped, large **cutting tables** on which patterns are made

Figure 14.6 This technical drawing for the character of Clarice in *The Servant of Two Masters* shows the kind of information a costume designer provides. The costume shop manager consults with the designer and then interprets the designs for the first hand and for the cutters and drapers.

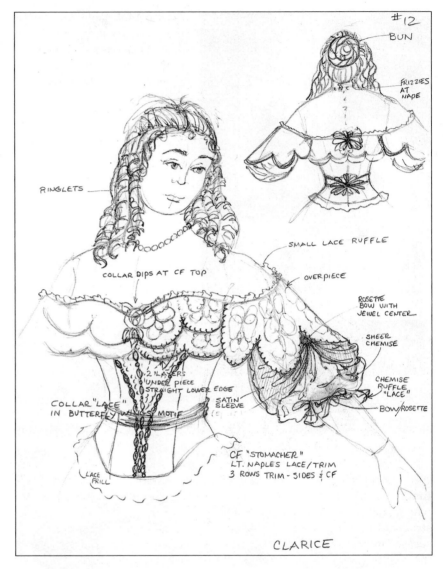

and fabric is cut, and a great variety of specialized sewing machines. Here is where the costume shop manager presides, ordering materials and supplies, administering budgets, establishing schedules, and assigning the work of the **cutters** (who make flat patterns and cut fabric), the **drapers** (who shape costumes on dress forms), the **tailors** (who construct tailored costumes for men and women), the **first hand** (who directly supervises the work of the cutters and drapers), and the **stitchers** (who sew together the pieces of fabric and turn them into costumes).

The costume designer provides a color rendering of each costume, swatches of the fabric to be used for each part of it, and technical drawings

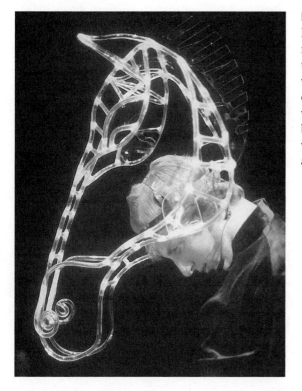

Figure 14.7   The horse heads for *Equus* were made from Plexiglas so they would be light-weight. The costume crafts artisans built them with the front and back balance equal so they wouldn't fall off the actors' heads.

showing how the costume will look from different angles and how it should be constructed (Figure 14.6).

The costume shop manager also supervises a subset of workers in the costume department, such as the **dyer,** who alters the color of fabrics or costumes in a separate, well-ventilated **dye room;** the **costume crafts artisans,** who work in a **crafts shop** with leather, plastics, and other materials to construct millinery, masks, footwear, armor, jewelry, and other costume accessories (Figure 14.7); and the **hair, wig, and makeup designer,** who works in the **hair, wig, and makeup studio,** which sometimes is a separate room and sometimes is a segregated part of the larger costume shop (Figures 14.8). Specialty items such as prosthetic noses are designed and built in the hair, wig, and makeup studio (Figure 14.9).

The costume shop manager coordinates with the stage manager to schedule the fittings. Actors are excused from rehearsal to try on their costumes so the costume designer can make artistic decisions (for example, how short the sleeves should be) and request alterations that will make the costume fit the actor's body more perfectly. These fittings take place in the **fitting room,** which can be a separate room nicely equipped with shelves, chairs, and floor-length mirrors, or only a curtained-off corner of the costume shop.

Stage actors are responsible for their own makeup, except when there's an unusual requirement like a false nose or an elaborate wig.

Figure 14.8 The costume designer designs the entire "look" for each character. This sketch for Brighella in *The Servant of Two Masters* provided the hair, wig, and makeup designer with clear instructions on how the false wig and facial hair should look.

PLATINUM BLONDE COLOR FAKE "HAIR" WIG

MUSTACHE - TINY, TURNED UP

IMPERIAL - TINY

STIFF BOW - NYLON NET?

LIMP LACE CRAVAT

IF CADENETTE, ON LEFT SIDE

BRIGHELLA

ASIDE   If actors haven't eaten before a fitting or they lock their knees for an hour while their costume is fitted on them, they sometimes faint. When this happens, the costume personnel know to immediately grab the actor's body so he isn't injured by hitting his head on the floor. When the actor returns to consciousness, he is always horribly embarrassed, but to the costume shop staff it's just another ho-hum day on the job.

Figure 14.9   The design and construction of Scrooge's nose for the Milwaukee Repertory Theatre's production of *A Christmas Carol* were the responsibility of the hair, wig, and makeup designer. The nose was made from rubber latex.

The costume shop manager also oversees the **wardrobe supervisor,** who supervises the **dressers** that assist the actors' costume needs and quick changes and who also ensures that the costumes are cleaned and maintained during the run of a production. Costumes not in use for a particular production are hung and shelved in a large storage space called **costume storage** or "the **racks.**"

Lighting

The master electrician heads the lighting technicians and supervises the electricians and the computer dimmerboard operator (Figure 14.10). While preparing for a production, electricians work with the lighting instruments on the stage, hanging and focusing the lighting instruments according to the instructions on the lighting designer's light plot. The lights are operated from the **control booth,** usually a small room behind a glass window at the back of the theatre; this is the job of the dimmerboard operator, frequently referred to as the "board op."

Computer technology has changed the work of the lighting technicians from when we were students. We used to wrestle with a huge number of levers and switches of all different sizes, and complicated shows required several operators. Today, **cues** are programmed into the lighting board, and all the board op has to do is push the green "Go" button to execute a cue. This is a great advancement, except that a computer dimmerboard is just like your computer at home. When it crashes, you lose your term paper. A wise dimmerboard operator has a backup disk of the show's cues ready to use when the board is functional again. A not-so-wise board op loses everything and spends a frantic day trying to re-create all the cues before that night's show.

The lighting crew at Radio City Music Hall is reported to have worn rollerskates on the job.

Sound

Sound uses the most mysterious backstage technology. The **sound engineer** has a special space in the control booth outfitted with wall-to-wall electronic

Figure 14.10 Lighting designer Angelo O'Dierno sometimes doubles as dimmerboard operator. He sets each cue on the computer board, and the monitor shows exactly what each light does for each cue. The dimmerboard operator hears the actors over a speaker in the control booth at the back of the auditorium and hears the stage manager's "Go" cue over the headset.

equipment. Technology has enabled the sound engineer to create sounds by using a **sampler,** which takes a sound and changes it into a set of numbers that are sent into a computer memory. A keyboard attached to the sampler has the capability to create any sound you want. Suppose you hit a key that creates the sound of a dog barking. Assign the same sound to more keys, and hit them one after the other as fast as you can. Now you have a pack of baying hounds. Assign a wind sound to another key. Now you're out on the moors on a windy night with a pack of baying hounds at your heels. The process is a mystery to us and highly addictive to sound engineers.

Among the most visually intimidating pieces of equipment backstage is the **mixer,** a big device covered with buttons and knobs. While it may look daunting, its job is quite simple. A mixer takes in sound, reorganizes it, and sends it out again sounding different. Ask your instructor to explain the workings of the mixer to you or to invite a trained sound engineer to the class to explain it.

The sound engineer assists the sound designer in placing speakers, cables, microphones, monitors, and other equipment according to the sound designer's plot and might also serve in the control booth as the sound board operator (Figure 14.11). For a large production with a live orchestra, a second sound engineer may be needed to operate a second computer sound board located at the rear of the auditorium, behind the audience. The second sound board operator hears the performance live, not distorted by amplification over a headset, and can precisely control the sound.

Stage Management

At last we come to the **rehearsal room,** where the actors and the director work and where the stage manager is in charge. Rehearsal rooms are empty rooms

Figure 14.11 The sound board operator watches the show from the control booth and takes cues from the stage manager over the headset.

about the same size as the stage. Some are quite tall, to permit actors to stand on platforms the way they will in performance. If the theatre puts on musicals that include energetic dance numbers, the rehearsal room usually has a cushioned or "sprung" floor like the floors in dance studios and basketball courts. It has a bit of bounce to it so the dancers don't hurt their knees and ankles while rehearsing. There are normally some racks or lockers nearby to store the actors' coats and backpacks and prop tables at the sides of the rehearsal room to hold items the actors use in rehearsal.

The stage manager has a difficult and important job backstage. Duties range from setting schedules to managing rehearsals to helping the director. The stage manager is "Information Central" during the entire production process. After opening night, the stage manager is the person in total charge of maintaining the quality of the production. During each performance, the stage manager watches the stage and gives cues over a headset to every technician with a specific cue to execute, because the stage manager is the only person who knows everything that's going on backstage (Figure 14.12). A good stage manager is essential to the success of any production.

A stage manager may have one or more **assistant stage managers,** commonly known as ASMs. They are present at every rehearsal and ready to do any task assigned by the stage manager. The stage manager is glued to the rehearsal room during a rehearsal, but an ASM is mobile and able to run errands or make phone calls. ASMs do whatever needs to be done. Everything lands in the lap of the ASM, a versatile, vital, and often underappreciated worker in the backstage world.

Figure 14.12 Stage manager Sara Jaramillo has her promptbook open in front of her as she calls a cue during New Harmony Theatre's production of the comedy *The Foreigner*.

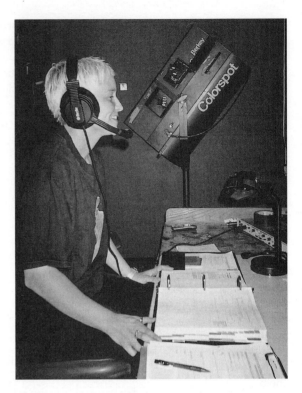

ASIDE   A man flying in a hot air balloon realized he was lost. He reduced altitude and called down to a woman on the ground. "Excuse me," he shouted, "can you help me? I promised a friend I'd be at his wedding dinner an hour ago, but I've forgotten if everyone's going to be dressed formally, and I don't know where I am."

The woman below replied, "You're in a hot air balloon hovering approximately 30 feet above the ground. You're an hour late for dinner, and since it's already 9 P.M., you certainly should be wearing a tuxedo. And you are at 42 degrees north latitude and 105 degrees west longitude."

"You must be a stage manager," said the balloonist.

"I am," said the woman. "How did you know?"

"Well," answered the balloonist, "everything you told me is technically correct, but I have no idea what to do with your information, and the fact is, I'm still lost. Frankly, you could have been a lot more help."

The woman called up to him, "You must be a director."

"I am," he replied. "How did you know?"

"Well, you don't know where you are or where you're going. You don't know what the people depending on you are wearing, and you have risen to where you are due to a large quantity of hot air. You made a promise which you have no idea how to keep, and you expect me to solve your problem. The fact is, you are exactly where you were before we met—but now, somehow, it's my fault!"

A LABOR-INTENSIVE INDUSTRY

Who's backstage? A large number of hard-working, well-trained, highly skilled, and dedicated people. We remember reading that for each U.S. Army soldier who goes into combat, there are twelve others working in support—providing supplies, transportation, strategy, and communications. Each actor on a stage, like a combat soldier, is supported by a large team the audience never sees. While lighting and sound technicians benefit from advances in technology and one person sitting at a computer can do the work of six or seven, other theatre technicians' jobs and working techniques haven't changed since the theatre of ancient Greece. Theatre is an individually hand-crafted industry that still requires people to do jobs machines can't do. The costumes must be custom-fitted to each actor, the scenery specially built for each production, the lights focused, the sound recorded, the props provided, and all the work coordinated by a stage manager who ensures that you have the best experience possible. All those people—that's who's backstage.

EXERCISES

1. Ask your instructor to lead your class on a backstage tour of the theatre on your campus.
2. After your class sees a production, invite the stage manager to visit your class and to describe his or her work on the production.
3. Invite a costume shop manager to your class to describe his or her work on a production your class has attended.

Theatre History

We learn about the present by studying our past. Some of you have studied the history of governments, of mathematics, or of film. We study the history of theatre to learn how plays have been presented down through the centuries in the world's many different cultures.

Courses in theatre history focus on topics like the physical buildings plays were performed in, the way theatre was produced (who paid for it), the sets and costumes that were used, and the theatrical conventions of the time (including what the acting was like and how the audience behaved).

Courses in the history of drama focus on the playwright's words. Drama is a branch of literature, and students in drama courses analyze themes, the kinds of characters used to tell stories, the techniques of language playwrights employ, and a play's genre, style, and structure.

Drama courses essentially are analytical and literary, while theatre history courses research how theatre was performed on stage. Both studies are fascinating.

In Chapters 2, 3, 4, and 6, you learned how to analyze a play as a form of literature. Now we invite you to join us for a sprint through an abridged version of theatre history. On your mark . . . get set . . . and aw-a-ay we go!

In the seventeenth century, Spanish playwright Lope de Vega wrote that all that's needed to create theatre is "Four trestles, four boards, two actors, and a passion."

CHAPTER 15

Theatre History

Theatre began long before any records of human activities were written down, and scholars debate the origins of theatre. With a little imagination, we can speculate about how theatre probably got started.

As children, we often make up games with our best friends. Our games include the dimension of time—they deal with things that happened yesterday or things that we want to have happen tomorrow. The structure of our games tends to be logical—each action causes a reaction that, in turn, leads to a result. Because we are self-conscious beings, we don't always enact ourselves in our games. Sometimes we represent characters different from ourselves. Best of all, our games tell stories that have a point to them. Our stories teach us lessons about how we should relate to other people, and they instruct us about ourselves and about ways we can influence the world around us.

Humans have been playing games for thousands of years. Our games are reminders of our past triumphs or preparations for the future, celebrations of our glories or rehearsals for our trials. In our games, we create images and fictions by representing people and places and objects, and people started doing this long before anything was written down or any pictorial records were made. Playing is a natural human activity through which we try to understand how our universe works and how to prepare for the future. The instinct to play led us to the creation of that activity we call "theatre."

THE BEGINNINGS OF THEATRE—PREHISTORY

Among the earliest and most amazing artistic representations we have are drawings by prehistoric cave dwellers (Figure 15.1). It seems sensible to assume that if these prehistoric artists could represent oxen and other animals in painted images of hunt scenes or rituals, they could also represent them in live imitations. They could have "played" at being animals. They could have made theatre.

Let's imagine what prehistoric theatre might have looked like. A clan is huddled around the fire that keeps their cave warm and frightens away wild animals. No one has eaten for two days, and everyone is hungry. Then a man comes into the cave, beaming with pride and dragging after him the hind leg

Figure 15.1 This cave drawing from Lascaux, France, shows the kind of bulls that were hunted for food and were an inspiration not only for painting but also for the storytelling that was an early form of theatre.

of a huge bull. Everyone flocks to him. Some put the leg over the fire to cook. Others go outside to get the rest of the bull. They skin it, hack it into pieces, and present the bull's horns to the hunter as a trophy. Everyone cheers. They eat. And then someone asks the hunter how he killed the bull.

The hunter begins the story of his kill by saying that he streaked his face with berry juice so that he would look fierce. Perhaps he even demonstrates by rubbing berries on his face as he talks. He goes on, probably embellishing the truth a bit like any good storyteller. He feels exhilaration from the attention he's receiving from his clanspeople, and that guides him to elaborate, to invent, to create a better story than strictly accurate reporting would provide (Figure 15.2).

This story features a man, but it could just as easily have been about a woman. Many legendary societies were led by women, from the Amazons of ancient Greek myth to the land of Xena, Warrior Princess, in contemporary TV lore.

> It started to get dark, and then out of the shadows of the forest he charged me. There was nothing for me to do but defend myself, so I broke off a branch from a tree, like this [*he picks up a long bone from the pile before him and handles it like a tree branch*], and I ran to a rock and scraped it into a point, like this [*he runs over to a large stone and scrapes the bone against it*], and just then the bull lowered his horns, like this [*he picks up the horns that had been presented to him*], and charged at me [*the crowd gasps with excitement*]. In the second before he reached me, I leaped over his horns and plunged my stick deep into his neck. He spun around and there was a horrible moment when I didn't know what he'd do. We were eye to eye. Then a great sigh came out of him, and he dropped where he stood!

The applause from the crowd is thunderous. The hunter is a hero and a celebrity. In addition to being a lucky survivor of the deadly bull's charge, he has discovered that he's a born storyteller. As he told his tale, he elaborated the details, drew out the suspense, and physically acted out his role, impersonating himself. He used berry juice for makeup, used the bull's horns for a

Figure 15.2
The hunter tells his story and demonstrates how he killed the bull.

costume, and even used a prop—the bone that represented the branch. His presentation was a simple form of theatre, for all theatre is impersonation and storytelling.

GREEK THEATRE

During the 2004 Olympic Games, Greece was once again the center of world attention. Tom reminded me that 2,500 years ago Athens was the political and cultural center of Western civilization. It was the birthplace of both democracy and theatre—the form of government we still live by and the kind of performance we still enjoy. The tragedies written by Aeschylus (ES-ki-lus), Sophocles (SOF-o-kleez), and Euripides (yew-RIP-i-deez) and the comedies of Aristophanes (air-iz-TOFF-a-neez) are still performed today. The large, open-air amphitheatres where those plays were originally performed are still standing and are still in use. By studying them, we can learn about both the Greeks' communal society and the importance they placed on the philosophical concerns that are the subjects of their dramas.

The best-preserved ancient Greek theatre is at Epidaurus (ep-i-DOOR-us). This theatre, located in a rural setting about a two-hour drive southwest of Athens, is still used today for performances of the ancient tragedies. We saw *Oedipus the King* (ED-i-puss) there a few years ago, and it was one of the most exciting experiences of our theatregoing lives. On a balmy summer evening, the theatre attracts crowds of up to twelve thousand—just as it did more than two thousand years ago. The theatre at Epidaurus seems to have evolved from the earthen threshing circles used by farmers (Figure 15.3). Many scholars believe the ancient Greeks first performed theatre by dancing and singing in their threshing circles after completing the harvest. From their celebrations was born the **chorus** of Greek theatre.

At Epidaurus you can see that the ancient Greek theatres were not freestanding buildings but were nestled against a hillside. The major playing

Figure 15.3   From ancient times to today, Greek farmers have built stone rings and filled them with newly cut wheat. When horses or people walk on the wheat, the seeds separate from the stalk. This procedure is called "threshing," and historians believe that the dancing, singing, and storytelling with which ancient farmers celebrated a successful harvest took place in circles like this. They conjecture that the threshing circle was the inspiration for the circular orchestra in ancient Greek theatres where the chorus danced and sang.

space was a circle, and the similarity to the farmer's threshing circle seems evident. The seating was carved out of the hillside, and the audience sat in the open air on the benches of the theatron (THEE-a-tron). We get our word "theatre" from this Greek word, which means "the seeing place." The seats followed the natural curve of the hillside and wrapped more than halfway around the performing space, similar to the seats in a modern thrust theatre. Most of the action took place on the large flat circle, the **orchestra** ("the dancing place"), where the actors who made up the chorus danced and sang (Figure 15.4). Many scholars believe that in the middle of the orchestra was the **thymele** (thigh-MEE-lee), an altar to the god Dionysus (dye-o-NICE-us). Behind the circular orchestra was a freestanding building called the skene (SKAY-nay). In front of the skene may have been a **proskene** (PRO-SKAY-nay), a narrow raised platform where the principal actors performed. Between the seating in the theatron and the freestanding skene was a large aisle, the **parados** (PAR-a-dose), where the chorus made its ceremonial entrance at the beginning of the performance (Figure 15.5). While Epidaurus's original theatron and orchestra are in fine condition today, the skene is no longer there. When plays are performed at Epidaurus today, unit sets are installed that often include a back wall to replace the missing skene.

The descriptions and diagrams in this introductory text don't reveal how the design of Greek theatres developed during the roughly eight hundred years from the Golden Age of Athens (fifth century B.C.E.) to the end of the Hellenistic Age (third century C.E.). We hope you'll want to learn more by taking advanced courses or reading books about theatre history.

Figure 15.4 The theatre at Epidaurus, Greece, is one of the best preserved of ancient Greek theatres, and performances are given there every summer. The orchestra is a perfect circle, the thymele is in the center of the orchestra, and benches for up to twelve thousand patrons are carved into the natural hillside.

EXPOSITION
• • • • • • • • • •

Photos of ancient Greek ruins make everything look white because the paint has been worn off by rain and wind. Historians assure us that the buildings, including the theatres, were colorfully painted. Sometimes pictures were painted on the skene showing where the action of a play was set. In later centuries, when theatres were built indoors and the entire theatre was covered over with a roof, the skene became the decorated back wall. From the ancient Greek word "skene" comes our modern word "scenery."

• •

The scripts of the ancient plays reveal that the Greeks used wagons and many of the other devices for moving scenery that we continue to use today. One of these devices was the **mechane** (our word "machine" comes from this Greek word), a large crane that could hoist characters into the air above the stage in much the same way we fly Peter Pan in our theatres today. It was frequently used to fly the actors playing the roles of the gods who resolved the conflict between the mortal characters in the play.

EXPOSITION
• • • • • • • • • •

A phrase heard frequently today is **deus ex machina** (DAY-ous ex MACK-ee-na). It means "god from the machine." The phrase metaphorically describes the cavalry riding in to save the settlers in a cowboy movie or the friend who helps you solve your homework problems—an unexpected person or event

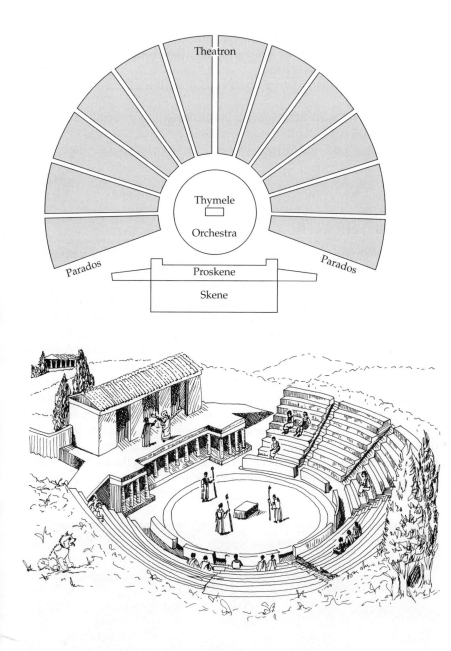

Figure 15.5 This ground plan (top) of a typical Greek theatre includes the names of the important parts of the theatre. The thymele (altar) is in the center of the orchestra (the dancing circle). The theatron (the seeing place where the audience sat) is divided into wedge-shaped sections. This illustration (bottom) of an ancient Greek theatre shows the theatron where the audience sat (the seeing place), the orchestra where the chorus performed (the dancing circle), the skene (the stage house), and the parados (the passage between the theatron and the skene that the chorus used for its ceremonial entrance and exit). The skene in this illustration has a raised proskene (the platform on which the main characters performed). Note how the theatron is carved into the natural hillside.

that comes to the rescue. This phrase describing the contrived ending of a play dates back to the use of the crane in the ancient Greek theatre.

• •

Several American campuses have imitation Greek theatres, and many universities perform ancient Greek dramas the way they were originally produced (though the actors speak English, not Greek). There are even some modern plays written to be performed in outdoor settings that have circular performing areas in the Greek manner, such as the pageant *TEXAS*, shown in Color Plate 22.

> **ASIDE**   The Greeks established a large colony on the island of Sicily, and the theatres they built there are still standing. Many scenes in Woody Allen's movie *Mighty Aphrodite* were filmed in a Greek theatre on Sicily.

ROMAN THEATRE

In the city of Orange, in the south of France, is the most completely preserved Roman theatre in Europe. The Romans succeeded the Greeks as the important civilization of Europe, and they must have loved drama because they built theatres everywhere. You can visit the ruins of Roman theatres in Turkey, North Africa, and Spain as well. Roman theatres are similar to Greek ones—large, open-air amphitheatres with no roofs. But the Romans built their theatres on flat ground instead of carving them out of hillsides, and they also built the seating area (Figure 15.6). The orchestra in Roman theatres is only a half-circle, and the seats are connected to the skene, making the theatre a complete and unified structure instead of a space made up of parts separated by a big aisle. The skene of this Roman theatre is huge. When it was colorfully painted, it must have made a spectacular backdrop for a play. In front of the skene is a platform large enough for a team of horses and a chariot. This platform is the proskene where the actors performed and is the earliest physical evidence we have of what today we call a stage.

Figure 15.6   The Roman theatre in the city of Orange, France, has an enormous skene and proskene and a half-circle orchestra.

When the Roman Empire collapsed, Western European civilization lost its centralized government and unifying culture along with its respect for intellectual activities like reading, writing, and theatregoing. The advent of the Christian era saw theatre return to its primitive state, as local storytellers and wandering musicians entertained audiences wherever they could attract a crowd. No permanent theatre was built for a thousand years, and plays were performed on makeshift stages that were set up in a found space, like a town square, and quickly dismantled after the performance.

THEATRE IN THE MIDDLE AGES

In the Middle Ages, some plays were performed by troupes of actors and acrobats who traveled in wagons that could be converted into temporary stages (Figure 15.7). The medieval actors' wagons were colorfully decorated to attract attention, and they were cleverly constructed to serve the needs of the performance. A platform could be attached to the side of the wagon for the actors to perform on, and a curtain could be hung off the top of the side of the wagon facing the audience. The curtain might have a street painted on it, and it could be drawn open to reveal a second curtain with a house painted on it in much the same way a drop is revealed in wing and drop scenery. The characters exited through this curtain and into the wagon to rest or to change costumes. The wagon served the same purpose as the Greek skene. It was the backstage area that became known in later centuries as the **tiring house.**

In the later Middle Ages, the traveling actors' wagons, now called **pageant wagons,** became very elaborate—think of them as the ancestors of the

Most scholars agree that the term "tiring house" is short for "attiring" and describes where actors change into their costumes.

Figure 15.7 Wagons like this one were used in the Middle Ages by actors who traveled from town to town. The side of the wagon could be lowered and used as a stage, and the inside of the wagon became the changing room. The curtain at the back of the stage could be painted to suggest a particular place.

Rose Parade floats you see on New Year's Day. The audience would gather at various points throughout the city, just as people today stand on street corners to admire parade floats as they roll by. Horses would pull the pageant wagons to a designated place, and the actors would set up their platform stage, roll down the painted backdrop, and give a short performance. Then the wagon rolled on toward its next destination while a subsequent wagon rolled up to take its place. Each wagon's performance was one short play in a long cycle of plays that told a story, and the audience remained in one place waiting for the next wagon to arrive with the next short play. The performances were presentational—the actors spoke directly to the audience and sometimes hopped off the stage to mingle with the spectators.

EXPOSITION
• • • • • • • • • • •

The short plays evolved from performances of short religious dramas that had been performed inside churches before each of the Stations of the Cross. Each station was called a "mansion."

• •

If you have ever seen the end of a homecoming parade, you will have some idea of how another popular form of medieval stage might have developed. The parade concludes in a parking lot, with all the floats lined up end to end. In the Middle Ages, all the pageant wagons may have ended up in the town square, where the largest gathering of people could admire them. They lined up side by side so that their individual platforms could be combined into one long platform. The players from each wagon did their sketches, one after another, using not just their own small platform but all the platforms that had been lined up. This kind of theatre is called a **mansion stage.**

Today the word "mansion" is used to describe a very large house, but it was simply the medieval French word for "house." The term "mansion stage" described a wide stage with a number of separate houses attached to the back of it, each depicting a unique location. These houses could be built of solid materials and give the illusion of being three-dimensional, or they could be painted on the curtains at the back of the pageant wagons. Because all these houses were visible to the audience at all times, some people describe a performance on this sort of stage as "simultaneous staging" and describe the stage itself as a **simultaneous stage,** though "mansion stage" is the more accepted term. Figure 15.8 is based on a drawing of the passion play performed in Valenciennes, France, in 1547 and shows what a mansion stage might have looked like.

You're not likely to see a mansion stage today, but the idea of performing in a town square is still alive, as you can see in Figure 15.9. The photo shows the temporary stage we saw in the town square of Bratislava, Slovakia, in 1995. You can see a mansion stage if you visit Oberammergau, Germany, where *The Passion Play* is presented every ten years. If you'd rather stay closer

Figure 15.8   A mansion stage could be set up in a town square. It had a wide platform for the actors to perform on, and at the back were houses that could be either two-dimensional painted scenery or three-dimensional structures. Each mansion (or house) suggested a particular location. The characters could enter from one of these mansions, and the wide platform was a neutral area that permitted the actors to move about without being limited to the space in front of a particular mansion. This drawing shows the mouth of hell (and the devils coming out of it) at one end of the stage and an angel coming from heaven at the other. In the middle is the character who symbolizes humankind. This illustration is based on a drawing of a 1547 passion play.

Figure 15.9   This temporary platform stage was set up in the town square of Bratislava, Slovakia. The curtain has been painted to represent a house, and the actors standing backstage, at the rear of the platform, wore costumes from the fifteenth century.

Figure 15.10 A modern mansion stage is used for *The Great Passion Play,* a religious drama presented to tens of thousands of spectators each year in Eureka Springs, Arkansas. All the different settings for the play are visible to the audience throughout the performance.

to home, you can visit Eureka Springs, Arkansas. Each summer *The Great Passion Play* is performed there, and in its twenty-five years more than six million people have attended (Figure 15.10).

ELIZABETHAN THEATRE

The newly built Shakespeare's Globe Theatre in London is a round wooden building with an uncovered courtyard in the middle. From above, the theatre has the shape of the letter "O." Shakespeare's Globe Theatre is built along the lines of the theatre Shakespeare acted in and is called an Elizabethan public theatre. Color Plate 23 shows a recent performance in Shakespeare's Globe Theatre. Many Shakespeare festivals across America perform in theatres based on what we think the Elizabethan public theatres were like. Two of the best known are the Oregon Shakespeare Festival and the Utah Shakespearean Festival. Elizabethan-style theatres have recently been built in Staunton, Virginia, and Lenox, Massachusetts.

No original Elizabethan theatre is still standing, so no one knows precisely what these theatres were like, but scholars agree that they were as different from both the Greek and Roman theatres as they were from the mansion stages of the Middle Ages. The primary sources for an imaginative reconstruction of an Elizabethan public theatre include a rough sketch by a seventeenth-century tourist, a business contract listing the dimensions of a theatre, and the texts of the plays themselves, which imply certain things about the stage. For example, when Shakespeare describes the theatre as

Figure 15.11   This drawing shows what an Elizabethan public theatre might have looked like.

a "wooden O," it's fair to guess that the original Globe Theatre was round. The drawing in Figure 15.11 may help you follow our description.

Elizabethan public theatres were freestanding buildings constructed of wood and plaster. They were either round or multisided, and in the center was a large courtyard that was open to the elements. This openness meant that audiences in the courtyard were vulnerable to the sun and rain, just as you are today if you go to a football game. The buildings were three stories tall, and protruding into the center of the courtyard was a three-sided stage about 5 feet tall. The stage had at least one trapdoor in it so that characters could enter from below. High above the stage was a sheltering roof that gave the actors some protection from the sun and rain. The roof, beautifully painted to suggest the sky, was called "the heavens." The poorer members of the audience, who paid only a one-penny admission charge, stood on the ground to watch the performance. In *Hamlet,* Shakespeare refers to them as **groundlings** and has his title character complain that they respond only to coarse humor and vigorous action. The richer members of the audience paid a second or third penny for admission to the seats on the second or third tier, where they were protected from the elements. The platform stage thrust itself into the center of the open courtyard, creating the exciting relationship between actors and audience that we have today in a thrust theatre. The platform stage was set up against one side of the courtyard, which formed a back wall for the actors to use for entrances. This wall had two or three doorways

Both Laurence Olivier's Academy Award–winning Henry V *and* Shakespeare in Love *(the movie that made stars of Gwynneth Paltrow and Joseph Fiennes) show what theatregoing was like in Shakespeare's time.*

and probably a small, elevated stage above the center doorway to serve as a balcony or to suggest that the characters were standing on a hill.

What is most unusual about the stage of an Elizabethan public theatre, compared to our modern theatres, is that the architectural facade remained neutral throughout the performance. The theatre building itself was a unit set that didn't require any decorative scenery. All parts of the architectural stage were continually in the audience's full view, but no part of it suggested a particular locale. Instead, the dialogue described where the action took place, and the audience imagined whatever location the characters said they were in. For example, when Romeo wooed Juliet, she was standing on the balcony and the audience imagined an Italian courtyard. Indeed, Shakespeare's plays do not depend on an illusion created by scenery, costumes, or lighting. Their performance conventions were quite different from today's. To change the location of the action, one set of characters exited as another set entered through a different door. The audience immediately understood that the scene had changed. A presentational performance on an Elizabethan stage is very compelling. Once you have experienced the performance of one of Shakespeare's plays in the kind of theatre he wrote them for, you will truly appreciate how exciting his plays are.

In 2004, a replica of Shakespeare's Globe Theatre in London opened in Rome, Italy, with a performance of Romeo e Giulietta.

Shakespeare died in 1616. In 1642, a civil war broke out in England during which the king was beheaded and the victorious Puritan government made theatre illegal. All the wood-and-plaster theatres fell into disuse or were torn down. By the time King Charles II was restored to the throne in 1660, no Elizabethan public theatres were left. This unique and functional theatre that had served Shakespeare so well was not seen again until the twentieth century, when scholars began to research what it had looked like. Their research led to the construction of many Elizabethan-style theatres in America and to the 1996 opening in London of Shakespeare's Globe Theatre.

EXPOSITION
• • • • • • • • • • •

Spanish theatres in the seventeenth century were similar to English theatres. They were built in the courtyards of inns, and the Spanish used their name for a courtyard, **corrales** (ko-RAH-laze), to describe the theatre as well. Our word "corral," used to describe a fenced-in area for horses, comes from the Spanish word. Figure 15.12 shows a corrales still in use in Almagro, Spain.

• •

RENAISSANCE THEATRE IN ITALY

About the same time the English were building their wood-and-plaster theatres, the Italians were rediscovering the glories of ancient Rome. In literature, painting, and architecture, the Renaissance was in full flower. Architects

Figure 15.12 The theatre in Almagro, Spain, looks like Shakespeare's Globe Theatre, except that the audience is seated facing the end stage platform instead of standing on three sides of a thrust stage. This seventeenth-century corrales was rediscovered in 1953, and a festival of classic Spanish drama is performed on this stage each year.

saw the ruins of ancient Roman theatres all around them, and they rediscovered *De Architectura* (ar-key-tek-TOO-ra), a book by a Roman named Vitruvius (vi-TROOV-ee-us) that included lengthy descriptions of what ancient Roman theatres were like. The book was translated from Latin to Italian in 1486, and in the next few years a lot of new theatres were built. Instead of slavishly imitating the ancients, however, the Italian architects made what they believed were improvements. To begin, they built their new theatres indoors so that the rich nobles who paid to have them built didn't have to sit outside in the rain or sun. Then they made the new theatres smaller, because they weren't open to the general public. Just as the White House in Washington, D.C., has a small movie theatre for the exclusive entertainment of the president's guests, these Italian theatres were for the exclusive entertainment of the nobleman's guests.

Just north of Venice, in the town of Vicenza (vi-CHEN-za), is the Teatro Olympico (tay-AH-tro oh-LEEM-pee-coe). It was built in 1580 and designed by the famous architect Palladio (pa-LAH-dee-oh), and it remains in perfect condition (Figure 15.13). The ornately decorated theatre looks as if it's made out of white marble, except for the ceiling, which is painted to look like the sky, complete with fluffy clouds. The theatre is small, yet it's similar in some ways to the Roman theatre in Orange, France. The seating is in a half-circle, as is the space in front of the stage. The small stage is raised slightly off the floor. You couldn't bring a horse and chariot onto it, but then this whole indoor theatre seems like a miniature.

Figure 15.13 The Teatro Olympico, built in 1580, remains in perfect condition today. The theatre is indoors and very small. It has an ornate facade at the back of the stage and a half-circle orchestra.

The facade of the stage is covered with columns, niches, statues, and architectural details. The Teatro Olympico is more ornate than any theatre we've discussed so far. The Greeks painted the front of their skene, and the Romans made it three-dimensional with ornate columns and sculptures. The Italians added something new: they let you see through the three archways in the facade of the skene, into the distance. The archways are like picture frames, and the vistas take your eye to the horizon. The facade and the stage in front of it in the Teatro Olympico are an unchanging unit set, just like the ancient Greek skene and the facade of the Elizabethan public theatre. The vistas, painted three-dimensional wood and plaster, were designed by Palladio's contemporary Scamozzi for a production of *Oedipus the King*. The vistas are unchangeable during a performance, though in theory they could be replaced with other vistas for the performance of a different play.

EXPOSITION

Renaissance Italian painters were fascinated with the theory and practice of perspective drawing. We are so accustomed to perspective drawing today

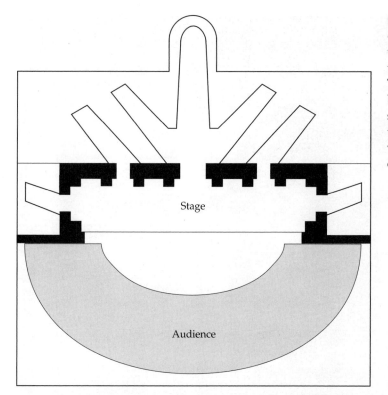

Figure 15.14 This ground plan of the Teatro Olympico shows how the audience could see through the three archways in the stage wall. The scenery down each corridor was built and painted so that the vista suggested streets reaching far into the distance. The Teatro Olympico was a step toward the development of the proscenium arch theatre.

that we can't imagine drawing in any other way. But Renaissance artists like Scamozzi were captivated by the new idea that mathematically precise rules of spatial relations could enable the artist to draw something that appeared to have depth. What better way to present the illusion created by perspective drawing than to put the painting in a frame! As with drawing, so with theatre. The archways in the facade of the Teatro Olympico are like the frame on a painting, and they permitted Scamozzi to create a three-dimensional vista that could represent a "real world" spectators could peep into.

• •

If we moved from one seat to another, we would discover that the center arch reveals three different vistas. No matter where we sit, we look down a long street (Figure 15.14). The floor is on an incline and the three-dimensional scenery on those streets gets smaller and smaller as it gets farther away from the audience. This device, called **forced perspective,** makes the distance seem great. By making things progressively smaller, the artist can make them seem farther away. If you were to walk up the central street shown in Figure 15.15, you would look like a giant, because you would be taller than the buildings.

In Parma, the Teatro Farnese (far-NAY-zay) was another experiment by the Italian architects. It is famous for having the earliest existing proscenium arch in theatre history. It's also an indoor theatre, but it's a little bigger than

Figure 15.15 The classically inspired ornate facade of the Teatro Olympico has three archways; this photo shows the vista beyond the central arch. Note that the floor is raked upward and that the scenery along the corridor grows smaller to create the illusion of great distance.

the Teatro Olympico. The Duke of Farnese probably wanted to outdo the Duke of Vicenza. The Teatro Farnese, built in 1618, originally was as ornate as the Teatro Olympico. But Parma was bombed during World War II, and the theatre was badly damaged. While photos show what it looked like before 1945, today only a few parts of the walls retain their ornamentation; the rest is a plain wooden structure.

The seats in the Teatro Farnese and the large orchestra in front of the stage are in a horseshoe shape (Figure 15.16). On some occasions, seats may have

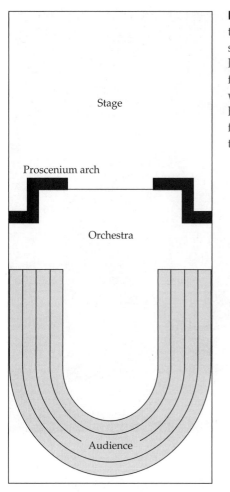

Figure 15.16 This ground plan of the Teatro Farnese shows the horseshoe seating for the audience, the large orchestra that could be flooded for mock sea battles, and the stage with its proscenium arch. Seats may have been placed in the orchestra, facing the stage, for performances that took place on the stage.

been placed in the orchestra so the audience could see a performance on the stage; on other occasions, the orchestra was flooded and used for mock sea battles. The major feature of the Teatro Farnese is the proscenium arch that separates the stage where the actors performed from the auditorium where the audience sat. It's as if the central arch in the facade of the Teatro Olympico had been made wider and taller and the audience was asked to watch the play through the frame around it (Figure 15.17). The scenery on the stage of the Teatro Farnese would not have been a box set—that type of set wasn't invented until the nineteenth century. On some occasions it might have been a unit set, but most frequently it would have been wing and drop. We know this because of the existence of drawings that show where the wings were placed. The proscenium arch was used with wing and drop scenery that was painted in perspective to create illusions, preparing the way for today's realistic theatre.

Figure 15.17 Italy's Teatro Farnese, built in 1618, is the earliest existing theatre to have a proscenium arch. Much of the ornate decoration shown here was destroyed during a bombing raid in World War II. The large orchestra in front of the stage may have been flooded for the presentation of mock sea battles.

BAROQUE COURT THEATRE

The proscenium arch theatre quickly became the only kind of theatre in Europe. People loved the idea of peeking through a picture frame into the magical world on stage. The rich lord of almost every castle had a proscenium arch theatre built for his family and friends, and the merchants of almost every town built one for the townspeople's entertainment. A couple of elegant court theatres remain in perfect original condition today, nearly two hundred years after they were built. The one in Cesky Krumlov (CHES-ski KROOM-lov), the Czech Republic, is particularly exquisite.

The Cesky Krumlov theatre is so beautifully preserved that you feel like you're in a museum. This theatre was built in the eighteenth century, during a period that art historians call the Baroque, and everything is covered with elaborate ornamentation, Color Plate 24. The ceiling is painted with angels flying through the sky, and the walls are painted to look like sculpted marble—as are the proscenium arch, the balcony railing, and the lord's box in the center of the balcony. Notice that the orchestra in front of the stage is small and filled with benches for the audience. Over the centuries, the full circle of the orchestra in the Greek theatre became a half-circle in the Roman theatre and now is used for the audience, not the actors. The half-circle or horseshoe shape is still used for the balcony, but the main floor is filled with seats facing the stage—the better to see the action through the picture frame of the proscenium arch. The floor of the auditorium is flat, and the spectators sitting on benches might have had trouble seeing over one another, so the stage floor is on an incline, raked upward away from the audience.

A large portion of the stage, the **apron,** sticks out in front of the proscenium arch. In this theatre the apron is flat at the front, but in many theatres it is curved. Before the days of electric light, theatres were lit by candles. If the actors walked very far upstage it was hard to see them, so they did most of their acting close to the audience, on the apron.

The scenery at Cesky Krumlov is wing and drop. There still exist beautifully painted eighteenth-century original wings and drops that depict outdoor and indoor scenes, and on occasion performances are given on this stage in the same manner as they were two centuries ago: the theatre is lit only by candles, and the actors use the ornate costumes and the wing and drop scenery of that era. The performance creates a kind of theatrical magic that gives you goose bumps.

THE EARLY MODERN AGE

New theatres built in Europe and the Americas throughout the eighteenth and nineteenth centuries retained essentially the same spatial arrangement as the Baroque theatres, though there were three developments worth noting: an increase in size, the introduction of raked seating to improve the audience's view of the stage, and the steady improvement of stage lighting.

Theatres grew in size from the small court theatres of the Baroque age to enormous halls seating several thousand. This expansion was driven by the demand for seats from the growing middle classes. Instead of being an elite entertainment for the local aristocrat and his guests, theatre became the popular form of public entertainment. Theatres seating several thousand divided their seats by price so that all strata of society could attend. Affluent people sat in the box seats and the dress circle, the middle-classes sat in the orchestra (or "stalls," as they're called in England), and those who couldn't afford the more expensive seats sat in the balcony and the gallery. As theatres grew larger, their interior decoration remained ornate (Figure 15.18).

The raked seating in the orchestra (main floor) and in the balconies made it easier for audiences to see the action on stage and also permitted audiences to be reasonably close to the stage. While it may be true that spectators in the balcony saw the tops of the actors' heads more than they saw their faces, the balcony's proximity to the stage made it possible for everyone to hear the actors' dialogue.

The great Italian actress Eleonora Duse was celebrated for speaking softly, yet she could be heard by audiences of more than three thousand in huge theatres like New York's Metropolitan Opera House.

Figure 15.18   The Teatro Communale in Bologna, Italy, is typical of the huge theatres built in the eighteenth and nineteenth centuries in many European and American cities. These theatres influenced the size and architecture of the American "movie palaces" built in the 1920s and 1930s. As the fashion for multiplexes of smaller movie theatres developed, many older movie theatres were renovated and are used today for tours of Broadway musicals.

In Baroque court theatres, candles lit both the stage and the auditorium. The players and the audience shared a commonly illuminated space and interacted openly. Characters spoke "asides" to the audience, acknowledging their presence, and spectators sometimes spoke back to the characters (and if they didn't like a performance, they sometimes spoke to the *actors* just as you might yell at a baseball player who has made an error). By the mid-nineteenth century gas lighting was in common use, and by the end of the nineteenth century electric lighting had been introduced. These technological developments made it possible to influence the mood of a scene by illuminating it with a chosen color, to focus on the important actors by increasing the brightness on their part of the stage, and to separate the audience from the world on the stage by darkening the auditorium. The first audience to sit in a darkened auditorium was astonished by the innovation. Today's audience sits in the dark and peeps through the proscenium arch at the brightly lit actors on the stage. We are so accustomed to this convention that we are astonished if the auditorium remains lit during a performance.

A major development of the early modern era was the degree to which theatre became a commercial business. No longer dependent on the patronage of a rich noble, theatre became a profitable enterprise, and the man (or sometimes the woman) who headed the acting company was the attraction that drew large crowds. This was the era of actor-managers, as described in Chapter 8, and the conventions of performance were shaped to celebrate the reigning star.

The first half of the nineteenth century saw a growing interest in the study of history among Europeans. Scholars—and then the general public—strove to learn how life was lived in earlier times. They were curious about what buildings looked like, how people dressed and behaved, and what kinds of furniture they used. A passion for historical accuracy developed in the theatre, and dramatic characters like Julius Caesar were dressed in Roman togas instead of the clothing of the audience's era, as had been the custom. This was an early stride toward the style of Realism. Within a few years, the startling innovation of the box set was introduced, replacing the wing and drop scenery that had dominated theatrical scenery for two hundred years.

As Realism took hold in the design of costumes and scenery, the style of acting changed. Actors sought to represent characters rather than to present them, and the personality of the star became less important than the credibility of the character. With this change came experiments with performing in small theatres. This "little theatre" movement began with the Théâtre Libre (tay-AH-tre LEE-bre), or "Free Theatre," founded by André Antoine in Paris in 1881. Small theatres produced plays that replicated and studied "real life." This fashion spread throughout Europe and ultimately to America, where in the early part of the twentieth century the first important American playwright, Eugene O'Neill, and the first important American scene designer, Robert Edmond Jones, were involved in the founding of the Provincetown Playhouse in New York City.

Whether plays were produced in large theatres or small, the style of Realism dominated the final decades of the early modern age. Theatre, like all aspects of culture, thrives on change, and when Realism was firmly established, theatre artists rebelled against it and sought alternative ways to write and produce theatre. They sought alternative spaces in which to gather audiences for the theatrical experience.

THE MODERN AGE

The history of twentieth-century theatre is a study of continual experimentation in the way plays were written and performed. That experimentation led to changes in theatrical design and theatre architecture. The styles you read about in Chapter 4 were reactions against the limitations of Realism, a style that succeeds best when the audience watches the play through the picture frame of a proscenium arch stage. Twentieth-century playwrights' efforts to put a "truer" reality on the stage led to experiments in the size of theatres and in the relationship of audience to stage. Their stylistic experiments broke the rules that had prevailed for nearly three centuries and led to the introduction of arena stages, thrust stages, and black box, found space, and environmental theatres. A quick review of the illustrations in Chapter 13 will refresh your understanding of the many exciting changes that happened in twentieth century theatre.

> **ASIDE**   Year-long courses in theatre history and drama are offered at most colleges, and we encourage you to learn more than we can touch on in this brief chapter.

THE FUTURE

Linda tells me that if we could predict the future, we would abandon theatre, get rich in the stock market, and retire to the south of France. Unfortunately, none of us can predict what's ahead, and we admit that the future of theatre is as difficult to predict as the future of the stock market. However, we're optimistic folks, and we have great hopes for advances in theatre just as we have hopes for world peace.

People have predicted the death of theatre ever since the movies started drawing away a large percentage of its audience. Some people predicted the death of the movies when television won over the popular audience. Today DVDs, the Internet, virtual reality games—all the exciting electronic experiences that are a part of our contemporary culture—have led some to predict the death of television. Yet the movies endure, and theatre has not disappeared.

We believe theatre will remain a vital element of your future for the obvious reason that there's something unique about the authentic experience of live theatre that we humans find compelling. We need it. We want it. We have always had it. We will make certain it's a part of our future.

Theatre has been a part of human experience from the beginning of civilization. Every time somebody thinks theatre is dying, it bounces back to the center of human experience by embracing the newest changes in society and technology. That's why it has earned the nickname "the fabulous invalid."

We believe live theatre will embrace technological inventions and thrill large audiences and at the same time will be produced very simply in small theatres and enthrall small audiences. Theatre architecture may focus on small interior spaces that encourage a concentrated experience, or it may adopt the newest modern technology of architectural engineering. For example, retractable roofs previously were used only on buildings where aircraft were built and maintained or on major sports venues. This cutting-edge movable architecture was applied to theatre for the first time in 2003 when Rock Valley College's Starlight Theatre unveiled a star-shaped roof that opens and closes like the petals of a flower. Large audiences enjoy an evening of theatre under starry skies; when the rains come, the roof closes and the show goes on (Figure 15.19).

Inside the theatres of the future, productions may adopt new technologies like virtual reality (see Figure 13.22), or they may return to the philosophy of the great seventeenth-century Spanish playwright Lope de Vega (LOPE-ay day VAY-ga), who wrote for the simple platform of the corrales stage. Lope

Figure 15.19 The Starlight Theatre at Rock Valley College in Illinois has a 100-foot star-shaped roof that opens to let patrons enjoy an open-air performance. The hard plastic, translucent curtain divides in the center and slides to the sides, revealing the stage.

claimed that all you need to create theatre is a place to stand and something important to share with an audience. "Four trestles, four boards, two actors, and a passion" is how he described the minimal essentials needed for theatre to happen. As long as people live, they'll have a place to stand and something to care about. And long as we have those two things, we'll have theatre.

EXERCISES

1. Teams of three to five students should research the theatres in your community. One team should research the earliest theatre built in your community, a second team should research the oldest theatre still in use, a third team should research the largest movie palace, and a fourth team should research the theatres on your campus. Each team should prepare a report for the class that shows pictures and tells the following:

    a. When the theatre was built
    b. By whom it was built (city, church, private business, individual)
    c. How large it is/was (the size of the stage, the number of seats)
    d. What kind of theatre it is/was (proscenium arch, arena, thrust)

2. Pretend you are a reporter for your community's largest newspaper and have been assigned to write a feature article describing the history of the

major theatres built in your community. Share with the class the outline for the article you would write.

3. Using the Internet for your research, create an album of images showing examples of each of the following types of theatres:

   a. The ruins of an ancient Greek theatre on the island of Sicily
   b. The ruins of an ancient Roman theatre in Asia Minor (Turkey) or North Africa (Libya)
   c. The mansion stage at the theatre in Oberammergau, Germany
   d. An Elizabethan-style public theatre in North America
   e. The interior of a Baroque court theatre, *excluding* the theatre in Cesky Krumlov
   f. The interior of a large opera house in America
   g. The interior of an arena theatre, *excluding* the Alley Theatre in Houston
   h. The interior of a thrust theatre, *excluding* the Guthrie Theatre in Minneapolis
   i. The interior of a black box theatre
   j. A performance in a found space

Theatre in America Today

The first three acts introduced you to how you can understand and evaluate theatre, how the creative process leads to a theatrical production, and how audiences and backstage workers contribute to the creation of the theatrical experience. The brief overview of theatre history in Act 4 created a context for learning more about the theatre of your own time.

Act 5 explores theatre in America today. It's such a large subject that we are limiting ourselves to the two topics students have told us they are most curious about and most enthusiastic about: the business of show business and American musical theatre.

To put yourself in the mood for the two chapters in this fifth and final act, recall the words and music of the anthem of American musical theatre that Irving Berlin wrote for *Annie Get Your Gun:* "There's no business like show business . . . so let's go, on with the show."

CHAPTER 16

Show Biz Is Big Biz

It's a mistake to describe theatre as "one-size-fits-all." Whether it's in New York or in Des Moines, whether it's on campus or in a warehouse, and whether it's produced on a big budget or a low budget, show biz is big biz. Understanding how and why theatre is produced can help you decide which kind of theatre you want to see. Theatre in America is produced in one of four ways: as a commercial enterprise, as a not-for-profit cultural service, as an amateur activity, or as an educational experience.

● *FORESHADOWING*

Four Ways Theatre Is Produced

1. Theatre as a commercial enterprise
2. Theatre as a not-for-profit cultural service
3. Theatre as an amateur activity
4. Theatre as an educational experience

THEATRE AS A COMMERCIAL ENTERPRISE

Some History

There's a historical reason why theatre is a business in America. The Puritans who founded the Massachusetts Bay Colony in 1620 believed that theatre was immoral. They shared the religious beliefs of Oliver Cromwell, who headed the English government that made performing theatre against the law. The Puritans believed that work was moral and play was immoral, and they equated theatre with the sort of idleness that is "the devil's plaything." Any public activity that took people away from work was immoral, so the playhouses in England were torn down or nailed shut.

The Puritans, like many Americans today, believed in a literal reading of their Bible, and they also understood that people must be honest. To pretend to be other than what you are is to lie, to do the devil's work. Puritans believed that an actor who pretended in a play to be someone else must be lying and therefore was an agent of the devil. This early American belief kept theatre from developing as a part of our cultural mainstream.

A second and conflicting belief was held by many early Americans (and is held by many modern Americans). These Americans believed that profit is a sign that the person making the profit is smiled on by God. This belief, developed from the Calvinist strain of Protestantism, was adopted by many sects in our capitalistic nation. Early Americans who believed that profit was a good thing were eager to enter into businesses that made money, and when they discovered that theatre could turn a profit, they introduced it into the colonies. As early as 1716, a theatre was built in Williamsburg, Virginia.

These conflicting beliefs of early Americans banged against each other and created the belief that theatre is immoral unless it turns a profit and therefore is a demonstration that God is smiling. This conundrum reveals two enduring truths of American culture: that theatre is immoral and should be prohibited by law, and that the only good theatre is theatre that makes money. Americans approve of *Cats* because it ran for sixteen years on Broadway and made a huge profit, but they disapprove of *Waiting for Godot* because it lost money at the box office even though our most respected thinkers describe it as a masterpiece.

ASIDE   When Linda went to her first basketball game, she asked Tom, "Is this like Broadway or more like regional theatre?" He explained that the NBA is the best basketball in the world, that it's like going to the Royal National Theatre of Great Britain. We needed some way to classify the level of entertainment we were about to see, and we used theatre as a measuring stick. Once Linda was exposed to the best basketball, she became an avid fan, just as we know people who have become theatregoers for life once they were exposed to great theatre.

Commercial Theatre Today

Commercial theatre has a single purpose: to make money. Like any other economic venture—a fast-food chain, an automobile factory, a pharmaceutical laboratory—the people selling the product expect to turn a profit. Commercial theatre producers believe their production will attract ticket buyers in sufficient numbers for everyone in the company to make money. The actors, ushers, and stagehands will earn a **salary;** the playwright, director, and composer will receive a **royalty;** and the investors will earn a substantial return on their investment. When commercial producers are right, they make a lot of money for themselves and for everyone connected with the venture. When they are wrong, they lose everything. Theatre is a highly risky business.

Though profit is its primary aim, this highly risky business sometimes makes art as a welcome by-product. In its effort to attract ticket buyers, commercial theatre engages the finest talents. Just as an automobile manufacturer hires the most skilled designers, engineers, and workers, the commercial theatre hires the most talented writers, performers, and directors. Sometimes the product these people create is what the world admires and calls "art," and sometimes it is not. Just as Ford Motor Company could invest its wisdom and financial resources in the 1950s to develop an ugly, unwieldy, and unpopular car called the Edsel, so can the commercial theatre produce flops, such as the musicals based on the popular movies *Carrie* and *The Sweet Smell of Success*. *Carrie* lost its entire $6 million capitalization when it closed after only one performance!

The corporate structure of commercial theatre parallels other businesses. A producer (or a group of producers) comes up with an idea for a product (a play) and convinces people with money to invest in it. A corporation is formed by the producer (the CEO, or chief executive officer) who attracts **angels,** investors, who stand to make a profit if the public buys the product. The producer engages all the people who will create the product—playwright, actors, stagehands, and so on—and rents the rehearsal hall and the theatre in which the product will be presented. When the product is ready, tickets go on sale. If the public buys lots of tickets, everyone makes money. If the public does not buy tickets, the show folds, the corporation declares bankruptcy, the salaried employees are out of a job, the royalty earners don't see a penny, and the angels lose all their money.

How much money is risked? In America today, a commercial theatrical venture requires an investment of somewhere between $2 million and $18 million, depending on the play to be produced. A big musical such as *The Producers* spends about $11 million to open on Broadway (Color Plate 25). A small play with four actors and one set spends around $2 million. On top of the initial investment is the weekly expense of operating the show, the **nut.** The weekly nut includes the costs of renting the theatre, paying the salaries and royalties, and advertising the production. For a large musical, the nut can be $600,000 a week. Where does the money to cover it come from? From ticket sales.

The cost of making a movie like Pirates of the Caribbean *exceeds $100 million.*

A Broadway musical—again, let's use *The Producers* as an example—can sell up to $800,000 in tickets each week, which means it can turn a profit of around $200,000 a week. How many weeks of $200,000 profit does it take to pay back the $8 million investment? Forty weeks. Late in the first year's run of a hit musical, the investors might begin to see some profit. After the angels have recouped their investment, the producer can keep half the profit. In our example, that leaves $100,000 to be distributed among the investors each week. At that rate, the angels see a lot of profit—more than $5 million a year. The greatest commercial successes run for many years, turning out $100,000 a week profit from the original production. An additional $100,000 a week profit is seen from each touring production, and with long-running hits like *The Phantom of the Opera* as many as three productions will tour America simultaneously. On top of the profits earned from national tours, additional profits of $100,000 a week can be realized from international productions as well as from sales of the original cast CD. Even more profit is realized if a movie studio buys the rights to make a film, and even after the Broadway run has ended and every touring and foreign production has closed, profits can be made from the fees paid by resident professional theatre companies or amateur theatres. In short, the money to be earned from a commercial hit is enough to make the producers and investors very, very rich.

Before you get excited and rush off to invest in a commercial theatre venture, you should know that 90 percent of these ventures lose 100 percent of their investment. It is a painful truth to tell, but the wisest producers in the theatre business can engage the most proven writers, the most attractive stars, and the most talented directors and still come up with a flop that closes after one night. Successful commercial theatre is more difficult to achieve than is a championship basketball team. Too much can go wrong, and there is no guaranteed formula for success.

ASIDE   *Seussical the Musical* and *La Bohème* are two recent flops that illustrate the perils of investing in theatre, and *Les Miserables* illustrates the enormous profit that can be realized from a hit.

Seussical, based on the stories of Dr. Seuss, was created by very experienced writers, composer, director, choreographer, and stars, but the producers' expectations of a multiyear run proved wrong. *Seussical* received poor critical reviews, failed to attract large audiences, and closed in less than six months. Its investors lost $11 million. They may yet recover some of their investment, however, because *Seussical* is now touring the country, and audiences who love Dr. Seuss and don't know or care that the show was a flop on Broadway may buy enough tickets for the show to turn a weekly profit and ultimately recover its investment (Color Plate 26).

La Bohème won't, however. Directed by Baz Luhrmann and designed by his wife, Catherine Martin—the team that created the hugely popular movies *Moulin Rouge* and *Romeo and Juliet*—*La Bohème* received rave reviews from the critics and won two Tony Awards but failed to sell enough tickets to recover its investment, let alone turn a profit. It closed after six months. The producer told the *New York Times*, "We got young hipsters, Manhattan art lovers, kids and cognoscenti. What we didn't get was the *Showboat* audience from New Jersey." The weekly running costs for *La Bohème* were $560,000, so it won't be going on tour. The investors lost three-quarters of the $8.5 million investment—over $6 million.

Les Miserables ran for sixteen years on Broadway, the second-longest-running musical in history (after *Cats*). It cost $4.5 million to produce in 1987, and when it closed in 2003 *Les Miz* had taken in $390 million on Broadway and $1.8 *billion* worldwide. Now that's a profit!

Where Commercial Theatre Is Produced

Commercial theatre can be produced anywhere somebody thinks money can be made, but you are most likely to find commercial theatre in New York or in a large city with a theatre where touring productions of Broadway hits are presented.

● **FORESHADOWING**

Five Places Commercial Theatre Is Produced

1. Broadway
2. Off Broadway
3. Off Off Broadway
4. Touring productions
5. Cruises, casinos, and theme parks

Broadway   In America, the center of commercial theatre is **Broadway.** We use the term "Broadway" to mean many different things. To begin, Broadway is the name of a street in the middle of New York City that runs diagonally through Manhattan Island. Most of the commercial theatres in New York are located on or within three blocks of Broadway, between 41st Street and 54th Street and between 6th Avenue and 9th Avenue. This small section of midtown Manhattan—three blocks by fourteen blocks—is the geographic district that carries the legendary name "Broadway." This area has been called the "street of dreams," the "great white way," and the place where "if you can make it there, you can make it anywhere" (Figure 16.1).

Employees of a Broadway show are given an employment contract that the theatrical unions classify as a "First Class Production" to distinguish it from contracts that don't guarantee the artists as high a salary. Actors, designers, ushers, and stagehands all earn more money working on Broadway than on any other theatrical contract, so for them Broadway is the best.

EXPOSITION
● ● ● ● ● ● ● ● ● ● ●

Labor unions for people who work in the theatre protect their members in the same way labor unions protect carpenters, nurses, firefighters, and professors. Theatrical unions establish the minimum salaries their members may be paid, provide health and retirement plans, determine the number of hours in a working day and the number of days in a working week, ensure safe and sanitary working environments, protect members from sexual harassment or financial exploitation, establish the legal grounds for termination from a job, provide a procedure for grievances, and so on. Stage actors belong to Actors' Equity Association (called "Equity"), and those who act on the big and little screens also belong to the Screen Actors Guild (SAG) and the American Federation of Television and Radio Artists (AFTRA). Stage managers also belong

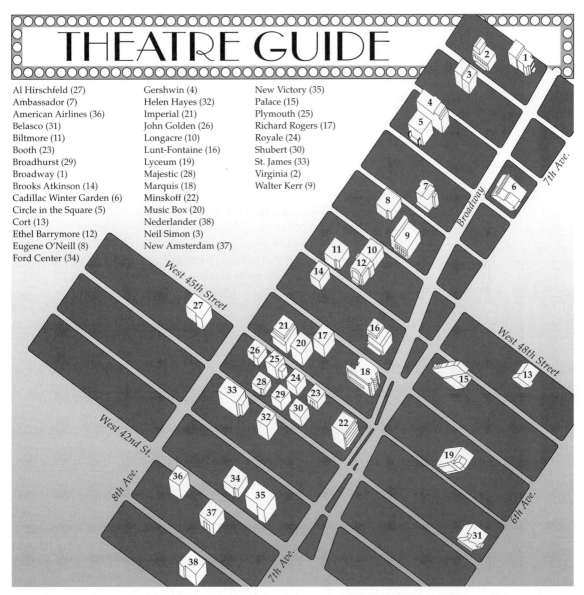

THEATRE GUIDE

Al Hirschfeld (27)
Ambassador (7)
American Airlines (36)
Belasco (31)
Biltmore (11)
Booth (23)
Broadhurst (29)
Broadway (1)
Brooks Atkinson (14)
Cadillac Winter Garden (6)
Circle in the Square (5)
Cort (13)
Ethel Barrymore (12)
Eugene O'Neill (8)
Ford Center (34)

Gershwin (4)
Helen Hayes (32)
Imperial (21)
John Golden (26)
Longacre (10)
Lunt-Fontaine (16)
Lyceum (19)
Majestic (28)
Marquis (18)
Minskoff (22)
Music Box (20)
Nederlander (38)
Neil Simon (3)
New Amsterdam (37)

New Victory (35)
Palace (15)
Plymouth (25)
Richard Rogers (17)
Royale (24)
Shubert (30)
St. James (33)
Virginia (2)
Walter Kerr (9)

Figure 16.1 Broadway cuts diagonally through midtown Manhattan and is the center of the Broadway theatre district, which reaches from 41st Street north to 54th Street.

to Equity, but the Society of Stage Directors and Choreographers (SSDC) serves that constituency. Scene, costume, lighting, and sound designers belong to United Scene Artists (USA), a union affiliated with the larger and more powerful International Alliance of Theatre Stage Employees (IATSE), representing stagehands, electricians, and other behind-the-scenes workers. Theatrical unions serve their members in many ways, and those who work on Broadway are guaranteed the highest minimum wage in the industry.

Many theatregoers also think Broadway produces the best theatre, and sometimes that's a fair judgment. When the finest artists create a successful work, the result can be breathtaking. Examples that come to mind include Al Pacino in Oscar Wilde's *Salome* and the revival of the great American musical *Fiddler on the Roof* that starred Alfred Molina. But a great deal of bad theatre also is presented on Broadway—failures like *Gandhi,* the play Tom acted in that closed after a single performance. Nevertheless, Broadway remains in the American consciousness as a synonym for "excellence," and as long as Broadway continues to stage excellent productions, that meaning will endure.

"Broadway" has still another meaning. The theatre district, which for decades produced the works of serious playwrights like Tennessee Williams, Arthur Miller, and Edward Albee, has today become a synonym for feel-good theatre. When people today say that something is "like a Broadway show," they usually mean that the play is lighthearted entertainment. This new meaning has a good economic basis. Theatre tickets cost $100 each, and people who pay that much money want to leave the theatre feeling happy—that's why people go to musicals like *The Little Shop of Horrors.*

Specifically what kind of theatrical production do these ticket buyers wish to see? At the end of a hard day, those shoppers, business executives, and camera-carrying tourists want diversion, not confrontation. They want spectacle and singing and dancing. They also want to see what they can't see back home—they want to see what's new on the theatrical scene. American culture values the new over the old. A new-model car is more popular than an old-model car, and this year's new fashion always supplants last year's. In a similar vein, the commercial theatre in New York is dominated by new shows or by revivals with big-name stars. An "all-singing, all-dancing new spectacle" is the pinnacle of American commercial theatre. *Cats, Les Miserables, Beauty and the Beast, The Lion King, 42nd Street, Rent,* and *Kiss Me, Kate* are all perennially popular Broadway musicals.

Off Broadway   The second place you might see commercial theatre is **Off Broadway.** This term describes a kind of theatrical production that began in New York City in the 1950s and has evolved into a primary way to present serious drama. For a century, every important new American play began its life on Broadway, but after World War II ended, in 1945, the American theatre began to change. Some theatre artists became frustrated by the increasingly popular spirit of Broadway; they wanted to do plays that were artistically rewarding even if those plays didn't appeal to large audiences. These artists were prepared to earn smaller salaries in order to present plays that nurtured their spirit. A few courageous and adventuresome theatre professionals presented serious plays in small theatres that were not located in midtown Manhattan. They sold less expensive tickets to smaller audiences who lived in the neighborhood or who sought out theatre that challenged audiences to think and feel deeply. When Brooks Atkinson, then the critic for the *New York Times,* went to see Tennessee Williams's *Summer and Smoke* at a Greenwich Village theatre and then wrote a rave review in the next day's paper, Off Broadway was born. For the next several decades, Off Broadway was the vital "engine room" for serious American theatre.

Producing a play Off Broadway is less expensive than producing one on Broadway, so investors risk smaller amounts. The potential earnings from ticket sales are also lower, however, so the amount of money to be earned is smaller for investors and artists alike. A common practice today is to open a play Off Broadway and, if it is a success, to move it to Broadway, where more money can be earned. The hit musical *Rent* is a good example of this (Color Plate 27).

Like the term "Broadway," the term "Off Broadway" has several meanings, the first of which is geographic. It refers to theatres that are not located in midtown Manhattan. Most Off Broadway theatres are either in Greenwich Village, the section of lower Manhattan below 14th Street that has been the home of artists and writers since the early 1900s, or in the Upper West Side, the region west of Central Park and north of 59th Street where many artists and professionals reside today (Figure 16.2).

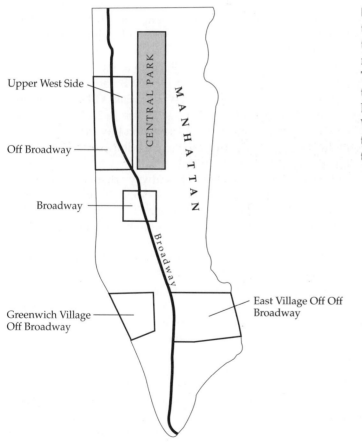

Figure 16.2   Manhattan Island is the center of New York City, and the thoroughfare of Broadway runs diagonally through the length of the island. This illustration shows the Broadway theatre district in midtown, the Off Broadway theatre districts on the Upper West Side and in Greenwich Village, and the Off Off Broadway theatre district in the East Village.

Off Broadway is also the name for a specific kind of union contract. The minimum salaries for an Off Broadway contract, though established by the same unions, are lower than those for a first class production on Broadway.

From your point of view as a member of the audience, Off Broadway describes a kind of theatrical experience that is substantive and controversial and that appeals to an intellectually inclined audience. Today, commercial productions of serious plays are more frequently found Off Broadway, while lighthearted musicals are more frequently seen on Broadway. The prestigious Pulitzer Prize for drama has been awarded to Off Broadway hits like *Angels in America* (later an HBO movie starring Al Pacino) and *Dinner with Friends* (later an HBO movie starring Dennis Quaid).

Off Off Broadway   By the 1960s, with Off Broadway well established, a few courageous and adventuresome theatre artists who wanted to do even more challenging and avant-garde work than could be commercially successful Off Broadway started producing their work in even smaller venues, charging even lower prices for tickets, and presenting work that appealed to an even smaller audience. **Off Off Broadway** became the "in place" for experimental theatre. Many of today's important theatre artists began their careers Off Off Broadway: playwrights like John Guare, Sam Shepard, and Terrence McNally (who wrote the book for the musicals *The Full Monte* and *Ragtime*); and actors like Al Pacino and James Earl Jones.

The description "Off Off Broadway" soon came to have its own set of meanings. Like Broadway and Off Broadway, Off Off Broadway began as a geographic description. The movement started in the East Village, the hippy haven of the Lower East Side of Manhattan (see Figure 16.2), but very soon Off Off Broadway productions were being presented in tiny theatres all over Manhattan. Off Off Broadway also has come to describe a kind of contract, though most early productions were so modest that there were no union contracts involved (indeed, many early Off Off Broadway artists worked for no pay). Most important, Off Off Broadway became synonymous with experimentation. Some productions, like Richard Schechner's Environmental Theatre production of *Dionysus in 69*, experimented with theatrical styles. Others confronted society's taboos and tried to make audiences think and feel and *change*; sexual taboos were central to this kind of theatrical fare, which began in the 1960s when the contraceptive pill first came into wide use and the "sexual revolution" began. Off Off Broadway plays like *Hair* and Terrence McNally's *Sweet Eros* celebrated sexual liberation and had performers acting in the nude (Figure 16.3). Political taboos were equally confronted, with plays like *Viet Rock* and *In White America* exposing the hypocrisy in American governmental policies.

Today, Off Off Broadway is so well established that its productions are included in the Theatre Listings in the *Sunday New York Times*, but it remains the arena for presenting plays that challenge audiences' political, religious, social, and stylistic expectations. Some innovative productions are so successful that they transfer to Off Broadway, like Moises Kaufman's *The Laramie*

Figure 16.3 *Hair,* the antiwar musical, was the first show on a Broadway stage in which actors were totally nude in a scene. There's no nudity in the movie version. This photo of the musical number "Black Boys/White Boys" is from the 1968 Broadway premiere.

Project (more recently seen as an HBO movie). Some transfer all the way to Broadway, like the musical *Urinetown* (Color Plate 28), which began in a tiny Off Off Broadway theatre, transferred to Off Broadway, and then moved to Broadway, where it won three Tony Awards. At the time we're writing this, *Urinetown* is in its third year on Broadway and has a touring production playing in almost every large American city.

The future of Off Off Broadway seems bright. Within the past two years, no fewer than nine new theatres have opened in Manhattan. Many are in the area immediately west of the Broadway theatre district, and most of them are Off Off Broadway venues seating audiences of fewer than 199. Despite the devastating impact on the American economy of the September 11, 2001, attack on New York's World Trade Center, with theatre particularly vulnerable because it depends on tourism for much of its audience, commercial theatre is thriving today—On, Off, and Off Off Broadway.

Touring Productions   While you may not be traveling to New York in the immediate future, some commercial theatre may be traveling to your hometown. Many midsize cities boast a theatre that hosts **touring productions,** plays or musicals that have succeeded commercially in New York and then go on the **road,** as theatre folks call it. The production will be very much the same as it was in New York, although the scenery sometimes has to be simplified to fit into a wide variety of theatres and the cast frequently is different. A touring production travels from city to city, from theatre to theatre. A **first-class tour** travels by plane and stays for three or four weeks in larger cities like San Francisco, St. Louis, and Philadelphia. First-class tour artists are handsomely paid. A **bus-and-truck tour** travels by bus (with the scenery loaded in a truck) and frequently plays split weeks or one-night stands. Artists traveling in a bus-and-truck tour receive much smaller salaries. The quality of a touring production of a Broadway hit in your city may depend on the kind of tour your city attracts, and the performance might be significantly less impressive than what you would have seen in New York.

People buy tickets to these commercial touring productions for one or more of four reasons. First, it's too expensive for most of us to hop off to New York to see theatre. Second, some people love theatre and hope for the opportunity to experience excellence in their own hometown. Third, some people may be familiar with a particular show's reputation and are eager to see this newest hit from New York. Fourth, people want to see the stars. Indeed, to help ensure the success of a commercial tour, producers often will cast a star whose name will help sell tickets even if that star is not particularly right for the role. Because many stars from the New York stage are unknown to the audiences across America, producers hire television celebrities. Sometimes the stars of a touring production are fine actors, and sometimes they are not. Because the production will play only a short engagement in each town and will sell almost all its tickets before the local critics and audiences have formed a judgment about it, the star's name is a major marketing tool in this business venture.

Cruises, Casinos, and Theme Parks   Commercial theatre is produced on cruise ships, in casinos, and on theme park stages. Most of these productions are musical revues, not dramas with a plot, but these spectacles give many audiences their first exposure to professional theatre and also give many talented young singers, dancers, and comedians their first professional job.

Whether you pay to attend these shows as a part of the cost of your cruise or your admission to the amusement park or you buy a ticket for the performance, you are experiencing commercial theatre. The shows, though not often considered "great art," can be quite entertaining. Because the artists are paid and the producers intend to make a profit, they are commercial theatre.

THEATRE AS A NOT-FOR-PROFIT CULTURAL SERVICE

The notion that theatre is something other than a profit-making business—that theatre should make an important contribution to the quality of our life—is an idea that is resisted by many Americans, although it is enthusiastically embraced by the citizens of most industrialized nations, from France, Germany, and Russia to Japan, where their leading actors are officially designated as "national treasures" by the government. Happily for those of us who want more from theatre than light entertainment, the concept of theatre as an important cultural resource began to gain acceptance in America during the second half of the twentieth century. With this acceptance, alternative ways of producing theatre developed.

Many theatres in America are described as **not-for-profit.** Not-for-profit professional theatre is different from the commercial offerings of Broadway in more than just the way it does business. In its June 2, 2003, issue, *Time* described America's regional theatres as "Bigger than Broadway!" LORT theatres frequently produce plays with larger casts than commercial producers can afford and regularly produce new plays that challenge the audience's values and expectations. *Time* argued that the boldest theatre in America is produced in our hometowns more often than it is on Broadway—unproven new American plays, unfamiliar classics, plays that confront audiences with unfamiliar styles and conventions. An example is *Macbeth* done as if it were a Japanese **Kabuki** (ka-BOO-kee) performance (Color Plate 29).

In the 1950s, about the time Off Broadway theatre was getting started, some theatre artists determined to create theatre anywhere but in New York. These artists didn't like the economic pressures that dictated the kinds of plays they could do in the commercial arena, and they didn't like living in New York—so they started theatres in their hometowns. But they also didn't want to do amateur theatre, with all the qualitative limitations the phrase implies. They wanted to do the great plays from the history of world drama, and they wanted to do them with fine professional artists. These intrepid pioneers wanted to rescue theatre from the clutches of commercialism and restore it to its proper function—enriching people's lives. They decided to found permanent theatre companies. These theatres, called **regional theatres, repertory theatres,** or **resident theatres,** have become a major part of America's cultural landscape.

EXPOSITION
• • • • • • • • • • •

In the 1960s, resident theatres organized themselves as the **League of Resident Theatres,** known by the acronym **LORT.** By the 1980s, America had more than 80 LORT companies. Today, more than 250 LORT companies present professional theatre across America.

• •

The Alley Theatre in Houston and the Arena Stage in Washington, D.C., were two of the earliest professional theatre companies outside New York. In a few short years, similar theatres were founded in many cities. Most of these theatres imitated the only model their founders knew—Broadway—and so they were commercial ventures. Rather quickly, their founders discovered that it was almost impossible to make a profit from a resident theatre; most were losing money. About as quickly, they became aware of the many not-for-profit institutions in America—schools, churches, and hospitals. Because these institutions provide people with services that our society believes are valuable, they qualify as not-for-profit businesses. When the Internal Revenue Service designates them as qualifying for **501(c)3** status, these businesses cannot distribute profits to their stockholders the way profits from a commercial production may enrich an angel, do not have to pay taxes, and can accept charitable contributions. Because these theatres weren't making a profit anyway, it was easy for them to seek not-for-profit tax status.

501(C)3 is the Internal Revenue Service's designation for a business that may not disburse profits to its investors, that does not have to pay taxes, and that may accept charitable contributions.

A not-for-profit corporation is governed by a board of trustees, made up of citizens who volunteer their time and expertise to provide guidance to the executive who actually runs the institution—the university president, the hospital administrator, the theatre's artistic director. The trustees hold the institution "in trust" for the citizens of the community and are responsible for its finances and its basic policies.

How much money does it take to operate a not-for-profit theatre? Where does the money come from? Not-for-profit theatres vary widely in size and budget. Small ones like the New Harmony Theatre in Indiana operate on less than $500,000 a year. Large ones like the Guthrie Theatre in Minneapolis have annual operating budgets in excess of $7 million. The trustees work with the theatre's managerial staff to create a realistic budget, estimating how much will be spent and how to bring in an equal amount so that at the end of the season the theatre's costs and income balance.

The theatre's expenditures are projected by the staff, based on their experience of the true costs of producing the season's plays. The theatre's projected income is divided into two categories: earned income and contributed income. Earned income describes all the money that the theatre gets from the sale of tickets (subscriptions, single tickets, and group sales) and from incidental sources like concessions sales and costume rentals. A rule of thumb is that a theatre must earn about 65 percent of its expenditures and must attract the remaining 35 percent in charitable contributions. If a theatre has a budget of $3 million, approximately $1,950,000 must be earned income and $1,050,000 contributed income. Each theatre's success in attracting contributions is different, but two very important questions are what happens if the total of earned and contributed income exceeds the amount expended and what happens if the total falls short of the amount expended.

The first question is easier to answer. Because a not-for-profit business is prohibited by federal law from distributing its profits to the trustees, any surplus is either kept in reserve against the shortfall that is likely to occur in some future year or used to purchase needed equipment for the theatre—anything from a new roof to a new computer lighting board.

What happens when the annual report shows that the theatre has lost money? The trustees can experience everything from grumbling to panic. In a best-case scenario, the institution makes up the shortfall through an earlier year's surplus, through an endowment, or—out of desperation—through gifts from rich trustees or their friends. The normal scenario is that a theatre borrows money from a bank, adds the payments on that loan to next year's expenditure budget, and struggles forward. The worst-case scenario is that the theatre's loan increases over several years until the accumulated debt becomes impossible to repay. At that point, the trustees may decide that the not-for-profit corporation must go out of business and the theatre's doors must close. A theatre's closure is a sad day for the citizens of that city, but it does happen.

ASIDE   A theatre's crisis doesn't always come at the end of the season. Tom once served as artistic director for a Shakespeare festival in Maine, and every Wednesday evening the trustees gathered to add up how much contributed income had been donated that week. They had to decide if we could meet the payroll the following day, or if we had to close. The theatre didn't close, but it is hard to go about your business calmly when you fear the coming week will be your last.

Sources of Contributed Income

To keep their doors open, the staff and trustees of not-for-profit theatres seek to attract contributions. A not-for-profit theatre has four sources of contributed income, described next.

⬤ FORESHADOWING

Theatre's Four Sources of Contributed Income

1. Foundations
2. Corporations
3. Individuals
4. Government grants

Foundations   You've probably heard of the Ford Foundation or the Rockefeller Foundation, but you might not know about thousands of smaller **foundations** that annually make gifts to worthy causes. Some of these smaller foundations support not-for-profit theatres. A foundation is a financial entity that has been created to protect accumulations of wealth from heavy taxation. The foundation's money is used for charitable ends—to support education, medical research, or the arts. A foundation gives away money for purposes that our society views as worthy.

Corporations   Businesses give money to various deserving causes, and some contribute to not-for-profit theatres. A profit-making **corporation** has several good reasons to give away money instead of disbursing it to the stockholders. For one thing, charitable contributions are in a company's best business interest. To succeed, corporations must have high-caliber persons running them, and corporations recruit nationally for personnel at the managerial and executive levels. One inducement corporations offer is the quality of life in their city. Corporate executives, like other educated and cultured people, want to live in areas with good golf courses, quality schools for their children, and professional theatre companies.

Corporations also give money to theatres as a form of advertising. When you read that a theatre's production is "sponsored" or "coproduced" by a corporation, you are reading an ad. The corporation has given money to the not-for-profit theatre in exchange for promoting its name to people who might buy its product.

Individuals   Wealthy people can write a check for $50,000 without blinking, but the rest of us can support theatres in smaller ways. **Individual donors** are the largest group of contributors to not-for-profit theatres. Why? Because we are a nation of philanthropists. Part of the American ethos is that we give our time and money to help those who are less fortunate. Through our churches, through service organizations such as the Red Cross, and as alumni of colleges, we help support our society with gifts of money and time.

You will be asked at some point to contribute to the arts. You might receive a phone call from a dance company asking for a donation, or when you purchase a season ticket to your local LORT theatre you may be encouraged to round your check up to a higher amount and so make a contribution.

Government Grants   In America today, theatres (and other charitable institutions) may receive **government grants** from their city, state, and federal governments. Many people argue over whether theatres should be supported with tax dollars, but those of us who work in the theatre believe not-for-profit corporations that provide a basic service to the community should be supported. The question is, How do we define basic services? Where, if at all, should not-for-profit theatres fall within the list of basic services?

Some large cities award grants to not-for-profit arts organizations as a way of encouraging a tourist attraction that brings lots of tourist dollars into the local economy. State governments frequently have arts councils that make grants to artists and arts institutions. But the federal government's **National Endowment for the Arts (NEA)** is the most prominent of all government arts agencies. This federal agency was created in 1965 to disburse federal tax revenues to artists and arts organizations.

EXPOSITION
• • • • • • • • • • • •

The law creating the NEA was signed by President Lyndon B. Johnson. At the signing ceremony he said, "Art is a nation's most precious heritage, for it is in our works of art that we reveal to ourselves, and to others, the inner vision which guides us as a nation."

• •

Government grants for the arts total a surprisingly small amount of money. Our federal government's per capita spending for the arts is less than that of Germany, England, Canada, or France. More of our federal tax dollars are spent each year to support the musicians in military bands than to support all the artists and arts institutions in America. In 1991 the U.S. government disbursed only 67¢ per American to support the arts, and in 1996 that sum was cut nearly in half. Today, you pay more for a candy bar than the government disburses per person for the arts.

Though our government does not support our theatres with much hard cash, the American people have undergone a change in attitude over the past half-century. We are learning to demand theatre as a vital element of society that can be more than entertainment, more than a profit-making business. We are starting to believe what people have known since the first prehistoric hunters gathered—that theatre is good for the life of the community. America's not-for-profit theatres nurture artists, develop the voices of new playwrights, and serve us all by keeping alive the insights of the great artists of the past.

THEATRE AS AN AMATEUR ACTIVITY

Amateurs are people who do something because they love it. The word comes from the Latin word "amare," meaning "to love." There are amateur athletes in your parks, amateur singers in your choirs, and actors performing in **amateur theatre** all across America.

Community theatre is the term for amateur theatre sponsored by local organizations and performed by volunteers who do it for love, not money. Churches, service clubs, and civic organizations are the major producers of community theatre, and you have probably attended one of their performances at some time in your life. These plays are done for the friends and neighbors of the people putting them on and most frequently are entertaining and proven favorites that affirm the values of the audience. Community theatre produces the same feeling of goodwill between audience and performers that is produced between the cheering fans and the neighborhood softball team. Everyone knows that the pros play better, just as everyone knows that the Cleveland Symphony plays better than the Friends of St. Michael's Church, but the personal relationship between the audience and the players engenders an excitement that makes it every bit as much fun to go to the amateur performance as it is to go to the softball game. You may even find that you'd rather go to community theatre than any other kind.

The cost of producing amateur theatre is very modest, because no one is being paid. A few hundred dollars usually will cover the royalties to the playwright, the advertising, and the costs for building the scenery and costumes. These costs are commonly paid by the sponsoring organization. If a modest admission is charged, that money goes back to the school, the church, or the service club. Amateur theatre is an activity, not a business.

THEATRE AS AN EDUCATIONAL EXPERIENCE

Many Americans' first experience of live theatre is at a school. Most colleges and universities, many high schools, and even some primary and middle schools have auditoriums and present plays. **Educational theatre** is used to describe plays presented in schools, and educational theatre's primary reason for existence is to provide training to students who wish to study theatre as an academic discipline. Just as students of chemistry need a laboratory in which to concoct evil-smelling potions while they are studying to become researchers in pharmaceutical firms, so students of theatre need a laboratory in which to botch the classics while they are learning to become professional actors. In many countries this training is offered exclusively by vocational schools. In America, students also have the option of going to universities where people of varying levels of skill and commitment learn the fundamentals of acting, designing, directing, and playwriting (Figure 16.4).

Other students study theatre as an intellectual discipline in much the same way you might study economics or history. These students study the ideas of the great playwrights, the political function of theatre in a society, and the history of culture as it has been reflected in written drama and live performance. To serve these students, colleges and universities put on plays. Just as music students must hear music to learn about music, so theatre students must experience theatre to learn about theatre. Theatre as an intellectual pursuit is a second reason why schools do plays.

There's a third reason. Many American cities are too small to support a professional not-for-profit theatre or a commercial touring production, so colleges serve the population by producing theatre. People in Hattiesburg, Mississippi, or Normal, Illinois, want the enriching experience of theatre, and their local college is best equipped to provide it for them. Indeed, hundreds of thousands of Americans' primary experience of live theatre is plays presented by the theatre students at their local college.

The audiences for these plays—whether drawn from the student body or from a city's intellectual community—seek enrichment more than diversion, so it is not surprising that a typical season will include plays rarely produced in a commercial or not-for-profit theatre. Instead, educational theatre provides you with a chance to see the classics from earlier ages and the experimental plays of today (Figure 16.5).

Because educational theatre's two principal reasons for existence are to provide students with a laboratory in which they can learn their craft and to offer a forum in which other students can study the dramatic literature this entire field of academic study is founded on, educational theatre is—or at least should be—supported by the college or university. The work students do in educational theatre should not be self-supporting any more than is the work engineering students do in a computer lab or the work law students do in a moot court. Unhappily, the administrations of most American colleges and universities fail to provide appropriate financial support for the academic discipline of theatre. Too often, educational theatre is as box-office driven as

Figure 16.4   A student develops her acting skills playing the role of Amanda in Florida State University's production of *The Glass Menagerie*.

Figure 16.5   High school students at Salt Lake City's Waterford School perform *Ivona, Princess of Burgundia* by avant-garde Polish playwright Witold Gombrowicz, directed by Roger Benington and designed by Rodney Cuellar.

commercial theatre and must plan its repertoire with a keen sense of what will appeal to the ticket-buying public. Much educational theatre has to be self-supporting because of the fundamental dichotomy in American thinking that separates serious work from frivolous play and judges theatre to be worthy only when it is profitable. The overwhelming proportion of college and university administrators, the very people who ought to understand that educational theatre is education and not commerce, share with the general American public a confusion about the nature, purpose, function, and potential benefit of theatre.

THEATRE AS FESTIVAL AND OUTDOOR DRAMA

A **festival theatre** can be a commercial venture, a not-for-profit cultural service, an amateur event, or an educational experience. It is defined not by how it does business but by the kind of theatre it presents. Festivals produce plays that celebrate a particular kind of drama or represent a particular author. Some festivals focus on American drama, others on comedy, musical theatre, or previously unproduced plays. The festivals that focus on the works of a single playwright include the many Shakespeare festivals that people flock to in summer.

EXPOSITION
• • • • • • • • • • • •

Among the oldest of America's festival theatres is the Oregon Shakespeare Festival, now one of the largest theatre companies in America. It maintains more than three hundred employees while producing ten or more plays annually in three theatres for an audience that exceeds a hundred thousand. The Oregon Shakespeare Festival is a multimillion-dollar not-for-profit business that has replaced logging as the major industry in the region. It has spawned dozens of imitators; the most successful include the Shakespeare festivals in San Diego, California, and Montgomery, Alabama.

• •

A festival theatre is also distinguished by its audience. Although most other theatre audiences are made up of people who live nearby, festival theatre audiences are made up of enthusiastic and dedicated travelers unconcerned with the social importance of being seen at the theatre or of seeing the latest Broadway hit. Rather, these theatregoers come to view the festival theatre's specialty. They frequently plan their summer holiday around a visit to an out-of-the-way place like Stratford, Canada, or Cedar City, Utah (Figure 16.6). As a result, festival audiences are enthusiastic. They are knowledgeable but are not unduly critical or demanding. These people are there to have a rewarding time, and they encourage the actors to perform their best with their enthusiastic laughter and applause.

Outdoor dramas are a wonderfully American phenomenon seldom encountered elsewhere in the world. You may have had a wonderful experience

Figure 16.6 You can see the festive atmosphere here as Revels Company performers Jason (left) and Erick Shelly entertain patrons in the Utah Shakespearean Festival's 1999 production of *The Greenshow.* Singers, dancers, magicians, and puppeteers perform preshow events on the Festival's grounds.

at one. Many Shakespeare festivals are performed in open-air theatres, but outdoor dramas based on historical events or religious stories are also performed each summer in open-air theatres all across the country. Outdoor dramas include *The Lost Colony* in North Carolina, which dramatizes the lives of the first English settlers in North America, and *The Hill Cumorah Pageant* in Palmyra, New York (Figure 16.7). Tens of thousands of Americans enjoy outdoor drama each year, and these performances are a vital part of the total picture of American theatre.

ASIDE   Many local residents volunteer to perform in *The Lost Colony.* TV star Andy Griffith got his start playing Sir Francis Drake in the pageant. A few years ago, a blond teenager was assigned to play a Native American, and the director told him to dye his hair black, shave it off, or "do something." The boy found an old wig his mother had worn when she played a Native American woman years earlier. In a performance, he drew back his bow to shoot an arrow, but the string caught his wig and sent it flying toward the middle of the stage. As he crept out on the stage to retrieve it, his embarrassment helped him decide to become a lawyer instead of an actor.

Figure 16.7 *The Hill Cumorah Pageant* in Palmyra, New York, is an outdoor religious pageant that provides both theatrical and spiritual experiences for an audience of eight thousand. More than five hundred performers are onstage. For a rich description of this theatrical experience, see pages 63–66 in Jon Krakauer's best-selling book *Under the Banner of Heaven.* (New York: Doubleday, 2003.)

EXERCISES

1. Using the Internet to do your research, prepare and give the class a 10-minute presentation describing an *organization* that serves one of these:
   a. LORT theatres
   b. Shakespeare festivals
   c. Educational theatres
   d. Community theatres
   e. Outdoor religious and historical dramas

2. Students should form into groups of five and have one person in each group research a different kind of theatre in their community: commercial, not-for-profit professional, community, educational, or festival or outdoor theatre. At the next class meeting:
   a. Each group makes a presentation of its research.
   b. All the students who researched a particular kind of theatre gather to discuss the differences among the theatres of that kind they researched.

3. Tabulate the number of students in the class who have attended each of the five kinds of theatre during the past year: commercial, not-for-profit professional, community, educational, and festival or outdoor theatre. Have the class discuss *why* the largest number of students attended the most frequently attended kind of theatre and *why* the smallest number attended the least frequently attended kind.

17

Musical Theatre

Millions of people love American musical theatre. They love the romantic stories, the astonishing dancing, the gorgeous voices, the dazzling costumes, the spectacular scenery, and, above all, the way the music lifts their emotions—musical theatre makes them feel terrific. Musical theatre is synonymous with the best of American theatre. The ancient Greeks gave us tragedy, the Elizabethan English gave us Shakespeare's verse dramas, the French gave us some wildly funny farces, and we Americans have developed musical theatre to a level where audiences around the world celebrate it.

HOW DID MUSICAL THEATRE EVOLVE?

● FORESHADOWING

The Development of Musical Theatre

1. Prehistory and ancient Greek drama
2. Opera
3. Operetta
4. Ballad opera
5. Musical comedy
6. The musical

Prehistory and Ancient Greek Drama

Musical theatre is older than recorded history. Early storytellers may have sung or chanted parts of their performances, and their friends probably beat on drums to add to the excitement. Archaeologists recently discovered flutes in China more than ten thousand years old carved from animal bones. These instruments may have accompanied stories told around a campfire. Though we have no written records to prove it, it is highly likely that music has been part of theatre from its beginning.

Many paintings and sculptures illustrate how ancient Greek dramas were sung and chanted. They suggest that the chorus danced to the accompaniment of a musician who used percussion and wind instruments to maintain the rhythm and underscore the mood with melody. Music contributed significantly to the total effect of ancient Greek drama.

Opera

Opera was invented in the Renaissance. When the theatre artists of fifteenth-century Florence rediscovered the ancient Greek plays, they weren't sure how to produce them. Singing and dancing obviously had been part of the performance, but in the absence of written notation, nobody knew what the ancient music sounded like or what the dance looked like. So the Italian artists invented a new form of theatre in which the entire performance was set to music. These operas (the word means "works") were entirely sung, from beginning to end, and the music was considered far more important than the lyrics. Opera lovers go to listen to the music, and if they can't understand the language in which the performers are singing, they often don't mind. Their attention is on the music.

From the beginning, opera was an elaborate and impressive kind of musical theatre. The diary of an English diplomat who attended an opera in Venice in 1645 is amazingly similar to what we might write if we went to see a musical like *The Phantom of the Opera.* He wrote that the performance was accompanied by excellent musicians and singers, the scenery was beautifully painted, and there were machines that flew the actors through the air. He felt that it was one of the most magnificent and expensive entertainments the wit of humans could invent.

Opera has some obvious traits that will help you distinguish it from other forms of musical theatre. The music is very complex, and only the best-trained singers and musicians can perform it. The stories of operas usually are set in a distant time and place and frequently are based on ancient Greek or German myths. Further, the stories of operas are almost always tragic. The main characters often die, and the operas invoke deep sadness in the audience.

Operetta

As a balance to the sad stories and complex music of opera, composers and writers collaborated to create a kind of lighthearted musical theatre called **"operetta"** (the word means "little opera"). Operetta is sometimes described as "comic opera" because the plots include comic characters who make the audience laugh with their witty lyrics and antic behavior and because the stories end happily. Operettas appeal to a less intense audience than does opera because the music is not quite so complicated and because more attention is paid to the lyrics. The words in an operetta are easier to understand, partly because it's standard practice to translate them into the audience's language and partly because some of the words are spoken, not sung. Most operettas contain brief sequences of spoken dialogue.

Music of Ancient Greece, *a CD made by* Christodoulos Halaris, *reconstructs the music accompanying the ancient Greek dramas.*

Figure 17.1 Kevin Kline, Angela Lansbury, and Linda Ronstadt starred in a Broadway revival of Gilbert and Sullivan's *The Pirates of Penzance.* Typical of operettas, the action is set in a bygone time and in an exotic locale, and each dashing and handsome pirate finds true love with a beautiful maiden in a pretty dress.

Operettas became popular in the nineteenth century with compositions by Offenbach, Strauss, and the English team of Gilbert and Sullivan, whose works include *The Mikado, HMS Pinafore,* and *The Pirates of Penzance* (Figure 17.1). Americans wrote operettas as well. John Philip Sousa, best known as a composer of military marches, composed "El Capitan March" for his operetta about the Spanish-American War. Today's musical theatre evolved more from the operetta than from opera, but its heritage includes both.

ASIDE   The melody for "The Marine Corps Hymn" comes from a comic French operetta by Jacques Offenbach. When Marines sing "From the halls of Montezuma to the shores of Tripoli," do you think many of them know they're singing a song from a stage comedy that featured pretty girls in frilly costumes?

Some recognizable traits of operettas distinguish them from other kinds of musical theatre. To begin with, the music is lush and Romantic and frequently is in ¾ waltz time. Because an operetta's music is not as complex as the music for an opera, the demands on the singers and musicians are not as great—and the audience can more readily remember the emotionally pleasing tunes. Though you may not know where they come from, you probably know several melodies from operettas, like the energetic music for the French cancan. Also, the stories of operettas are usually set in exotic and Romantic locales—far away places with strange sounding names—and the plots are usually love stories that end happily ever after. Probably the most obvious trait is that operettas include jokes and comic characters.

Ballad Opera

During the centuries when opera and operetta developed in Europe and were imitated in America, a separate form of musical theatre became popular in England. This English form also came to America and helped shape the kind of musical theatre we know today. In both opera and operetta, music is the most important element, and the words take a back seat. By way of contrast, the most important element of English musical theatre was the words, with music only a secondary embellishment. Quite simply, the English wrote comic plays, inserted some songs into them, and called them **ballad operas.**

The songs in a ballad opera were entertaining interludes more than integral parts of the story, and frequently the songs were not composed specially for the occasion. Instead, the authors took well-known popular songs and wrote new lyrics for them, which made the ballad operas audience-friendly because people already knew the melodies. But this practice did not provide an opportunity for music to help tell the story or to make a major contribution to the ballad opera's emotional impact.

The best-known ballad opera, written in 1728 by John Gay, is *The Beggar's Opera.* It is about a dashingly attractive highwayman named Macheath who lives among petty thieves and prostitutes in contemporary London. The provocative setting introduced scandalous characters and made the show titillating and shocking. Sex and violence proved to be big box office attractions, and *The Beggar's Opera* ran for one hundred consecutive performances—a feat that had never before been achieved. In eighteenth-century London, theatres normally presented a different play each night, rotating some dozen or more plays so that audiences would return to buy tickets for the different productions. *The Beggar's Opera* introduced the idea of the long run that today finds musicals like *Beauty and the Beast* running for more than ten years.

Ballad operas like *The Beggar's Opera* toured America starting in 1735. The ballad opera form of a spoken play with songs interspersed through it took strong root and joined with the Romantic tradition of operetta to help shape the indigenous American musical theatre.

The words in musical theatre are commonly called the "libretto," the Italian word for "book." The word comes from the same stem as "library," and it is used to mean all the words in a script, including the song lyrics and the spoken dialogue.

The producer of John Gay's The Beggar's Opera *was named John Rich. The commercial success of the show led a wit to remark that* The Beggar's Opera *"made Gay rich and Rich gay."*

Musical Comedy

Theatre historians describe the 1866 production of *The Black Crook* as the first example of American **musical comedy.** *The Black Crook* was a corny melodrama that the producers feared would be a flop if it was presented straight, so they took a big risk and hired a French ballet troupe to appear in the show. Without much concern for their relevance to the plot, the producers inserted songs and dances and turned the dull melodrama into an exciting spectacle that ran for 475 consecutive performances. *The Black Crook,* without anyone thinking about it in advance, introduced two factors that altered the ballad opera and moved it in the direction of what we now call musical comedy. The first factor was dance. In addition to the songs that the actors sang, *The Black Crook* introduced a chorus of dancing girls. Before too many more years went by, a male chorus was added to the evolving form of the musical comedy. An obvious characteristic of musical comedies today is a large singing and dancing chorus. The second factor, and the biggest attraction of *The Black Crook,* was the appearance of those dancing girls in flesh-colored tights. While we might not be titillated by that spectacle today, in 1866 it was pretty daring. Sex appeal has remained a major trait of American musical theatre ever since.

American musical comedy came into its own in the twentieth century. Writers, blending the lighthearted and Romantic spirit of European operetta with the form borrowed from English ballad opera, invented the **book musical.** A book musical is a play with a plot and characters that tells part of its story through songs and dances. What distinguished musical comedy from its predecessors was that the authors, instead of inserting songs and dances into an existing play, collaborated with the composers from the beginning so that the songs belonged in the play and added to its emotional arc as they helped tell the story and develop the characters. In operettas music was the most important element, and the ballad opera's script was its most important element. The men who wrote the book musicals, on the other hand, believed that the story and the music were equally important and that the two could

Never Gonna Dance is the title of a musical based on Jerome Kern's well-loved songs that opened on Broadway in 2003.

work together to enrich the audience's experience. The best of the early book musicals were by composer Jerome Kern and playwrights Guy Boulton and P. G. Wodehouse, often called "the fathers of American musical comedy." Their hit musical comedies *Very Good, Eddie; Leave It to Jane;* and *The Band Wagon* are sometimes revived today (Figure 17.2).

ASIDE   Watch the 1946 bio-pic about Jerome Kern, *Till the Clouds Roll By.* It may not be accurate biography, but it is a wonderful anthology of Kern's great hits. It stars Judy Garland, Van Heflin, Lena Horne, and (in a surprise appearance) Frank Sinatra.

Several traits of musical comedy distinguish it from operetta and ballad opera. To begin with, the settings and characters are American. Whether the works are set on a college campus *(Good News)* or in the wild West *(Girl Crazy),* they are filled with recognizable American characters and take place in our familiar world. An even clearer indicator of musical comedy is that the songs are American popular music. They use the 32-bar structure, and they're in $\frac{2}{4}$ rhythm more often than in the $\frac{3}{4}$ waltz rhythm of European operettas. The songs sometimes embrace the "ragged" syncopation that came to be called **ragtime,** and there's a pretty good chance you'll recognize one or more of the old standards and say, "So that's where that song came from." The naive and slightly corny boy-meets-girl plots always end happily ever after—another trait of musical comedy. Yet another is that the secondary plot is about broadly comic characters whose jokes and comic routines enliven the show.

Figure 17.2   In 2003, *Never Gonna Dance* brought back to Broadway the songs of Jerome Kern and the elegant style of dancing introduced by Fred Astaire in the 1931 Broadway musical *The Band Wagon,* shown here. Astaire starred in a movie version of *The Band Wagon* in 1953.

The surest sign of all that you're seeing a musical comedy is that the songs and dances seem to belong in the play. They may not do a lot to help tell the story, but there will be a justification for why they're in the show—they aren't just shoved in or tacked on.

American musical theatre took an important first step toward the kind of show that dominates Broadway today when *Show Boat* opened in 1927 (Color Plate 30). The plot of *Show Boat* is serious even though there is a light-hearted secondary plot, and Jerome Kern's music includes deeply moving songs like "Old Man River" alongside traditionally lighthearted musical comedy numbers like "Life upon the Wicked Stage Ain't Nothing for a Sweet Young Girl." The plot deals with interracial marriage, which was a volatile concern in 1927. Indeed, *Show Boat* remains a classic of American musical comedy. It has been made into several films and has been revived on Broadway frequently.

The team of Richard Rodgers and Lorenz Hart wrote some of the finest musical comedies of the 1930s and paved the way for the maturation of the form into the musical in the 1940s. *Pal Joey* may be their finest show. It starred Gene Kelly and introduced many songs that are now American popular classics, including "If You Asked Me, I Could Write a Book" and "Bewitched, Bothered, and Bewildered" (Figure 17.3).

Figure 17.3   Gene Kelly sang and danced the title role in Rodgers and Hart's *Pal Joey.* The show has had several Broadway revivals and was made into a film starring Frank Sinatra.

The Musical

It's impossible to say when the word "comedy" fell from common use and the musical comedy matured into the **musical,** but theatre historians usually cite Rodgers and Hammerstein's *Oklahoma!*, which opened in 1943, as the first modern musical. Both descriptive terms are used today, but there does seem to be a difference between these two kinds of musical theatre.

The major advances introduced by *Oklahoma!* include the psychological complexity of the characters and the integration of dance into both character development and storytelling. A dream ballet in the middle of *Oklahoma!* shows the audience the complex psychology of the central characters without dialogue being spoken or lyrics being sung (Figure 17.4). The dance sequence also foreshadows the serious events that happen later in the plot. By replac-

Figure 17.4   Dance became a central part of both character development and storytelling when musical comedy matured and evolved into the musical, as demonstrated in the dream ballet in *Oklahoma!* Broadway's most recent revival of *Oklahoma!* transferred from a successful revival in London, where it starred *X-Men*'s "Wolverine," Hugh Jackman. That version is now available on DVD and video. *X-Men* fans may be delighted to learn that Jackman is an accomplished singer and dancer who starred on Broadway in *The Boy from Oz*.

ing lighthearted tap numbers with the more serious dance form of ballet, *Oklahoma!* contributed to the maturation process of the musical. The introduction of the villainous, sexually repressed character Jud, whose dangerous threat to the happiness of the hero and heroine is overcome when he dies in a knife fight, also lends a serious tone to the musical.

Oklahoma! began what many theatre historians call the "Golden Age of American Musicals." In addition to Rodgers and Hammerstein, teams like Lerner and Loewe or Kander and Ebb were joined by solo composer-lyricists like Frank Loesser in producing a flood of memorable Broadway musicals: *Brigadoon, My Fair Lady, Camelot, Guys and Dolls, Cabaret, Fiddler on the Roof*— the list could go on and on, but it must include Cole Porter's *Kiss Me, Kate* (Figure 17.5).

The two most influential figures in musical theatre of the past three decades are Stephen Sondheim and Andrew Lloyd Webber. Both men are composers, and Sondheim is also his own lyricist. These two men have stretched the boundaries of musical theatre through their choice of subjects, the complexity of their music, and the sophistication of their theatrical vision. Sondheim's *Sweeney Todd* and *Sunday in the Park with George* introduced intellectual density and compositional intricacy to the musical (Figure 17.6). Andrew Lloyd Webber's soaring melodies in *Cats* and *The Phantom of the Opera* reintroduced the lyricism of the Italian opera to the modern musical.

The 2004 movie De-Lovely, *starring Kevin Kline, is a bio-pic about Cole Porter.* Night and Day, *the 1946 film about Porter's life starring Cary Grant, was less candid about Porter's private life, but it includes wonderful musical numbers performed by Mary Martin and Monte Woolley.*

Figure 17.5   Cole Porter's *Kiss Me, Kate,* based on Shakespeare's comedy *The Taming of the Shrew,* is one of America's greatest musicals. The recent revival starring Brian Stokes Mitchell is available on video and DVD.

Before these two artists arrived on the musical scene, a major change occurred in the late 1960s that expanded the nature of the musical. For decades, musicals had provided America with most of its popular songs. Old standards that some of us know today originated on Broadway stages. "Only Make Believe," "Smoke Gets in Your Eyes," and "Long Ago and Far Away" are melodies by Jerome Kern. George Gershwin, Irving Berlin, and Cole Porter contributed the hits "I Got Rhythm," "Alexander's Ragtime Band," and "Anything Goes," among others. But when rock and roll became popular, things changed. Broadway embraced the new 1960s musical idiom with the 1968 hit *Hair.*

The dawning of the Age of Aquarius was the dawning of a new era for musicals. Not only did the beat of the music change, but the idea of the book musical was on the way out. *Hair* had no spoken dialogue, nor did *Jesus Christ Superstar, Cats, Les Miserables,* or *The Phantom of the Opera.* The age of the **sung-through musical** had begun. It's interesting that our modern musicals share this characteristic with the Italian operas from the Renaissance—we seem to have come full circle in our development of the musical!

WHAT IS MUSICAL THEATRE?

Here's our best effort at a definition: musical theatre is a theatrical performance of a play in which all or part of the text is sung and in which visual spectacle joins with music and dance to tell the story and to express the characters' larger-than-life emotions.

The musical components of musical theatre are evident, but what about its visual and emotional components? When you go to a musical, you often

Figure 17.6 Pointillist painter Georges Seurat is the central character in Stephen Sondheim's musical *Sunday in the Park with George*. This photo shows Seurat at work while two rich people look at one of his paintings.

say you're going to see a "show," and that means you're excited by the visual spectacle you're about to enjoy. When the helicopter descends in *Miss Saigon,* when the chandelier falls in *The Phantom of the Opera,* or when the kickline of identical dancers reaches the thrilling finale in *A Chorus Line* (Figure 17.7), the visual spectacle in musical theatre takes on central importance. In just the same way the seventeenth-century English diplomat was excited to see the opera in Venice and the nineteenth-century American audiences thrilled to look at the gorgeous girls in *The Black Crook,* today's audiences want to be dazzled by spectacle in a modern musical. They want moving scenery and fantastical costumes and a light show worthy of a rock concert. Spectacle has become an equal partner with music in shaping a musical, as exemplified by the visually most exciting Broadway show of recent years—*The Lion King* (Color Plate 31).

Together, music and spectacle lead us away from the problems of our day-to-day lives and encourage our escape into an imaginary world in which

Figure 17.7 The cast of *A Chorus Line* performs in unison, and the mirror behind them increases the visual spectacle.

the emotions are large and the rewards rich. A musical's soaring music and sparkling spectacle create a world in which emotions are exalted. As we enter that world for an evening's entertainment, we know that we're going to feel terrific and that we'll have an experience we will remember for a long, long time.

WHY IS MUSICAL THEATRE AN *AMERICAN* ART FORM?

● *FORESHADOWING*

Three Reasons Why Musical Theatre Is a Particularly American Art Form

1. The American spirit
2. The artistic and ethnic melting pot
3. The assembly-line approach to creativity

The American Spirit

From the times of our earliest settlers, the spirit of Americans has been optimistic, exuberant, expansive, and sentimental. The "new world" of North America abandoned the cynical and tradition-bound thinking of Europe and embraced the future-thinking and democratic optimism that has shaped our culture. The wide expanses of our unconquered continent contributed to the development of our national temper, and we have always understood that there was a new place to move, a new life to begin, and a brighter future ahead. In the nineteenth century, Americans embraced the concept of "Manifest Destiny" as our civilization expanded geographically across the continent. We reveled in knowing that the twentieth century was "The American Century," and our economic wealth and military power were unchallenged. As we begin the twenty-first century, we Americans hold onto an exuberant belief that the future will be better. Our children will be richer and will live in nicer homes. New medical discoveries will rid us of disease. The conquest of space will give us new horizons. This optimism also permits us to be sentimental. Because we know in our hearts that everything will work out for the best and that we will all live happily ever after, we are free to concern ourselves with the plight of others who are less fortunate and to forgive those who hurt us.

Musical theatre is a quintessentially American art form because the mirror it holds up reflects the world as we want it to be. We look at the stage and see the world that we believe ought to be true, the world that we believe will come true. The Romantic stories acted out by attractive performers, the elaborate costumes and spectacular scenery, and most of all the heart-lifting lyricism of the music all support our inherent beliefs, and we feel good. Musical theatre is celebratory theatre for a culture that thrives on celebrating our emotions.

The Artistic and Ethnic Melting Pot

American culture has absorbed the contributions of the many peoples who have emigrated to our shores, and the musical and visual arts these peoples brought with them have helped shape American musical theatre into a unique form that no other culture could have developed.

Although America began as a European—in particular, an English—culture, its music quickly expanded beyond the ¾ rhythm of the ballad and the ¾ rhythm of the waltz to embrace the syncopated rhythms from Africa that evolved into ragtime and later into jazz, soul music, rock and roll, and hip hop. A musical like Scott Joplin's *Treemonisha* could only have been created in America. American musicals also embraced the Latin American rhythms of the tango and reggae. A musical like *Once on This Island* (Figure 17.8) also could only have been created in America. The score of a modern musical is likely to use all these musical idioms, all these artistic expressions of the peoples who make up the melting pot of America.

Likewise, America's visual arts, though rooted in a European culture of representational painting and sculpture, quickly expanded beyond landscapes and portraits to explore the wonders of traditional art from Africa and minimalist art from Asia. The visual designs for the Broadway musical *Pacific Overtures* show the influence of Japanese art (Figure 17.9). Today, the designs for a Broadway musical reflect an amalgamation of visions and sounds that could only have developed in America.

The Assembly-Line Approach to Creativity

Our American genius is best exemplified by the efficient system introduced by Henry Ford for the manufacture of automobiles in the early twentieth

Figure 17.8 The musical *Once on This Island* reflects the color and music of one of the many cultures that make America a unique nation. In this production by The Children's Theatre Company in Minneapolis, actress Paris Bennett dances to the rhythms of her Caribbean home.

Listen to the cast recording of A Chorus Line *and discover for yourself the variety of musical idioms in that hit show.*

Figure 17.9 The two-dimensional style of traditional Japanese painting was adopted by the scene designer for Stephen Sondheim's Broadway musical *Pacific Overtures.*

century—the assembly line. We may retain a sentimental admiration for the quality of "old world craftsmanship," in which one artisan makes a unique object, but that is not the American way. Instead, we follow Ford's lead, assembling various parts and pieces into our final product whether that "product" is a new car or a new musical. Just as the parts of an automobile are added to the chassis as it moves along an assembly line, the parts of a musical are added as the show moves through the rehearsal process.

Traditionally, we see artists as solitary workers, as one person creating in front of a blank canvas, a sheet of paper, a block of marble. We think of a composer as sitting at the keyboard waiting for inspiration, then playing the melody, writing down the notation, orchestrating the composition, and finally playing it before an audience. That practice still exists, of course, but not in the creation of a musical. Musicals are assembled by a team. Each person contributes his or her expertise and collaborates with the others to assemble the final product.

FORESHADOWING

The Ten Players on a Musical's Creative Team

1. The producer
2. The book writer

3. The composer
4. The lyricist
5. The director
6. The orchestrator
7. The musical director
8. The choreographer (and the fight choreographer)
9. The designers
10. The stars

The Producer   The producer launches the project and oversees all aspects of the show from beginning to end. He or she (or, more frequently, a group of producers) decides what show is going to be assembled, raises the capital to finance it, and chooses which artists to hire, where the work will be done, and how and when it will be presented to the ticket-buying public. The producer, acting as CEO of the corporation that is hoping to make a profit from the venture, oversees the entire assembly line and makes certain that everything is moving forward wisely and steadily.

The producer's first decision is to choose what is going to be made, that is, what the project will be. Producers may use their own ideas or may accept ideas proposed by someone else, but the assembly line doesn't start until the project is chosen. Only a rare and brilliant musical like *Urinetown* is based on a writer's original idea (see Color Plate 28). More frequently, a musical is based on existing material. For example, *Cats* is based on a collection of poems by T. S. Eliot, *Les Miserables* is based on a novel by Victor Hugo, *Oklahoma!* is based on a play, *Thoroughly Modern Millie* is based on a movie, *Gypsy* is based on an autobiography, *Parade* is based on a real historical event, *Movin' Out* is based on the songs of pop singer Billy Joel, and *Joseph and the Amazing Technicolor Dreamcoat* is based on the Bible (Color Plate 32).

> **ASIDE**   A play or a musical is often called a "property." A property is anything that can be owned or protected by copyright. A house or other piece of real estate is described in law as "real property." A new computer software, like a playwright's script or the book, score, and lyrics of a musical, is described as "intellectual property." An inventor or artistic creator of intellectual property can protect work while it is still in development. The authors and composers of musicals do just that, so they frequently refer to the project they are working on as the "property."

Once the project is decided on, the producer hires the key creative artists: the book writer, the composer, the lyricist, and the director. In the early stages of a musical's assembly, these four work together to plan the show, usually in a long sequence of meetings. Their work may go on for several years. The producer guides this team to agreement on the spirit or tone of the project. Will it be lyrical, like *The Sound of Music,* or cynical, like *Chicago?*

The Book Writer   In collaboration with the other members of the creative team, the **book writer** figures out how the story will be told, establishing the main characters and the plot. In collaboration with the composer and lyricist, the book writer figures out where the songs will be placed to best advance the story and reveal the characters. Later, the book writer writes the scenes of dialogue that help tell the story. (In a sung-through musical, the function of the book writer is absorbed by the lyricist, because there is no book.)

The Composer   In consultation with the director and the book writer, the **composer** determines the musical idiom for each song and then writes the music. You may wonder which gets written first, the words or the music. If both jobs are done by one person, like Stephen Sondheim in writing *Sweeney Todd,* they are written simultaneously. When a team writes the songs, it can work either way. When Richard Rodgers worked with Lorenz Hart on *Pal Joey,* the music came first, but when Rodgers teamed with Oscar Hammerstein on *South Pacific,* the words came first.

The Lyricist   The **lyricist** writes the words for the songs and sometimes also writes the book. When separate artists create each of these parts of a show, they have to make certain that the spoken and sung words both sound like they come from the same character. It is common for a composer and lyricist team to write many musicals together.

　　The assembling of a musical permits and requires trial and error, and as the show moves along the assembly line, the creators often discover that some parts don't fit and should be replaced. Sometimes the creators cut a song from one show and use it in another show years later. On other occasions, they might add a song during rehearsals or out-of-town tryouts. Sondheim's famous song "Send in the Clowns" was written while *A Little Night Music* was being performed in out-of-town tryouts and was inserted into the show before it opened in New York. This notion of the interchangeability of parts truly illustrates the way musicals are assembled.

The Director   The fourth member of the central team of creators is the director. Through the early meetings, the director leads the book writer, composer, and lyricist toward a common vision of what the show will be like when it opens. The director is a guide in these early stages of the work, but the director's work speeds up when the project is further along and the script and songs have been added.

　　In this second phase of planning, the director becomes the most important person. He or she supervises the preparatory work of the secondary team of artists: the orchestrator, the musical director, the choreographer, and the designers. The director works closely with each of these artists to give the show coherence.

Figure 17.10 Roger Miller wrote the words and music for the songs in *Big River,* the musical version of Mark Twain's great American novel *Huckleberry Finn.* Linda designed the costumes for this production at The Pioneer Theatre Company.

The Orchestrator   The composer usually writes the melodies on a piano, but the audience hears the score played by a full orchestra. Because some composers are not trained musicians, the **orchestrator** selects the instruments that will be included in the orchestra and arranges the music, writing out the parts for each instrument. Country singer and composer Roger Miller was dependent on an orchestrator after he wrote the songs for the musical *Big River* (Figure 17.10).

ASIDE   Irving Berlin, who wrote Broadway musicals and hundreds of popular songs including "God Bless America," couldn't read music. He composed in only one key. He bought a "transposer" that fit over his keyboard so that when he hit the notes in the one key he knew, they were played in whatever key he wanted. Berlin was very talented, but he needed an orchestrator to turn his melodies into arrangements that could be played in his shows.

The Musical Director   The **musical director** teaches the music to the performers and to the orchestra and conducts the performances.

The Choreographer   The **choreographer** invents the dances, teaches them to the performers, and is responsible for a sizable amount of the show's total

Figure 17.11 Jerome Robbins, one of America's greatest choreographers, staged the athletic fight for both the stage and film versions of *West Side Story.* This photo is from the original Broadway production.

performance time. Sometimes the director is also the choreographer. If not, the choreographer consults with the director as well as the orchestrator and creates the choreography in a dance studio. The choreographer also consults with the designers to ensure that the space for the dances is appropriate and that the costumes enhance the dances. Later on, the choreographer will put the dancers through their paces. If you have seen the stage or film version of *A Chorus Line,* you have a good idea of what this hard work looks like. Rehearsals are fun to watch but tough on the dancers.

Some shows include elaborate fights, and these are choreographed as carefully as the dances. Think of the switchblade rumble in *West Side Story,* choreographed by Jerome Robbins (Figure 17.11). A fight choreographer has a special place on the assembly line.

The Designers   The scenery, costume, lighting, and sound designers consult with the four central creative artists (composer, lyricist, book writer, and director) and then imagine, draw, and supervise the construction and decoration of the show's scenery, costumes, and lights as well as prepare the show's sound design. The scene designer consults with the director to ensure that the visual look expresses the right tone and permits the director to stage the scenes and the songs and dances. The costume designer makes sure that the costumes express each of the characters correctly, that the colors and textures are harmonious with the scene design, and that the dancers can execute the choreography in those costumes. The lighting designer consults with the director, the choreographer, and the scene and costume designers to determine how to enhance the visual spectacle of the production with lighting.

The sound designer shapes what the audience hears, from the singers' amplified voices to the special effects that create aural illusions on the stage. To do this, the sound designer consults with the director about the desired emotions for each sequence, with the costume designer about placement of microphones, with the scene designer about placement of speakers, and with the musical director about the balance between the orchestra and the singers.

The Stars   Sometimes a musical does not have a **star** performer. **Ensemble musicals** like *A Chorus Line, Cats,* and *Rent* have succeeded without the charismatic central performance of a star like Hugh Jackman or Antonio Bandaras (Color Plate 33). Audiences, however, love star performers. Early in the musical assembly-line process, the producer usually gathers the director, choreographer, composer, and book writer to select the artists who will play the major roles. The producer knows that the popularity of the stars will impact box office sales, and the entire creative team knows that the unique talents of the stars will influence all their preparatory work. Today, we can't think of the musical *The King and I* without thinking of Yul Brynner, but Brynner was not the producer's first choice. Once Brynner had been engaged, however, all the songs, choreography, dialogue, and designs were adjusted to take advantage of his unique talents and charismatic persona.

ASIDE   Never underestimate the box-office power of stars. After Nathan Lane and Matthew Broderick had performed for a year in the hit musical *The Producers,* they moved on to other jobs. Ticket sales fell off, even though well-known actors like Jason Alexander, Martin Short, Henry Goodman, and Louis Stadlen gave wonderful performances. Early in 2004, Lane and Broderick returned to the show for fourteen weeks (earning $100,000 a week each), and ticket sales increased immediately. *The Producers* has the potential to earn $1.3 million a week, so paying $200,000 to the stars is a wise business decision. However, when Lane and Broderick completed their return engagement, ticket sales fell below $900,000 a week. The current stars are giving wonderful performances, but they are paid far less than Lane and Broderick were.

When the performers come on board and rehearsals begin, the assembly line speeds up. For the next six weeks, more and more elements are added to the show. The director guides the actors in the book scenes. The musical director helps the singers and musicians learn the songs. The choreographer's dances are added. At the same time, the scene designs are being finished and installed in the theatre. Then the technical rehearsals and dress rehearsals begin, when all the work of the independent artists—the actors and dancers and musicians, the scenery and costumes and lights, the orchestra and backstage crews—comes together in the final phases of rehearsal. The show gets more complex each day as it races toward opening night. That night, the actors wait backstage, the orchestra plays the overture, and the curtain goes up on another magnificent product of our uniquely American genius. It's "another opening of another show."

EXERCISES

1. Choose available videos or DVDs of a book musical, like *Kiss Me, Kate,* and a sung-through musical, like *Les Miserables.* In class, compare the two, examining what is gained and lost by the deletion of spoken dialogue in a sung-through musical.

2. Research the meaning of the term "the eleven o'clock number," and bring an example from a well-known musical to the class on cassette or CD. After three or four examples have been played, discuss the nature of this kind of song and its importance in the structure of a musical.

3. Pick two musical comedies from the 1920s and compare their musical forms with those in musicals written after 1970.

4. Research the history of the box-office impact of the stars Matthew Broderick and Nathan Lane on the weekly gross income of *The Producers* and compare it to the impact on the gross income of *Hello, Dolly* when original star Carol Channing was replaced by another actor. (*Hint:* Information can be found in books about the history of American musical theatre.)

CURTAIN CALL

● ● ● ● ● ● ● ● ● ●

Aristotle argued that we all seek pleasure and that our greatest pleasure comes from knowledge, from knowing the truth. In this book, Linda and I have tried to provide you with some knowledge about theatre, to share some truths with you, and to entertain you along the way. We hope that your increased knowledge has enriched your appreciation of theatre and that the next time you see a play or musical you will have a wonderful experience. We love the theatre, and we want everyone to love it as much as we do.

At the beginning of an introductory theatre course, students frequently say they're afraid to learn how theatre works because then they won't be able to enjoy it. They fear that their theatre experience will be hurt by paying attention to how the actors prepare their roles, how the theatre is financed, and what kind of dramatic genre and theatrical style they are experiencing.

At the end of an introductory course—and, we hope, after you've read this book—most students discover that they enjoy the theatre *more* than they did previously. They discover that they can enjoy and appreciate theatre at the same time. We hope that's true for you.

501(c)3   A designation by the Internal Revenue Service for not-for-profit businesses, like hospitals, schools, and arts institutions, that provide a public service; a 501(c)3 designation authorizes a business to accept charitable contributions, relieves it of the obligation to pay certain taxes, and prohibits it from distributing profits to investors.

act   A lengthy segment of a play, comprising several scenes.

action   (1) An event that changes the status quo in the plot of a play; (2) something done by a character; (3) what a character does to overcome an obstacle to achieving his objective; a part of the Stanislavsky System of acting.

actor   A person who performs a role in a play or film.

aesthetic distance   A description for the condition in which an audience is close enough to the stage to be emotionally involved in a play yet far enough away to be physically separated from it; the proper "aesthetic distance" gives the audience the most rewarding experience of a performance.

agent   A person who represents an actor by soliciting employment and negotiating contracts in exchange for 10 percent of the actor's salary.

agitprop   An adjective describing political drama; derived from "agitation" and "propaganda."

amateur theatre   Theatre produced and performed by people who are not paid and who do it for the love of doing it.

American seating   Theatre seats that are divided into sections by aisles running perpendicular to the stage.

anchor   To secure something, typically by tying it to the floor of the stage; the term derives from nautical use.

angel   An investor in a commercial theatre production.

apron   The portion of the stage that protrudes closer to the audience than the proscenium arch.

arbor   A cage that stageweights are placed into as part of the counterweight system for lowering scenery from the fly loft to the stage.

arena theatre   A theatre with seats completely surrounding a stage that is circular, oval, square, or rectangular; sometimes referred to as theatre-in-the-round.

artistic director   The administrative head of a not-for-profit theatre company whose responsibilities include selection of the plays to be produced and the directors, designers, and actors.

aside   Lines spoken by a character directly to the audience that the other characters pretend they don't hear.

assistant stage manager   A person who assists the stage manager during rehearsals and performances and has a wide range of responsibilities.

associative logic   A description of how a mind moves from one idea to another through the associations between the two ideas instead of through direct cause and effect.

audience   One or more persons gathered to participate in a performance.

audition   A process by which actors are selected for roles; it involves actors performing short portions of a play or song; the word is derived from "audio" meaning "to hear."

auditorium   The portion of a theatre where the audience sits or stands; derived from "the hearing place" in ancient Roman theatres.

backdrops   Large, two-dimensional painted scenery hung from battens in the flies.

backstage   The stage house space of a theatre that the audience does not see, and any support spaces in which scenery and costumes are constructed and stored.

balcony   Seating on a level above the main-floor orchestra seats.

ballad opera   An eighteenth-century English form of play with songs inserted into it; *The Beggar's Opera* is the best-known example.

batten   A pipe or pole hung in the fly loft of a stage house on which scenery and lighting equipment are hung; one part of the counterweight system.

beat   The smallest segment of an actor's role; a subdivision of a "unit" during which a very simple objective is achieved.

black box theatre   A theatre space that is an empty space painted black and that may be adapted to whatever play is performed in it; it is usually small and used for experimental theatre.

blocking   The patterns of movement of the actors on the stage, developed in rehearsal under the director's supervision.

book musical   A form of musical that tells part of its story through songs and dances; an American contribution to the development of musical theatre.

book writer   The person who writes the dialogue, nonmusical scenes in a musical.

box seats   Seats in a specially partitioned section of the auditorium, usually on the side wall and close to the stage and usually more expensive than other seats.

box set   Three-sided scenery used in a proscenium arch theatre to create the illusion of a real room with the "fourth wall" removed.

breakdown   A list of the characters in a play that is sent from a casting director to actors' agents as part of the process of casting the roles in a play.

Broadway   (1) The wide avenue that runs diagonally through Manhattan from southeast to northwest; (2) the section of midtown Manhattan in which most commercial theatres are located; (3) a description of commercial theatre; (4) a description of high-quality theatre; (5) a description of popular theatre that does not challenge the values of society.

bus-and-truck tour   The name of a commercial tour in which the actors travel by bus and the scenery travels in a truck.

call-back   An audition for which actors have been "called back" by the producer and director for a second reading.

carpenter   A scene shop technician who builds scenery; the name dates from a time when most scenery was constructed from wood.

casting director   A person hired by a producer or theatre to organize auditions and to select actors from among those submitted by agents.

causal logic   A deductive way of understanding a sequence of events that discovers the way each event is caused by another; it is the most common way an actor analyzes a role and a critic analyzes a play.

changing booth   A temporary or permanent place close to the stage where actors change their costumes; sometimes called a "quick change booth."

character   (1) The second in Aristotle's ranking of the six elements of theatre, which he described as "the agent for the action"; (2) a fictional being in a playwright's script.

character/scene plot   A chart, usually in the form of a grid, that shows which characters are in each scene of a play; used by directors, costume designers, and stage managers.

charge artist   The supervisor of the scene-painting crew.

choregus   (1) Ancient Greek name for the wealthy citizen who financed the production of a play; (2) the leader of the speaking chorus in Greek drama.

choreographer   The person who creates the dances in a production; a fight choreographer creates the moves for stage violence.

chorus   (1) The characters in ancient Greek drama who spoke, sang, and danced portions of the drama not spoken by the main characters; (2) the singers and dancers in a musical.

cinematic structure   The arrangement of the plot of a play that presents flashbacks and subjective scenes in other than chronological order.

circuit   The path of electricity from an outlet to a computer dimmerboard.

Classicism   A theatrical style in which the artist strives to imitate an idealized reality based on the power of reason; Classicism commonly is associated with the ancient Greek notion of "the golden mean," in which excess is considered improper and balance and proportion are considered desirable.

coaching   The advice, instruction, and encouragement a director gives an actor.

color media   A thin sheet of colored plastic placed in front of a theatrical lamp; called a "gel" in earlier times because it was made from gelatin.

comedy   The genre of play that makes you laugh, has plots that end happily, and reaffirms the values you hold to be important.

comedy of manners   A comic play that derives its humor from the language and behavior of the characters; see also "high comedy."

commercial theatre   Theatre produced for the primary purpose of making a profit on the financial investment.

community theatre   Theatre produced by and for people in a local community who volunteer their time and work.

complex plot   A plot that interweaves more than one story, that includes "subplots."

composer   A musician who creates the score for a production.

computer dimmerboard   A computer-driven control system used in theatre lighting.

computer dimmerboard operator   The technician on the lighting crew who operates the dimmerboard based on commands from the stage manager.

conclusion   The final segment of a play in which all subplots are resolved.

context (actor's)   The space, people, and time that influence an actor's preparation of a role.

contextual structure   The arrangement and sequence of scenes in a play that is determined by their relationship to a central theme instead of by a chronological or cause-and-effect logic.

continental seating   An arrangement of seats undivided by aisles, with each row of seats reaching from one side of the auditorium to the other.

continuous linear plot   A plot with a linear structure that unfolds without any gaps in the chronology of events.

control booth   A small booth, usually located at the back of the auditorium, where the stage manager and the sound and light board operators work during a performance.

convention   A rule or procedure in the theatre that is understood by actors and audience alike, in the same way that the rules of a sport are understood; the "convention of the fourth wall" is a good example.

convention of the fourth wall   The mutual understanding between audience and performers that there is an invisible "fourth wall" at the front of the stage and that the audience pretends the actors do not know it is there and the actors pretend they don't know the audience is present; this convention developed with the style of Realism and the use of a box set.

corporations   Profit-making businesses; one of the sources of contributed income for not-for-profit theatres.

corrales   Open-air theatres in seventeenth- and eighteenth-century Spain that were similar to the public theatres used in Shakespeare's England.

costume crafts artisans   Specialized craftspersons on the costume crew who do millinery and other specialty work.

costume list   A list of what each actor will wear from the skin out.

costume plot   A list showing the order in which costumes are worn.

costume shop   The area of a theatre where costumes are built.

costume storage   The area where costumes are stored when not in use; sometimes called the "racks."

counterweight system   A system of battens, cables, pulleys, and weights that facilitates raising and lowering scenery.

crafts shop   A subdivision of the costume and property shops where specialty items are built.

crew   The backstage workers in any of a theatre's departments; the name is a carryover from the eighteenth century, when backstage workers were recruited among mariners.

crisis   The moment in the unfolding of the plot when a change happens that leads inevitably to the resolution of the dramatic question; also called the "turning point."

critic   Someone who analyzes, describes, and offers an evaluation of a play or performance.

crossover   A passage actors use to get from one side of the stage to the other.

cross section   A scale line drawing of the scenery seen from the side of the stage showing how each piece of scenery will be installed in the theatre.

cue   (1) The theatrical term for any change in lighting or sound effects; (2) the moment when any scenery moves; (3) the line of dialogue or physical activity that comes immediately before a character speaks.

cue sheet   A list of things to be done by a crew member during a performance, referenced to lines in the script or actions on the stage.

curtain call   A post-performance ritual in which the actors bow and the audience applauds.

cutter   A specially trained person in the costume crew who makes paper and fabric patterns and cuts the cloth from which the costumes will be built.

cutting table   A high table in the costume shop on which patterns are made and cloth is cut.

deck   Another name for the floor of the stage.

description   The portions of a playwright's script that are not dialogue.

Determinism   A philosophy that holds that humans are shaped by genetic and environmental forces.

deus ex machina   A Latin phrase meaning "god from the machine," used to describe the resolution of the plot of a play by external means.

dialogue   The speeches the characters say; the playwright's primary material.

dianoia   The Greek word for "the process of thought," used by scholars to name the third-ranked of Aristotle's six elements of theatre.

diction   The choice and arrangement of words by the playwright that give a play its distinctive tone; not to be confused with "articulation," the preciseness of an actor's speech.

didaskolos   A specialist in ancient Greek theatre who instructed the chorus in speech and movement (the first part of the word "didaskolos" comes from the same stem as the word "didactic" and suggests our word "teacher"); an antecedent of the modern director.

direct mail   A form of marketing used by not-for-profit theatres.

discipline (actor's)   The conscious application of an actor's skill, time, and talent to achieve an optimal performance.

dissertation   A lengthy scholarly work required of Ph.D. candidates.

domestic comedy   A comic play with a domestic setting and middle-class characters.

drama   A category of play that is serious but not tragic.

dramatic question   The question posed early in a play's plot that keeps the audience interested until it is answered at the plot's resolution.

dramaturg   The literary consultant to a theatre; the word is borrowed from German.

draper   A specially trained person in the costume shop who shapes costumes on a dress form.

dress circle   A name for the first balcony of seating; commonly used in England.

dresser   A member of the wardrobe crew who helps actors change costumes.

dress form   A freestanding human shape on which costumes are fitted.

dressing room   The backstage room where actors change into their costumes.

dress rehearsal   A rehearsal near the end of the rehearsal period when the actors first wear their costumes; a dress rehearsal normally is scheduled after the technical rehearsals have been completed.

drop   A large painted cloth hung from a batten as part of the scenery.

dyer   A member of the costume crew whose specialty is dyeing fabrics.

dye room   A ventilated room near the costume shop with dye vats and equipment to change the color of fabric.

dynamics   The changes in tempo and volume that a director uses to shape the emotional impact of a play.

educational theatre   The name for theatre produced in schools, whose primary function is to train students.

electrician   A technician on the electrical crew.

elevators   Machines used to raise and lower scenery.

emotional recall   A tool of the Stanislavsky System of acting by which an actor remembers how he or she felt in a similar situation in real life and substitutes that feeling for the character's emotional state during the performance of a role.

empathy   The human capacity for experiencing another's emotion.

end stage theatre   A theatre with the stage at one end of a large space but without a proscenium arch formally separating the stage from the auditorium; commonly built in rooms not originally intended for performance.

ensemble musical   A musical that does not have starring roles, such as *Rent* or *A Chorus Line.*

environmental theatre   A kind of theatrical performance popularized by Richard Schechner, two traits of which are multiple actions happening simultaneously and continual readjustment of the performers' and the audience's spaces.

episodic linear plot   A plot with a linear structure made up of a sequence of scenes that have time lapses between them.

exposition   Background information revealed in the dialogue to help the audience understand the unfolding plot.

Expressionism   A theatrical style in which the artist strives to imitate subjective reality as it is experienced in nightmares and in which the visual world is distorted and abstracted to demonstrate how the central character feels about it; as a literary genre, Expressionism presents the story through the central character's vision and voice.

falling action   The portion of the plot that follows the crisis.

farce   A play that makes you laugh a lot and leaves you feeling liberated by the wildly anarchic and improbable things that happen.

festival theatre   A producing theatre with a particular focus to its repertoire, such as Shakespeare's plays.

first-class tour   Description of a commercial tour in which the artists receive salaries comparable to those in a Broadway contract.

first hand   A technician on the costume crew who supervises the cutters, drapers, and stitchers.

fitting   A session during which an actor tries on a costume and the designer makes any necessary adjustments.

fitting room   A special room or partitioned area of the costume shop where fittings take place.

flashback   A scene in a film or play that takes place in an earlier virtual time than its placement in the structure of the plot.

flat   A standard piece of theatrical scenery with a wood frame, usually covered in canvas.

flies   See "fly loft."

fly loft   The space in the stage house above the proscenium arch where scenery is flown.

focus session   A working period during which the lighting designer supervises the electricians who hang, circuit, and focus all the theatrical lights.

forced perspective   A drawing technique developed in the Italian Renaissance that makes two-dimensional drawings appear to represent a three-dimensional reality.

foreshadowing   Information included in the dialogue that the audience needs to know so it can understand later developments of the plot.

foundations   Charitable financial entities that contribute to not-for-profit theatres.

found space theatre   The name for a performance space that was not intended for that use; for example, the steps of a government building, the courtyard in a mall, a railroad station.

front elevation   A working drawing of the set that shows what the scenery looks like from the front.

front of house   The portion of the theatre used by the audience.

gallery   A name for the third or highest balcony in some theatres.

gel   See "color media."

genre   Categorization of dramas on the basis of their emotional impact on an audience; there are also literary characteristics of each genre; the six most common genres are tragedy, comedy, farce, melodrama, drama, and tragicomedy.

government grants   Tax revenues distributed through government agencies; a source of support for not-for-profit theatre.

green room   The actors' backstage waiting room, perhaps named after the green waiting room in London's Drury Lane Theatre.

grid   A network of steel beams high above the stage floor.

groundlings   The name for the audience in Elizabethan theatres who stood to watch performances; this audience paid the smallest entrance fee and is thought to have favored broad comedy.

ground plan   A scale drawing of the floor of the stage showing the placement of the scenery; used by the actors in rehearsals and by the stage crew for the installation of the scenery.

group tickets   Tickets sold at a reduced rate to groups.

guerilla theatre   Theatre of a political nature performed in unexpected public places.

hair, wig, and makeup designer   The designer who collaborates with the costume designer to complete the character's "look."

hair, wig, and makeup studio   A room or part of the costume shop where the hair, wig, and makeup designer works.

herd animals   Animals that live in a group; in some ways, humans are "herd animals."

high comedy   A comic play that derives its humor from the language and behavior of the characters; see also "comedy of manners."

hubris   The Greek word for excessive pride, which was considered to be a flaw in the character of an otherwise ideal person; the common flaw in the tragic heroes of ancient Greek dramas.

hybrid scenery   Scenery that merges many kinds of stagecraft.

idealized reality   An artistic expression of the artist's vision of truth based on either an intellectual or an emotional ideal of how the world ought to be; the reality of the theatrical styles of Classicism and Romanticism.

imagination (actor's)   The aspect of the actor's craft that exploits an actor's ability to think and feel as the fictional character.

imagistic design   Scene design that explores visual metaphors and striking images rather than representing observed reality; frequently associated with the theatrical style of Postmodernism.

inciting event   The moment in the plot when the dramatic question is asked; it marks the end of the introduction and the beginning of what is often called the rising action.

individual donors   One of the four sources of contributed income for a not-for-profit theatre.

instrument schedule   A list made by the lighting designer listing each piece of equipment and the color media that will be placed in front of it along with how it will be connected to the computer light board.

introduction   A term used in play analysis to describe the first scene or scenes of a play in which characters are introduced, exposition is provided, and the status quo is established.

Kabuki   A highly stylized form of Japanese theatre.

key collaborators   Descriptive term for the team of director and designers.

League of Resident Theatres   An organization of not-for-profit theatres across America that form a collective bargaining unit to negotiate with unions and that share common information.

light plot   A scaled diagram drafted by the lighting designer that displays all the lighting instruments to be used in the design and where they are placed.

linear structure   Description of the plot of a play that progresses without flashbacks to jumble the chronology; the action progresses "along a line."

live event   Theatre that happens when the audience is present; opposite of a recorded event.

load-in   The work period during which the scenery is brought into the theatre.

loge   An old French word for a booth of seats in the opera house, now used to describe theatre seats located at the very front of the first balcony.

LORT   Acronym for League of Resident Theatres.

low comedy   A comedy about characters we laugh at more because of what they do than because of what they say.

lyricist   The writer of the words in a script's songs.

mansion stage   A platform stage used in medieval Europe that consisted of a wide rectangular stage with a number of separate houses attached to the back of it, each depicting a unique location; see "simultaneous stage."

master electrician   The supervisor of the electrical crew.

meaning   The single dominant idea expressed by the plot of a play.

mechane   A large crane used to "fly" actors into the air in ancient Greek theatres.

melodrama   A genre of play that provides entertainment that has the appearance of being serious but ends with the protagonist victorious; melodramas usually have highly emotional scenes alternating with comic scenes.

mezzanine   The name for the lowest balcony, sometimes suspended from the main or "first" balcony.

mixer   An electronic audio device used by the sound designer to take in sounds, amplify and adjust them, and send them out to speakers.

Modern Art   An artistic movement of the first half of the twentieth century that expressed the deeper truth that outward appearances hide the truth of the human condition; Modern Art presents a visually distorted picture of the world.

multiple plots   Description of a play that tells more than one story.

music   The fifth-ranked of Aristotle's six elements of theatre; describes everything that is heard, from musical accompaniment to sound effects to the actors' voices.

musical   Description of the mature form of musical theatre that evolved in the middle of the twentieth century and that integrates song and dance with characters and plot.

musical comedy   Description of American musical theatre prior to the mid-twentieth century.

musical director   The person who directs the musicians and singers in a musical.

National Endowment for the Arts   Federal agency founded in 1965 to disburse tax revenues in support of the arts.

Naturalism   A theatrical style developed in the nineteenth century that is based on the philosophy of Determinism and that strives to present on stage an exact imitation of everyday life; Naturalism and Realism are closely linked, and sometimes the terms are used interchangeably.

NEA   Acronym for National Endowment for the Arts.

not-for-profit   Describes a business that serves the best interests of the public and is not required to pay certain taxes but is prohibited by law from distributing its profits to its investors; a not-for-profit corporation must be awarded a 501(c)3 status by the Internal Revenue Service.

nut   Slang term for the weekly operating costs of a commercial theatre production.

objective   A term in the Stanislavsky System of acting that describes what a character wants.

objective reality   A theatrical style, expressed in Realism and Theatricalism, that imitates the way things appear on the surface.

obstacle   A term in the Stanislavsky System of acting that describes what the character must overcome to achieve the objective.

Off Broadway   (1) The name for theatres and theatrical productions that are not presented in the Broadway district in midtown Manhattan; (2) a description of intellectually challenging plays; (3) a category of union contract that permits lower salaries than for Broadway productions and that therefore encourages less expensive productions.

Off Off Broadway   (1) The name for theatres and theatrical productions that are not presented in the Broadway district in midtown Manhattan or in the Off Broadway theatre districts; (2) a description of intellectually challenging plays; (3) a category of union contract that permits lower salaries than for Broadway or Off Broadway productions and that therefore encourages less expensive productions.

opera   A form of musical theatre developed in Italy during the Renaissance that is entirely sung, is serious in subject, and is musically complex.

operetta   A form of musical theatre that developed in Europe in the eighteenth and nineteenth centuries that is Romantic in subject, has scenes of spoken dialogue, and is less musically complex than opera.

orchestra   (1) The flat circle of earth at the center of an ancient Greek theatre where the chorus sang and danced; the word means "dancing place"; (2) the main-floor audience seating in a proscenium arch theatre; (3) the musicians who play during a musical theatre performance and who usually sit in front of and below the stage in a place called the "orchestra pit."

orchestrator   The musician who uses the composer's melodies to create the musical parts for the members of an orchestra.

outdoor drama   Theatre performed in outdoor theatres, usually in the summer.

pageant wagon   A wagon used by traveling actors in medieval Europe.

painter's elevation   A scale drawing painted by the scene designer to provide scene painters with clear guidance in painting the scenery.

paint frame   A wooden frame used in the scene shop to which drops can be fastened so the scene painters can paint them.

parados   (1) The passage between the audience seating area and the skene in ancient Greek theatre that was used by the chorus for entrances and exits; (2) the descriptive name for the choral ode sung by the chorus when it entered at the beginning of an ancient Greek play.

particular place   A unique place where theatre is performed live, at a particular time.

particular time   A unique time when theatre is performed live, at a particular place.

pass   A kind of ticket sold by not-for-profit theatres that is good for one or more admissions to one or more performances on a space-available basis.

pass door   A door from the auditorium leading backstage.

performance   The presentation of a play or musical before an audience.

photo/resumé   An 8 × 10 picture of an actor with a list of credits on the back, used by the actor when seeking a job.

playbill   The printed program distributed to the audience at a performance; it contains information about the play and the artists.

plot   The major action of the story that is told and that takes the audience on a journey from the status quo at the beginning to the changed circumstances at the end of a play; Aristotle described plot as "the life and soul of the drama."

Postmodernism   A theatrical style that evolved from Surrealism in the late twentieth century and that combines an imitation of the subjective reality of Surrealism with the objective reality of Theatricalism; Postmodernism is sometimes associated with imagistic theatre.

presentational performance   A style of performance in which the actors acknowledge the presence of the audience and sometimes speak directly to them; that is, the actors "present" the characters.

present tense   The time when a live theatre event is experienced by an audience.

preview   A rehearsal for which tickets are sold at a reduced rate and the actors and director learn how audiences will react to the performance so they can make adjustments before opening night.

producer   The businessperson (or venture capitalist) who heads the business aspects of a commercial production.

production concept   The result of the intellectual and creative process through which the director and the key collaborators determine how the script is to be interpreted and how that interpretation is to be realized on the stage.

production conference   A meeting of the director and designers to develop the production concept.

production manager   The middle-management supervisor of a theatre's production staff who is responsible for budgets, schedules, and personnel.

projections   Images projected by lights and used as part of a play's scenery.

promptbook   The stage manager's copy of the script that has all the cues that must be given to actors and crew members; sometimes called the play's "bible."

prop crew   The backstage staff responsible for the construction and maintenance of all properties.

property master   The supervisor of the prop crew.

prop shop   A special area or a part of the scene shop where properties are constructed.

prop table   A table in the wings where props are placed during a performance.

proscenium arch theatre   A theatre building that has a framelike arch around the stage; the most common kind of theatre today, it was developed in the seventeenth century; "proscenium arch" is the name for the architectural separation between the stage and the auditorium, frequently decorated very ornately; the audience looks through the arch at the performance on the stage the way you look through a picture frame at a painting.

proskene   A platform attached to the front of the skene in ancient Greek theatres on which actors stood.

public spaces   A term describing all the parts of a theatre building the public uses.

pulley   A slotted, round wheel that cables or ropes are pulled through; part of the counterweight system.

racks   A room for the storage of costumes.

radio drama   Plays performed for radio broadcast only.

ragtime   Syncopated music with a "ragged" rhythm that developed in the early twentieth century from African roots.

rake   The tilt of a stage from the lowest level, near the audience, to a higher level upstage; introduced when audiences sat on a flat floor, but still in use today to give a performance an unrealistic and dynamic quality.

reader   An actor hired to read all the other lines in a scene during an actor's audition.

Realism   A style of theatrical production and dramatic writing that imitates selected traits of the language and appearance of everyday life; it evolved from Naturalism, and today the terms "Realism" and "Naturalism" are used interchangeably.

realistic exterior scenery   Scenery that creates the illusion of a real place outdoors.

regional theatre   Description of a permanent American not-for-profit theatre company; also called "resident theatre."

rehearsal room   The room in which actors rehearse prior to rehearsing on the stage.

rendering   A colored drawing by a designer to communicate what a costume or set will look like.

repertory theatre   Description of a permanent American not-for-profit theatre company; implies that the theatre offers several productions concurrently; see also "resident theatre" and "regional theatre."

representational performance   A style of performance in which the actors pretend the audience is not there and the audience pretends the actors do not know it is there; the actors "represent" the characters.

resident theatre   Description of a permanent American not-for-profit theatre company; also called "regional theatre."

resolution   The moment in a play's plot when the dramatic question is answered.

reversal   A point in a play's plot when the protagonist suffers a temporary defeat.

reviewer   A person who writes or speaks an analysis and opinion of a play or performance; usually applied to a newspaper or television journalist who works against a deadline.

revolving stage   A turntable used to move scenery around in a circle.

rigging   The cables, ropes, pulleys, and winches used to fly scenery.

rising action   The segment of the plot between the point of attack and the crisis in which events complicate the plot and heighten suspense.

road   Slang term for the theatres a play tours to outside New York.

role   The entirety of a character's part in a play.

Romanticism   A theatrical style in which the artist strives to imitate an idealized reality based on the importance of emotion; Romanticism evolved in the early nineteenth century as a reaction to Classicism, and it values excess emotion.

royalty   A percentage of the gross revenue that is distributed to the creators of a production: author, director, composer, and so on.

salary   A weekly wage paid to theatre artists.

sampler   A device that electronically records a sound by transforming it into numbers; part of the computer and digitalized sound system used by sound designers.

scene   A short segment of the plot of a play.

scene painter   A specialist scenic artist who paints scenery.

scene shop manager   The supervisor of the carpenters and technicians who build scenery.

scenographer   A theatrical designer of scenery and costumes (and sometimes lighting) who works collaboratively with the director to create the visual world of the play.

scholar   In theatre, a researcher and theorist who writes about theatre.

screen test   An audition for a film or TV role.

season ticket   A reduced-rate ticket for a specific seat for each production in a season.

self   The actor's body, voice, and imagination; the actor's instrument.

sides   Selected pages of a script, used for an audition.

simple plot   A plot without any subplots.

simultaneous stage   A platform stage used in medieval Europe that consisted of a wide rectangular stage with a number of separate houses attached to the back of it, each depicting a unique location; see "mansion stage."

single ticket   A ticket for a specific seat at a specific performance.

six elements of theatre   The six elements listed by Aristotle in *The Poetics* as the constituents of theatre; in order: plot, character, thought, diction, music, spectacle.

skene   A freestanding building that was a part of an ancient Greek theatre; located behind the orchestra; actors made entrances from it and changed costumes in it; the word "scenery" is derived from "skene."

sketch   A drawing by a designer to communicate the basics of a design.

slapstick   (1) A prop used in the *commedia dell'arte* made from two boards fastened together at one end and loose at the other so they could be slapped together to make a loud noise when an actor was hit by it; (2) term used to describe any broad and physical farce action.

slip stage   A specially built stage floor that has narrow sections that slide sideways into the wings carrying actors or furniture on or off the stage.

sound board operator   The technician on the sound crew who operates the computer sound board during performances.

sound engineer   The technician on the sound crew who assists the sound designer in creating the sound effects, placing the speakers, and preparing for the production.

sound plot   A diagram showing the placement of all microphones and speakers.

spectacle   Sixth- and last-ranked of Aristotle's elements of theatre; includes all visual aspects of a production, from scenery to the movement of actors.

stage directions   The playwright's written instructions.

stage door   The exterior door used by actors to enter and exit the theatre.

stage house   The portion of a theatre building that includes the stage and all backstage spaces.

stage manager   The person in charge of all rehearsals and performances.

stageweights   Brick-shaped metal weights used in the counterweight system to balance the weight of scenery attached to battens.

staging   The arrangement and movement of the actors as supervised by the director.

stalls   English term for the main floor seats in a proscenium arch theatre.

Stanislavsky System   The organized method that actors use to analyze and create a character; invented by the Russian Constantine Stanislavsky.

star An actor whose name will attract ticket buyers.

status quo The stable situation at the beginning of a plot, before the dramatic question is asked.

stitcher A specialized member of the costume shop staff who sews together costume pieces.

storyboard A term borrowed from cinema to describe a sequence of rough drawings that show how scenes will look in performance; used by some lighting designers to communicate the effects they plan for in their design.

structure Description of the arrangement of the incidents of a play's plot.

student rush tickets Reduced-rate tickets sold immediately before a performance.

style (1) A categorization of artistic works by their literary or theatrical characteristics; (2) a categorization of plays by how they imitate reality; the six main theatrical styles are Realism, Theatricalism, Expressionism, Surrealism, Classicism, and Romanticism.

subjective reality The truth of human experience as abstracted in the unconscious, the primitive, and the irrational, expressed in the theatrical styles of Surrealism and Expressionism.

sung-through musical A form of musical theatre that tells the entire story through the song lyrics and has no spoken dialogue or "book."

super objective A term in the Stanislavsky System of acting that describes the main objective of a character in a play.

support spaces Nonpublic spaces in a theatre building where productions are built and rehearsed.

Surrealism A theatrical style in which the artist strives to imitate subjective reality as it is experienced in whimsical dreams; surrealism uses associative logic instead of cause-and-effect logic to move from one incident to the next.

swab Wash and mop (the stage); the term derives from nautical use.

tailor A specialist member of the costume shop staff who constructs tailored men's and women's costumes.

technical director The supervisor of the scene shop, who supervises budgets, schedules, personnel, and the construction and installation of scenery.

technical drawing A scale drawing illustrating how scenery is to be built and installed.

technical rehearsal A rehearsal at which the scenery, lighting, and sound are first added to the actors' performances; one or more technical rehearsals are scheduled toward the end of the rehearsal period, just before costumes are added for the dress rehearsal.

telemarketing Sale of theatre tickets over the telephone; commonly used by not-for-profit theatres for selling season tickets.

text The playwright's script, particularly as a source of the actor's performance.

theatre of the absurd A genre and style of European theatre that evolved in the mid-twentieth century and expresses the meaninglessness of the human condition in laugh-producing tragicomedies; Samuel Beckett and Eugène Ionesco are the best-known Absurdist playwrights.

Theatricalism   A theatrical style in which the artist strives to imitate objective reality as it is traditionally presented in the theatre; theatricalism is based on the belief that we are all self-conscious creatures who "act" our lives.

theatrical styles   Ways in which theatre productions express reality.

theatron   The seating area in ancient Greek theatres; we get our word "theatre" from this word, which means "seeing place."

theme   An intellectual idea examined in a play.

thesis   A lengthy research paper of scholarly content written by students seeking a Master's degree.

thought   The third-ranked element of Aristotle's elements of theatre; see "dianoia."

three unities   Organizing traits of a play as interpreted in the Italian Renaissance from Aristotle's *The Poetics;* unity of place, time, and action.

thrust theatre   A theatre without a proscenium arch in which the stage thrusts forward so the audience is seated on three sides; an excellent example is the Guthrie Theatre in Minneapolis.

thymele   In ancient Greek theatres, the altar to Dionysus, the god of wine, fertility, ecstasy, and theatre, that was erected in the center of the orchestra.

ticket   An admission to a performance, usually printed on paper or card stock.

tiring house   The room behind the stage where actors dress or "attire" themselves.

touring production   A theatre production that moves from one city to another; common in America today for commercial productions of Broadway hits.

tragedy   A serious play that makes you feel exhilarated because the hero's experience teaches you some profound truth about your life; a tragedy guides you toward feeling a sort of calm affirmation that your worst expectations about life are true, and you feel wiser for reaching this certainty.

tragicomedy   A genre of play that dominated mid- to late twentieth century drama and that inspires agitation, frustration, and anxiety; tragicomedies deal with serious topics but provoke laughter and express the lack of coherent values in the world.

training (actor's)   Formal instruction in the art and craft of acting that is offered in universities and professional schools.

trap room   A room beneath the stage floor from which scenery and actors can rise to the stage through a trap door.

turkey   A slang term for a theatrical production that fails commercially or artistically.

turning point   The moment in the unfolding of the plot when a change happens that leads inevitably to the resolution of the dramatic question; also called the "crisis."

two-dimensional painted scenery   Scenery, particularly cloth backdrops, painted to suggest three dimensions though obviously two-dimensional.

unit   A term in the Stanislavsky System of acting that describes a short sequence of a character's role in which a single objective is introduced and achieved.

unit set   A kind of scene design, made up of levels and platforms, that represents no single place and permits the audience to imagine many different locations.

unity of action   One of the three unities ascribed to Aristotle; an organizing trait of a plot in which a single story is told.

unity of place   One of the three unities ascribed to Aristotle; an organizing trait of a plot in which the story takes place in one location.

unity of time   One of the three unities ascribed to Aristotle; an organizing trait of a plot in which the story unfolds continuously.

virtual place   The fictional place in which the action of a play takes place.

virtual time   The fictional time in which the action of a play takes place.

wagons   Rolling platforms used to move scenery onto a stage.

walk-on   A slang term for a nonspeaking or small role in a play; sometimes called a "spear carrier."

wardrobe crew   The staff responsible for helping actors dress and for maintaining and cleaning costumes.

wardrobe supervisor   The head of the wardrobe crew.

white model   An unpainted, three-dimensional scale model of the set built by the designer; usually made from foam core, cardboard, or some other material.

willing suspension of disbelief   A phrase coined by the nineteenth-century English poet and critic Samuel Taylor Coleridge to explain the convention by which an audience can enjoy a theatrical performance by knowingly setting aside its objectivity.

winch   A mechanical device for pulling a rope or cable; part of the counterweight system.

wing and drop scenery   A kind of two-dimensional painted scenery developed in the eighteenth century and still used in musicals and dance concerts.

wings   (1) Frames with scenery placed on the side of the stage, parallel with the proscenium arch; (2) the areas on the sides of the stage floor that are unseen by the audience; where the actors stand before an entrance.

working drawing   See "technical drawing."

CREDITS

Text Credits

Page 10: "Color and Light" and "Putting It Together" by Stephen Sondheim. © 1984 Rilting Music, Inc. (ASCAP) All Rights Administered by WB Music Corp. (ASCAP) All Rights Reserved. Used by permission of Warner Bros. Publications U.S., Inc., Miami, FL 33014; **p. 21:** "dianoia" from *The Oxford English Dictionary, Second Edition,* 1989. By permission of Oxford University Press.

Photo Credits

All photos are courtesy of Tom Markus and Linda Sarver unless otherwise noted below.

Page 8: © Joan Marcus; **p. 9:** Shakespeare Theatre of Maine/Tom Marcus; **pp. 11, 13:** Courtesy of Robert Clayton; **p. 14:** Courtesy of Craig Schwartz; **p. 17:** Photograph by Donald McKague. Courtesy of the Stratford Festival of Canada Archives; **p. 19:** Archives of the University of Wisconsin-Milwaukee, Milwaukee Repertory Theater Photographic History, Mark Avery Collection 1977–1994; **p. 23 (left):** Courtesy of Robert Clayton; **p. 23 (right):** New Harmony Theatre; **p. 25:** Colorado Shakespeare Festival; **p. 28:** Colorado Shakespeare Festival; **pp. 29, 32, 34:** Archives of the University of Wisconsin-Milwaukee, Milwaukee Repertory Theater Photographic History, Mark Avery Collection 1977–1994; **p. 40:** Courtesy of The Cleveland Playhouse, Paul Tepley Photography, Inc.; **p. 41:** Archives of the University of Wisconsin-Milwaukee, Milwaukee Repertory Theater Photographic History, Mark Avery Collection 1977–1994; **p. 42:** Scenography and projection design by Beate Czogalla; slide by Justin Kasulka; **p. 43 (top):** Scenography and projection design by Beate Czogalla; slide by Justin Kasulka; **p. 43 (bottom):** George Karger—Pix, Courtesy of Getty Images; **p. 44 (top):** Courtesy of Photofest; **p. 44 (bottom):** © Brigitte Lancombe; **p. 49 (top & bottom):** Archives of the University of Wisconsin-Milwaukee, Milwaukee Repertory Theater Photographic History, Mark Avery Collection 1977–1994; **p. 50 (top):** Courtesy of Photofest; **p. 50 (bottom):** Photographer: Patrick Redmond. © Blue Angel Films; **p. 52:** Archives of the University of Wisconsin-Milwaukee, Milwaukee Repertory Theater Photographic History, Mark Avery Collection 1977–1994; **p. 53 (top):** Courtesy of J.M. Burian, photo by Josef Svoboda; **p. 53 (bottom):** Courtesy of F. Mitchell Dana; **p. 55 (left & right):** Courtesy of Photofest; **p. 57:** © The Museum of Modern Art; **p. 59:** Wayne State University; **p. 61:** Virginia Museum Theatre, © Virginia Museum of Fine Arts, Richmond; **p. 62 (top):** Courtesy of Richard Devin; **pp. 70, 86:** Courtesy of Robert Clayton; **p. 93:** Classic Greek Theatre Festival/Tom Markus; **p. 96:** Courtesy of Joseph A. Varga; **p. 101 (left & right):** Courtesy of Sam Sandoe; **p. 103:** Colorado Shakespeare Festival; **p. 106:** The Laboratory Theatre, Florida/Tom Markus; **p. 107:** © Joan Marcus/Shakespeare Theatre, Washington D.C.; **p. 110:** © Everett Collection; **p. 111:** Colorado Shakespeare Festival; **p. 116:** Courtesy of Noel True; **p. 125:** © Donald Cooper; **p. 128:** © Joan Marcus; **p. 130:** Archives of the University of Wisconsin-Milwaukee, Milwaukee Repertory Theater Photographic History, Mark Avery Collection 1977–1994; **p. 131:** Courtesy of Jane Page; **p. 133:** Rock Valley College Starlight Theatre; **p. 138:** Courtesy of Joseph A. Varga; **p. 143 (top & bottom):** Courtesy of Eric Fielding; **p. 149:** Courtesy of Eric Sinkkonen; **pp. 171 (top & bottom), 172, 173, 174:** Colorado Shakespeare Festival; **p. 181:** © Martha Swope; **p. 205:** National Park Service/Ford's Theatre NHS, Edwin L. Kesler, photographer; **p. 208:** Used by permission, Utah Historical Society; **p. 212:** Neuhause Arena Stage, photo courtesy of Alley Theatre, Houston; **p. 215:** Tyrone Guthrie's 1963 production of *The Three Sisters* at the Guthrie Theater. Photo provided by the Guthrie Theater; **p. 218:** Don Stowell Collection; **p. 219:** University of Connecticut, photo by Peter Morenus; **pp. 222, 224:** Courtesy of Joseph A. Varga; **p. 226:** Courtesy of Eric Fielding; **p. 227:** Courtesy of Joseph A. Varga; **p. 229 (top & bottom):** Courtesy of Pamela Howard; **p. 231 (top & bottom):** Courtesy of Mark Reaney; **p. 239 (top):** Colorado Shakespeare Festival; **p. 243:** Archives of the University of Wisconsin-Milwaukee, Milwaukee Repertory Theater Photographic History, Mark Avery Collection 1977–1994; **p. 244:** Rock Valley College Starlight Theatre; **p. 251:** Courtesy Comité Départemental du Tourism de la Dordogne; **p. 260:** Used by permission of The Great Passion Play of Eureka Springs, AR; **p. 263:** Courtesy of Franklin J. Hildy ©; **pp. 266, 268 (bottom):** © Alinari/Art Resource, NY; **p. 273:** Rock Valley College Starlight Theatre; **p. 285:** Don Stowell Collection; **p. 293 (top):**

INDEX

• • • • • • • • • • •

Boldface page numbers refer to figures and figure captions.